THE DISAPPEARING DAIS

The
Disappearing Dais

A STUDY OF THE PRINCIPLES AND PRACTICE OF ENGLISH TEACHING

By

FRANK WHITEHEAD

Senior Lecturer in English and Education
University of Sheffield Institute of
Education

1971

CHATTO & WINDUS
LONDON

Published by
Chatto & Windus (Educational) Ltd
42 William IV Street
London W.C.2

*

Clarke, Irwin & Co Ltd
Toronto

ISBN   7011 1204 2 (Hardback)
ISBN   7011 1414 2 (Paperback)

First Published 1966
Second Impression 1966
Third Impression 1968
Fourth Impression 1971

Printed photolitho in Great Britain
by Ebenezer Baylis and Son, Ltd.
The Trinity Press, Worcester, and London

Let the teacher stand on an elevated platform, and, keeping all the scholars in his sight at once, allow none of them to do anything but attend and look at him.

COMENIUS, 1657

English is never easy to teach; it becomes even harder when classes are large, classrooms bleak and unillustrated, and the desks rigid and constricting, with the master holding forth from a superior dais.

SCHOOLS COUNCIL MEMORANDUM, 1964

CONTENTS

ACKNOWLEDGEMENTS

The author makes grateful acknowledgement to the following for permission to include copyright material:

James Gould Cozzens, Longmans, Green & Co Ltd and Harcourt, Brace & World, Inc, for an extract from *The Just and the Unjust*; the Macmillan Company for an extract from *Experience and Education* by John Dewey; Captain W. E. Johns and Hodder & Stoughton Ltd for an extract from *Biggles' Second Case*; Edward Arnold Ltd for an extract from *Moonfleet* by J. Meade Falkner; Christopher Mayhew and Lincoln-Prager Ltd for an extract from *Dear Viewer*; the Trustees of the Joseph Conrad Estate and J. M. Dent & Sons Ltd for an extract from *Youth* by Joseph Conrad; Mr M. B. Yeats and Macmillan & Co Ltd for 'A Popular Personage at Home' from *The Collected Poems of Thomas Hardy*; Siegfried Sassoon and Faber & Faber Ltd for 'Morning Express'; the Estate of the late Mrs Frieda Lawrence and Laurence Pollinger Ltd for 'Bat' from *The Collected Poems of D. H. Lawrence*; Chatto & Windus Ltd for 'The Send-Off' from *The Poems of Wilfred Owen* and for an extract from *Proper Studies* by Aldous Huxley; Bernard Malamud and Eyre & Spottiswoode Ltd for an extract from *A New Life*; Henry Lee Smith, Jr, and the Harvard University Press for an extract from *Linguistic Science and the Teaching of English*; Norman Mailer and André Deutsch Ltd for two extracts from *Advertisements for Myself*; David Holbrook and the Cambridge University Press for an extract from *English for the Rejected*; David Holbrook and the Editor of *The Guardian* for an extract from an article; Tavistock Publications for an extract from *Our Adult World and its Roots in Infancy* by Melanie Klein; the Hutchinson Publishing Group Ltd for an extract from *Young Writers, Young Readers* edited by Boris Ford; Edmund Blunden and A. D. Peters and Co for 'Winter, East Anglia'; and the University of London School Examinations Council for the examination question relating to this poem.

AUTHOR'S NOTE

In writing this book I have become conscious of how much I owe to my former teachers in the University of Cambridge, to my former teachers, colleagues and students at the University of London Institute of Education, and to the many friends and acquaintances within the teaching profession who have discussed the teaching of English with me at various times during the past quarter of a century. I have to acknowledge, above all, a very special debt to Professor P. Gurrey and Miss Maura Brooke Gwynne, who first taught me to think coherently and critically about aims and methods in the teaching of English, and from whom I have continued, over the years, to learn so much. While they are certainly not to be held responsible for its defects, I believe that whatever merits the book may have are due primarily to their influence.

I am also most grateful to Mrs. Joan Goody, to Mr. Kenneth Pike and to my wife for allowing me to quote, and comment on, pieces of writing by their pupils. Parts of Chapters 4 and 7 have appeared in slightly different form in *The Use of English*, and I am grateful to the editor for permission to reprint.

F.W.

The traditional school could get along without any consistently developed philosophy of education. About all it required in that line was a set of abstract words like culture, discipline, our great cultural heritage, etc., actual guidance being derived not from them but from custom and established routines. . . . Revolt against the kind of organization characteristic of the traditional school constitutes a demand for a kind of organization based upon ideas. I think that only slight acquaintance with the history of education is needed to prove that educational reformers and innovators alone have felt the need for a philosophy of education. Those who adhered to the established system needed merely a few fine-sounding words to justify existing practices. The real work was done by habits which were so fixed as to be institutional.

JOHN DEWEY *Experience and Education*

'Don't work so hard at it, Ab. There is always theory and there is always practice. If you think you're going to change that you're wrong. Theory is where you want to go; and practice is how you're going to get there.'

'Yes,' said Abner, 'or else, theory is what you tell people you're going to do; and practice is what they catch you really doing . . .'

JAMES GOULD COZZENS *The Just and the Unjust*

Chapter 1

THE GROUNDWORK OF PRINCIPLE

ENGLISH is unique among school-subjects, though the nature of this uniqueness often goes unrecognised. When we stress the centrality of English teaching (as in the Spens Report's dictum that English should be the 'unifying principle' of the school curriculum) we are perhaps groping towards this recognition. Nearer to the heart of the matter is George Sampson's observation that English 'includes and transcends all subjects' since it is 'for English people the whole means of expression the attainment of which makes them articulate human beings, able to inherit the past, to possess the present and to confront the future' (Sampson, 1921). Certainly, I believe, we shall never reach a full understanding of what English teaching can and should be until we have grasped the peculiarly intimate relationship which exists between the individual human being and his mother-tongue; more particularly we need to have brought to clear focus in our minds the way in which a child's acquisition of his native language is inseparably intertwined with his developing conscious-ness of the world in which he is growing up, with his control of his inner phantasies and the feelings they give rise to, and with his possession of the values by which he will live his life in the civilisa-tion he forms a part of.

I can perhaps pinpoint the difference such an awareness makes to our theory and practice as teachers by referring to a representative statement from a couple of decades ago. In 1947 Professor I. A. Gordon wrote that English teaching has the task of developing 'a threefold skill: (1) the ability to express oneself in spoken or written speech and so to initiate communication, (2) the ability to understand the spoken or written speech of another and so to complete the communication, (3) the ability to feel or appreciate the appeal of literature'. At the time this seemed to me both helpful and en-lightened. It jettisoned firmly any lingering notion that English can be thought of as a 'content subject', and made plain that the acquisition of information (knowledge *about* the English language, or knowledge *about* English books or English authors) can never be of more than marginal importance to it. And it saw the abilities which the pupil has to develop not as separate isolable entities but rather as different aspects of a single unitary skill—the ability, one might say, to use one's native tongue effectively in all its modes, in listening and speaking as well as in reading and writing, in its everyday utilitarian functions as well as for the more subtle imaginative and emotional purposes which make up the province of literature.

Even now much English teaching has not caught up with this. Miss Groby is still with us, very much as James Thurber predicted. (Miss Groby, you will recall, was interested not in what prose said but in the way prose said it; she had a special penchant for the more recondite Figures of Speech, such as metonymy.) One can still find secondary schools where a form's English lessons are parcelled out, for administrative convenience, among several members of staff, one doing 'oral', another spelling and punctuation, and so on. And the dichotomy between 'language' (conceived in the limited terms dictated by external examinations) and 'literature' (a matter of knowing about set books) is still common enough, even to the point of separation on the time-table. By contrast, the best of today's English teaching has progressed far beyond Professor Gordon's definition, in ways which I hope to indicate.

From the standpoint of such teaching the notion of English as 'communication' is seen to be inadequate. Not only does the term suggest an excessive preoccupation with language in its referential function, as a means of transmitting information; it carries with it the unfortunate implication that what is to be communicated exists already in the mind, waiting only to be encoded in words. Left out of account by this are all the occasions when our language is a means of exploring and illuminating experience, of giving shape to an intuition which can crystallise only as the words grow together to define its inherent structure. This creative role of language can be identified at its most unmistakable in such a work as Eliot's *Four Quartets*, where we can watch a great poet engaged in what D. W. Harding has aptly called the 'creation of concepts'. Only rarely, of course, can the historic bounds of human consciousness be thus enlarged; but we should remember that for each of us (and especially for the child on his journey towards maturity) the old truths have to be rediscovered afresh if they are to be fully valid. There is a deeper significance than is always realised to E. M. Forster's much-quoted rhetorical question: 'How can I tell what I think till I see what I say?'

Similarly the word 'skill', as used by Professor Gordon, now seems to me far too limiting in its connotations. It manœuvres us into thinking of language as somehow external to the human being who uses it—a technique which can be mastered by intellectual effort, or a set of responses which can be 'learned' by a process of conditioning. Surely this completely fails to match the extraordinary delicacy, complexity and manysidedness of the processes that go on inside us when we acquire our native language. The fact is that our mother-tongue is something that is built into us at a very deep level of the whole personality. It is the medium in which we have evolved our most deeply-ingrained modes of interpreting the universe in which we live; and our capacity for human relationships, our ways of perceiving, understanding and mastering the phenomena of our everyday existence are shaped and coloured by it in countless ways of which we are seldom consciously aware. The work of certain Russian psychologists, notably Vygotsky and Luria, provides interesting indirect confirmation of the way in which the child's perception of reality takes its structure and patterning from language, as his acquisition of this enables him to sort out his impressions into generalised categories incorporating the accumulated experience of past generations. For a child, it is claimed, the word not only indicates a corresponding object in the external world, but also abstracts and isolates its essential features, thus bringing it into relation with a systematisation of experience which involves a reorganisation of the child's whole mental activity.[1]

I myself was vouchsafed a peculiarly forceful insight into this power of the word some years ago when one of my children was fifteen or sixteen months old. One fine spring afternoon we had made an expedition into the countryside and walked in bright sunshine through a green meadow filled with cows and birdsong. During the walk Stephen had added to his small store of vocabulary the word 'cow', which he repeated at intervals with evident satisfaction and every appearance of understanding. A day or two later we were sitting indoors when he puzzled us by insistently repeating the word 'cow' over and over again. There was no cow present, nor yet a

---

[1] See in particular Luria and Yudovich (1959), an account of work with a pair of identical twins who at the age of four to five were exceptionally retarded in their speech development. When disentangled from its Pavlovian jargon, the material is interestingly suggestive, even if a good deal less conclusive than the authors claim.

picture of one, and we were at a loss to account for his apparent conviction that the word and the occasion were matched in some way that we would surely understand. A few days later a similar outburst occurred, but this time we found the clue. We realised that the wireless was on and that a recording of bird-songs was being played from it. And on the earlier occasion, we now recalled, sparrows had been twittering from the eaves outside the window. Clearly the word 'cow' had been attached by Stephen not to the animals we adults had seen on our walk, but to the whole complex of impressions received on that sunny afternoon, a complex now revived by the recurrence of one element from it. The episode was for me a striking revelation of the terrifying deluge of unstructured sense-impressions which flood in upon the young child, unnamed, unsifted, and still waiting to be sorted out into categories. There is a very real sense in which 'knowing the word for it' enables us to place our sensations within a larger pattern which is systematised and which makes life intelligible.

Not only does the acquisition of language bring intellectual order into the 'buzzing, boooming confusion' of the child's earliest sense-impressions; it also introduces the possibility of ordered control into the child's inner world of impulses and feelings. During the first few years of life the child's hold on reality is still tenuous, but he has a rich phantasy life which is powerfully loaded with emotions, sometimes ecstatic, sometimes terrifying. This world of phantasy is seldom accessible to direct observation, but its existence and nature has been firmly established by psycho-analytical investigation, together with the fact that from the age of five or six it is driven largely underground, to appear thereafter in waking consciousness only in the disguised form of either sublimated achievement or neurotic symptom. A further anecdote may illustrate the role of language in bringing stability to these inner phantasies and in helping the child to reconcile them with his experience of outer reality. One morning when he was about two, Stephen was excessively, and at first inconsolably, frightened by an alarm clock which went off, unexpectedly and very loud, close to his ear. It was remarkable to observe the calming effect which followed when we reminded him of the picture and text of his first story-book, in which the Teddy Bear Coalman had 'a little alarm-clock which woke him early every morning'; in this case the word was able not only to connect the object with a familiar ordered context, but also to indicate and maintain a feeling-attitude towards it.

Because the child acquires his first language at a time when his inchoate emotional life is so vivid and insistent, the feeling-tone which attaches to it is exceptionally powerful and long-lasting. There is, in fact, a magical primitive element in our relationship with language which persists well into adult life. We can observe it at work in our attitude towards swearwords, or in the involuntary relief we feel when the doctor gives a name to our illness, even before we have had any chance to take the medicine he prescribes. Undoubtedly this irrational and semi-magical belief in the power of the word has its realistic component, since words do, in fact, enable us to control and manipulate our environment in manifold practical ways. No less important, however, is the power they give us to control ourselves— to bring order and coherence into the bewildering flux of wishes, impulses, and emotions which would otherwise submerge us. Here, indeed, lies the key to the supreme power of literature; it is able, through its symbolic representations, to insinuate stable forms of organisation into the feeling-aspect of our lives, and so help us maintain a balanced integrity between the conflicting claims of inner and outer reality. There is a discernible continuity of function here (from nursery rhyme through *Treasure Island* to the tragedies of Shakespeare) which, once we have grasped it, permits us to see our work with literature as the culminating aspect of our work in English in no merely arbitrary or accidental sense. All children, whatever their ultimate role in life is to be, need experience of literature; they need the uniquely valuable organisation of experience which is embodied in literature, if their personalities are to expand and flower into a capacity for fullness of living. As Matthew Arnold put it, 'The arts are our storehouse of recorded values. . . . In consequence there is a necessary relationship between the quality of the individual's response to art and his general fitness for a humane existence.'

The child's development of language is, then, very closely bound up with his whole development as a thinking and experiencing human being. Moreover, this power to participate through language in the accumulated experience of the human race is very far from being merely a mechanical or intellectual skill, and the process of acquiring it is no mere matter of habit-formation. It is proper to stress that the child's mother-tongue is, in fact, acquired rather than deliberately learned. It is 'picked up', for the most part unconsciously, by an intuitive process of assimilation, imitation and adaptation; and it is also 'picked up' for the most part outside school.

This is undeniably true of the spoken language, for the normal five-year-old comes to school already able to understand and employ almost all the common structures of his native language, together with a very considerable vocabulary. And even during his school years the lessons concerned directly with his reading, writing and speaking form only a tiny fraction of his total experience of the language, for this continues to expand and develop at many other times—during other kinds of lesson, in the playground, in the street, in the home. The English child, in fact, acquires far the greater part of his mastery of the English language *outside* English lessons, so that it would be wholly misleading to think of English teaching as concerned with implanting in him a hitherto non-existent skill or congerie of skills. No, the true task of English teaching is to help children to refine, polish, raise to a higher level of sensitivity, effectiveness and precision a language which they already possess in a highly developed form.

From this follows the key-principle of which all that follows will be an elaboration. The main business of the English teacher is not instruction in any direct sense, nor even teaching in the sense which may be applicable in some other subjects. It is the provision of abundant opportunity for the child to use English under the conditions which will most conduce to improvement; opportunity, that is, to use his mother-tongue in each of its four modes (listening, speaking, reading and writing) and for all the varied purposes (practical, social, imaginative, creative) which make up its totality; opportunity moreover to use it under expert guidance and in situations which will develop ultimately his power to be self-critical about his own efforts.

English, then, is central to the child's all-round growth towards maturity and its true objectives can be achieved only when his whole personality is involved, on a more than superficial level, in the activities of the English lesson. In English, therefore, even more than in any other subject, it is a *sine qua non* for the teacher that he should understand his pupils in depth, sympathise with their needs and aspirations, and be perceptively aware of their individual rhythms of growth and development. Of course good teachers have always recognised the central importance of knowing and understanding the children they teach, and it remains true now as ever that the kind of understanding which really counts is that which the teacher can gain only in the course of his intimate day-to-day contacts with his own pupils. Nevertheless, if his observation of individual children is to be comprehensive, accurate and unprejudiced, it needs to take place within a soundly conceived theoretical framework; and we are fortunate today in being able to draw for this upon the results of an extensive child-study movement.

As Susan Isaacs put it: 'The practice of education has always rested upon particular views, implied or asserted, as to the nature and course of the normal development of the child. The scientific study of child development for its own sake is nevertheless comparatively recent.' [Isaacs (1935), p. 374.] In the present century our infant schools have been radically transformed by the application of insights derived from this new field of child study; and the revolution has begun to extend upwards to an increasing number of junior schools. Secondary schools, on the other hand, are still slow to recognise the relevance of this work to their own problems, so that it seems advisable at this point to outline briefly the main findings whose implications will frequently be either referred to or assumed in subsequent chapters.

In the first place, systematic study of children has brought home to us more forcefully than ever before the fact that every child is a unique individual. Children of the same age differ enormously from one another in their physical maturity, their general level of ability, their special talents and interests, their personality structure and dominant motivations.[1] What is more the individual child's pattern of development is peculiar to himself alone, and is often markedly erratic, uneven or lopsided; his rate of growth is neither constant nor predictable, for it is liable to be characterised at one time by rapid spurts forward, at others by slow advance, or standstill, or even, in some respects, a slipping-backward. All children, when faced by severe stress from the environment, regress for a time to a less mature level of functioning and behaviour; and no childhood, however sheltered, can escape this altogether.

Yet within the diversity there are also uniformities. Despite the very important individual variations, we know that developmental growth is a continuous process which necessarily follows an orderly sequence. The orderliness of this sequence is often referred to by the term 'maturation'—a concept which underlines our recognition of 'the fact that during the developmental course all children follow a

---

[1] If this seems almost too obvious to need stating, we should ask ourselves whether it is not also one of those truths which are more often assented to than acted upon.

very similar order of development, irrespective of the environment to which they are exposed' [Anderson (1939), p. 16]. To take a very simple instance, we all know that 'no child . . . learns to walk without having first learned to stand, nor does any child speak clearly before he has passed through the babble stage of syllables in language' [Breckenridge and Vincent (1960), p. 11].

Of course in studying human development what we are concerned with is always and necessarily the *interaction* between the child and his environment, so that we must not slip into the error of thinking of development as a kind of 'unfolding' of predetermined innate characteristics. But the term 'maturation' is useful because it enables us to concentrate on the regularities of sequence which seem to be inescapable in all the circumstances and cultures we know of, and so to become aware of the limits within which the influence of the environment (including that deliberately planned environment which we call education) is bound to operate.

Understandably enough, the processes of maturation can be observed most clearly, its sequence traced most confidently, during the early years of childhood where within any given culture the environment differs relatively little from one infant to another. During these early years, it is the child's physical or motor activities that are developing most conspicuously. There seems to be little doubt, however, that similar maturational processes underlie and control the more complex and interdependent social and intellectual skills of later childhood and adolescence. At these later ages it will often be a particular type or amount of experience (rather than a particular level of functioning of nerves or muscles) which is necessary before the child can move on successfully to a new phase of learning. But however subtle and complicated the prerequisites for the new advance, it remains true that for any individual child there comes a particular time when one of his maturing abilities is 'ready' to move on to the next stage in its development;[1] and the importance of this 'readiness'

---

[1] We may speak of 'stages' in specific aspects of the child's development so long as we keep in mind that these stages are not separate discrete 'steps' and that the term is merely a convenient way of distinguishing periods of slow, steady growth from others in which observable growth is rapid or spectacular. There is dispute about the usefulness of the term in some fields, such as that of physical growth, where the data suggest rather a continuous growth rhythm with occasional periods of acceleration. It should be realised also that evidence is as yet lacking for the existence of any *general* stages of development in which the rhythms of growth in different areas (physical, motor, perceptual, cognitive, affective, electrophysiological) could be seen to combine together. See the very interesting interdisciplinary discussions in Tanner and Inhelder (1956a, 1956b, 1958, 1960).

is perhaps the most fundamental contribution which child study has yet made to education. There is a good deal of evidence to show that no advantage is gained in the long run by pressing the child on to the next stage before he *is* ready for it. It seems, in fact, that such premature 'forcing' is one of the most prevalent causes of backwardness and apathy later on. (Clearly much is lost also if the teacher fails to recognise and exploit the unique 'teachable moment' — though it is probable that in this case the ill effects will be neither so long-lasting nor so irremediable.)

Closely bound up with this recognition of the forces making for growth which are inherent in the child's own nature is our deepened realisation that growth for the child is essentially an active and not a passive process.

Even in the years beyond the nursery school age, *the children's own activity* is the key to their full development. Whether we are observing the great need of the child for active movement as a condition of physical growth and of poise and skill, the ways in which he is led out of the narrow circle of his own egoistic desires and naive assumptions about the world, or the situations which provoke thought and reasoning, we are brought back at every point to the view that it is the child's doing, the child's active social experience and his own thinking and talking that are the chief means of his education. The part of his teachers is to call out the child's activity, and to meet it when it arises spontaneously. The school can give children the means of solving problems in which they are actively concerned, but cannot fruitfully foist upon them problems that do not arise from the development of their own living interests in the world. [Isaacs (1935), p. 408.]

The principle of activity, as thus stated, is clearly not to be confused with the cut-and-dried formulae which sometimes go under the title of 'Activity Methods'; nor is it to be supposed that the activity referred to necessarily means physical activity, so that the children need to spend their time running round the class-room performing cartwheels in among the desks. A class of eleven-year-olds listening in hushed and rapt attention to the teacher reading a story may be engaged in an intensely active enlargement of experience; equally the same class busily employed in covering pages of their exercise-books with dictated notes about the parts of speech may be, contrary to all appearances, thoroughly passive and inert as far as any processes of growth and development are concerned. At the centre of any sound conception of English teaching, there must be this awareness that it is the child's own speaking, reading, writing, thinking and experiencing that really matters.

But surely, it is sometimes objected, if we encourage children to be active in ways which they choose for themselves, they will just want to play all the time. There is a deep and disabling misconception here. Child study has shown incontrovertibly that children's play is not a frivolous time-wasting occupation; it is on the contrary one of the central means by which the child extends his growing powers and fits himself ultimately to take his place in the adult world. Thus, in the early years 'the most fertile means of education . . . is the child's own spontaneous play . . . [which] provides the normal means of growth in manipulative skill and imaginative expression, in discovery, thought and reasoning . . .' [Isaacs (1935), p. 407]. And in the same way the play activities for which children show such zest in the later years of childhood – their competitive and team games, their dramatic play, their hobbies – need to be seen as important ways in which they develop their intellectual and imaginative experience, their powers of memory and persistence, and their capacity for social co-operation. Even at the secondary school stage the distinction between play and work (so obvious to most adults) has little real meaning to the child. The fundamental task for the teacher is to take hold of these powerful impulses towards growth and to guide them into the most fruitful channels, both in and out of school.

It is in this context, moreover, that the role of 'interest' in education assumes its true significance. It is no sentimental desire to coddle and indulge children, to protect them from the discomforts of hard work, that leads us to insist that they can learn most effectively and permanently only when their interest is deeply engaged. The fact is that, as Dewey was one of the first to recognise fully, 'Interests are the signs and symptoms of growing powers. . . . Only through the continual and sympathetic observation of childhood's interests can the adult enter into the child's life and see what it is ready for and upon what material it could work most readily and fruitfully' [Dewey (1941), p. 14]. Every teacher has encountered the thirteen- or fourteen-year-old who, though listless and 'lazy' in regard to school 'work', displays an amazing tenacity and retentivity in the pursuit of some chosen interest or hobby – whether it be bird-watching or fishing, making model aeroplanes, or merely the memorising of sports records and cricket averages. We need to enlist this energy in the service of 'lessons' as well as 'out-of-school activities'; and if it is objected that at the secondary level pupils' interests are commonly too trivial and superficial to be utilised in this way, perhaps I may quote an instance which dramatises vividly for me the possibilities which can so easily be overlooked. In his autobiography, Ernest Jones, the doyen of British psycho-analysts, recalls that when he was nearly twelve he developed 'a passionate interest in ciphers'; he even devised one which he was satisfied would baffle any opponent, though admittedly 'it would not have been a very convenient code for purposes of rapid communication, since it involved the interplay of so many sub-ciphers that it took the best part of a day to transcribe a sentence into it'. A common enough craze, one might say, in children of a certain age. Yet for Ernest Jones the absorption was able to transmute itself into a more useful form. Combined with a dawning interest in phonetics, it led him to study Pitman's shorthand; he absorbed the contents of the three Pitman manuals 'in a furor' and to such good effect that after a week he was able to pass the official examination, thus acquiring an accomplishment which he found immensely useful in later life. It is, of course, a tribute to Ernest Jones's quite exceptional gifts that he was able to effect this transmutation for himself. Most children need the hint or nudge of an adult shrewd enough to see where the immediate bent is capable of leading. To centre one's teaching upon transmutations of this kind is neither sentimental nor utopian; it is, essentially, realistic, for there is well-established evidence that strong motivation and keen interest can extend the span of a child's attention and carry him over formidable obstacles and difficulties.

These, then, are the five basic principles on which all my later argument will build: the extent of individual differences, the importance of 'readiness', the principle of activity, the significance of play, and the principle of interest. In the case of older boys and girls our conviction of their centrality needs to be supplemented by awareness of two further factors, one sociological, the other psychological. It is a commonplace that nowadays children aspire to become teen-agers early. (In one of our larger cities recently I watched the queue form for a Saturday morning 'Teen-Agers' Cinema Club', and noticed wryly that few if any of those queuing could have reached even their twelfth birthday.) Once their 'self-concept' has taken on this form, they are exposed immediately to unprecedentedly powerful pressures from the world of mass-communications outside the school. As a consequence the secondary school looms less large in the life of its pupils than it once did; it is now only one agency, one influence, among many, and the values it stands for have to meet an insistent challenge, both overt and covert, from those which crowd in stridently from the supermarket, the record-player, the large and small screen. Few English teachers, in these days, can be unaware of the disruptive force which this conflict can exert.

At the same time the cultural conflict does no more than accentuate certain tensions whose roots are independent of our contemporary social malaise. Despite what the more soothing of our educational psychologists have sometimes urged to the contrary, it seems that adolescence must always bring with it some renewal of tension between child and parent, and, as a reflex of this, between pupil and teacher. Within every boy or girl strong mixed feelings of love and hate towards father and mother were driven underground at the age of five or six, and as an accompaniment of puberty these re-emerge, to be worked through again both at home and at school. Even under the most favourable of circumstances we cannot expect to find in our older secondary pupils the same ready enthusiasm and 'biddableness' which is so characteristic of the primary school age. The fourteen- or fifteen-year-olds may go to school willingly and cheerfully enough; but their appreciation of it is centred not so much round their relations with teachers as round their contacts, in and out of school, with friends of their own age. A certain rebelliousness against adult control, however considerate and kindly; a resistance to adult judgments and valuations, however sensible or wise; an underlying unconscious rivalry with the adult—these are all inevitable at this stage, and they alter inescapably the relationship between pupil and teacher, introducing an acerbity, an element of resentment, which the teacher must learn to accept without being ruffled by it. The expressions of hostility and aggression serve a purpose; they enable the adolescent to free himself, ultimately, from dependence upon adults and to stand on his own feet. The transition can be made less painful to both sides by the more relaxed and friendly atmosphere which is increasingly common in secondary schools nowadays (symbolised, one might say, by the disappearance from most classrooms of the raised teacher's dais). Even so, we need an emotional security and maturity within ourselves if we are to be able consistently to meet this underlying hostility and envy and muted rivalry without excessive feeling—without, in fact, taking it personally. And if my argument has been accepted about the centrality of the mother-tongue in human growth and development, it will be evident that the teacher of English has, at this stage of education, both exceptional opportunities and an exceptional responsibility.

Chapter 2

READING AND LITERATURE

(i)

THE scene is the class-room of a first year form in a grammar school. The book lying open on each desk at page 85 is Masefield's *Jim Davis*. In this school the pupils are not 'streamed' until they enter the second form, so there is a wide range of ability in this class – at the top end of the scale one or two boys who will probably gain an honours degree at a university in due course, at the other end a number who, in another town or county, or given a slightly different turn of luck in the 11-plus examination, might have found themselves in a secondary modern school. Smith, who is reading aloud at the moment, is clearly not one of the abler members of the form. He reads in a listless lack-lustre tone, keeping his head bent anxiously over the page, and bringing out each word as a separate discon-nected unit of sound. When he comes to a long or unfamiliar word, such as 'frigate' or 'stanchion' he halts and mouths to himself silently, trying faint-heartedly to convert letters into sounds. Having reached the end of the paragraph, he lowers his book and looks pointedly at the teacher.

Robinson, the next reader, attacks his stint in a different spirit. He stands with shoulders squared and book held well up in front of him, and his reading comes out in bold ringing tones as a continuous stream of intelligible discourse, uttered with some variety of stress and intonation, if not of pace. But he is inaccurate over the details of his reading, often confuses or transposes unimportant short words, and when he comes to an unusual or difficult word he will miss it out if he can rather than pause over it. At one point instead of the word 'indecisively' ('Extry's hand travelled round for his sheath-knife, and yet it moved indecisively . . .') he says confidently 'indistinctly', and seems surprised when corrected. Before he comes to the end of the page the teacher stops him and guilefully instructs a boy in the back row to 'go on from there'.

This is not the first time that Brown's attention has wandered

during these lessons for he took *Jim Davis* home and read it right
through within the first week of term. When discreet prompting
from his neighbours has enabled him to 'find the place', he reads
with fluency and conviction, entering into the spirit of the passage
with obvious understanding, and dramatising with gusto the conversation between the boy and the smuggler. He seldom mispronounces
or falters over a word, and the teacher so far relents as to allow him to
read a couple of pages.

Now it is Jones' turn, and with him we come back to a quality of
reading-performance more like that of the average first-former. Jones
recognises and pronounces the words quite competently, his reading
proceeds at a fairly adequate pace, and the words flow into one
another in a way that is superficially plausible. But it soon becomes
clear that he is combining the words together in groups which do not
correspond to the demands either of meaning or of punctuation. One
sentence, for instance, comes out like this: 'I thought of Mims
(pause) waiting at home for me and of the jolly tea-table (pause) with
Hoolie begging for toast and Hugh's face (pause) bent over his plate.'

So the lesson proceeds, the pupils 'reading round the class' for
practice, the teacher interrupting at times to correct a mispronuncia-
tion, to ask or explain the meaning of a difficult word, or to say
simply, 'Try reading that sentence again.' At the end of the chapter
he will pause to ask a few questions about the events recounted in it,
to test whether the story has been understood so far, and perhaps to
underline with a brief comment some aspect of characterisation
which they should have noticed but may have missed. Lessons indistinguishable from this one (except that the book may be not *Jim
Davis* but *Treasure Island* or *Tom Sawyer* or *The Wind in the Willows*
or *A Christmas Carol* or even maybe *Robinson Crusoe*) could be
tracked down in almost any grammar school in the country; and the
pattern is commonly much the same for secondary modern forms,
except that here the same level of reading-performance will be
reached on the average two or three terms later, and the children are
more likely to be handicapped by a volume which is not a continuous
story, but an unsatisfying collection of extracts. Obviously a certain
amount is being achieved in such lessons. Everyone gets some practice in reading; the teacher can check up on individual progress (if
any); the book is (in some sense) 'read' by everybody; and (if the
story is any good) the class is probably a good deal less bored than in
many other lessons. Yet I fancy that most teachers must at some

time or other have asked themselves at the end of such a lesson: 'Yes, but . . . is it good enough?'

To answer this question we shall have to make a long detour. Perhaps the first point to be made, however, is the fairly obvious one that a lesson such as this is not concerned merely with a vocal accomplishment of the kind which might safely be entrusted to a speech-training specialist if the school happened to possess one. The fact is that 'oral reading, like silent reading, is essentially a re-thinking of the ideas on the printed page'; the only difference is that the oral reader has the 'additional responsibility to express what he is thinking in such a manner that those who are listening will think with him' [N.S.S.E. (1937), p. 309]. Lessons of the kind described above are properly thought of as 'reading lessons', not as 'reading-aloud lessons'; the stress falls on reading aloud only because at this age this is still the most effective means of developing and improving the children's ability to read in a much broader sense.

But surely, it will be objected, by the time they reach the secondary school children should be able to read. What on earth have the infant and junior schools been about? Things were very different (the objectors are likely to imply) in *our* young days.

As a matter of fact, the principal difference is not in standards of attainment (about which there is in any case very little satisfactory objective evidence which dates back beyond 1938) but in the meaning attached to the term 'able to read'. Fifty or sixty years ago reading was thought of as a fairly elementary mechanical skill; a child could be said to have mastered it when, on being confronted with the appearance of a word in print, he was able to produce the sound of the word aloud. To understand and interpret the meaning of what one read was regarded as a separate and supplementary mental process – not as an essential part of the reading act itself. Since that time a vast amount of experimental study has made this point of view wholly untenable. Reading, we now realise, is above all a 'thought-getting' process, involving at all stages the recognition by the reader of 'the important elements of meaning in their essential relations' [N.S.S.E. (1937), p. 25]. 'Learning to read' has in consequence to be seen as a continuing process which goes on throughout the child's school career, and which sets as its goal the power to read with understanding, appreciation and enjoyment – the power, in fact, to re-create as fully and accurately as possible the experience which lies embodied in the words on the printed page. In many

English lessons in the secondary school the pupil is still engaged largely in extending and refining his ability to read in this full sense of the word; he is applying the ability to more difficult and varied material (including literature), but there is an essential continuity with what has gone before. Thus, for infants and adults alike, reading is not a matter of producing (either aloud or subvocally) the 'sounds of the letters' or even the 'sounds of the words'; it is, on the contrary, a matter of relating printed symbols to the spoken language of which they are in any ultimate analysis a representation. When we read we are engaged in constructing from a series of such symbols a piece of continuous discourse which has meaning for us because we can perceive its resemblance to patterns of spoken language which are already familiar and meaningful. Consequently, in selecting and presenting reading-material for children the first consideration, at all stages, must be its interest—its power to draw forth strong motivation by its close relationship to the reader's most vital concerns and experience. In the best modern approaches to the teaching of reading this now takes precedence over the former preoccupation with presenting a carefully-graded sequence of sound-combinations which could be learnt and mastered a little at a time.

Moreover the experimental study of eye-movements in reading has shown conclusively that the competent reader, whether adult or juvenile, does not read continuously along the line of print, letter by letter—nor even, as a matter of fact, word by word. His eyes move from left to right along the line in a series of short, quick movements each movement being followed by a brief pause during which the eyes are at rest. At each such 'fixation-pause' he recognises words or groups of words as wholes, and how many pauses he makes depends a good deal upon the familiarity of the material, its difficulty, and the degree of interest it excites. Here is an example of an actual record of the eye-movements of a fluent adult reader, taken from Buswell (1937), p. 55. Each vertical line represents the centre of a 'fixation-pause'; the numbers at the top of the line indicate the order in which the fixations were made, and the numbers below show the length of each pause in thirtieths of a second:

<pre>
|1 |2 |3
Afte|r the war he gave t|he negro a little ho|use on
|9 |7 |5
</pre>

The less capable reader makes a greater number of pauses (the number may range from four to ten along a line of ordinary length), and he may also make some backward movements of the eye in order to pick up the meaning of words which he failed to recognise at the first attempt. In general, however, it is clear that the mature reader recognises most words instantaneously, and not by specific identification of each letter. Experimental studies have also shown that the pattern of expectation built up by the meaning of what is read offers the normal reader many short cuts to the recognition of individual words—so much so that a word which has been printed in an incomplete or distorted form can usually be read without any apparent difficulty or hesitation, so long as it occurs in a meaningful context. (Anyone who has wrestled to decipher illegible handwriting knows how much depends on getting the general sense of what the writer is likely to be saying; while it is well known that a major obstacle to efficient proof-reading is the tendency of the mind to supply the letters which *ought* to be there rather than those which the eyes actually perceive.) A sound approach to the teaching of reading seeks therefore to establish, from the beginning, habits of eye-movements along the line of print which are similar to those used by mature readers. It does this by using words which are already part of the child's own spoken vocabulary, by presenting them in complete sentences or meaning-units, and by ensuring that the pattern of these sentences seems idiomatic and natural to the child. At the same time the good infant teacher encourages the child from the beginning to make full use of meaning-clues from the context as an aid to identifying and recognising the words which are read. These clues may be contained in the pictures or situations to which the early sentences are attached, or they may be inherent in the emerging pattern of the story which is being read—a pattern which is often, for that matter, already familiar through previous tellings or readings.

It remains true, however, that when a reader (even a mature reader) meets new and unfamiliar words he must as a rule pause and attend to their details. An intelligent use of meaning-clues from the context is an important weapon of attack in dealing with such words, but it often has to be supplemented by the ability to break down the new words into its constituent parts, to perceive analogies with the shape and form of words already known and to utilise phonic analysis and synthesis in order to build up the word's probable sound-equivalent. Thus an understanding of sound-letter relationships (commonly known as 'phonics') is an essential element in learning to read, even though it is not, as was once thought, the whole story; and no child can complete the process of learning to read without mastering the system of correspondence (highly irregular in English) between written letters and groups of letters on the one hand, and spoken sounds or phonemes on the other. Complex though this system is, highly intelligent children often succeed in 'getting the hang of it' intuitively, without any systematic training. It is generally agreed, however, that the majority of children need planned and sustained guidance through its intricacies; what is still controversial is the stage at which such guidance can be given most effectively. While most infant teachers continue to supply it in small doses from the very beginning, others have found that many children make better and surer progress in the long run if training in phonics is deferred for some considerable time.

This is perhaps the point at which to stress my own conviction that the concept of 'readiness' has an importance in the teaching of reading which extends far beyond the initial stage. It has, of course, long been recognised that before a child can tackle the beginnings of reading successfully he needs to have reached a certain level of maturity in several directions. He needs, for instance, to be able to talk fluently and listen attentively, and to have had considerable experience of handling books and of being read to from them; his intelligence and powers of concentration, and his acuteness of sight and hearing must also have developed to the requisite degree. Moreover it is now widely admitted that individual differences are such that there is no single age at which all children can be assumed to be ready to begin reading. In consequence fairly elaborate formal tests of 'reading readiness' have been devised, and these are often found to give helpful guidance to the infant teacher; more frequently, perhaps, the teacher uses her own informal observations to gauge whether or not any particular child has reached the needed degree of maturity. The proved value of such careful attention to 'readiness' (accompanied where necessary by class activities which help to promote readiness) is well summed up by W. S. Gray when he writes:

It may seem on first thought that to delay the teaching of reading is a waste of time. Experiments show on the contrary that pupils who receive needed preparation more than make up the time devoted to it by the greater progress made later in learning to read; forcing a child to learn to read before he is ready usually results in confusion, failure, and a hostile attitude towards reading. [Gray (1956), p. 129.]

However, as was indicated in the previous chapter, maturation (with its corollary of 'readiness') is an aspect of human growth at all stages, and is not confined merely to those early phases in which its operation is most readily observable. And once we see learning to read as a single continuing process, we begin to perceive also that the process has its own orderly sequence of stages through which all children have to pass – in their own good time. There is naturally no sharp line of demarcation between these stages; inevitably they overlap and merge into one another. Nevertheless the experts' attempts to define them have revealed a fairly wide measure of agreement about their general nature: and W. S. Gray's summary statement [Gray (1956), Chapter VII] can be taken as sufficiently representative. The first stage (already referred to above) he describes as that of 'Preparing for Reading . . . the period during which children acquire the first-hand experiences and receive the training that prepares them to learn to read eagerly and with reasonable ease – the period before schooling begins until systematic training in reading begins'. The second stage, which would at one time have been thought of as the 'Reading Primer' stage, Gray refers to as that of 'Learning to read very simple material'. Within this stage he identifies at least three successive tasks which face the teacher: first, to establish initial reading attitudes and habits; second, to enable the children 'to engage in continuous understanding reading of very simple material' (i.e. within a vocabulary range of some 150 words) 'with a limited amount of teacher guidance'; third, to develop independence in reading until the children 'are able to read simple material independently with real interest in the content, and begin to engage in some self-initiated reading'. By the end of this stage children usually have acquired a reading vocabulary of about 300 words; and at some point during it they have been introduced to the basic principles of phonic analysis. At one time it would have been expected that all children should be ready to make the transition from the second to the third stage when they move from the infant to the junior school at the age of seven. In theory at least we are aware now that individual differences in children's rates of growth make this expectation wholly unrealistic; but in practice there may still occur at this point a sharp discontinuity of teaching approach which can be harmful to the confidence and future progress of many children. The third stage is certainly, however, most characteristically associated with the period spent in the English Junior School; according to Gray it lasts typically for about two years, and has as its aim the achievement of 'rapid progress in mastering the basic attitudes and skills involved in fluent, thoughtful silent reading and good oral reading'. By the end of it the number of words recognised quickly at sight should have increased to about 2,000, and the child should be.able to recognise and pronounce independently any new word that is within his speaking vocabulary. The fourth stage Gray describes as that of 'acquiring more mature reading interests and habits': it has also been referred to as the period of 'wide reading to extend and enrich experience'.[1] Its essential feature is that the child is now able, to a very large extent, to 'stand on his own feet' in his reading. He is able to read silently to himself 'real books' at a level of difficulty appropriate to his own emotional and intellectual maturity, and it is of the utmost importance that he should *want* to do so; for henceforth his progress in reading, and his consolidation of the ability so far acquired, will come mainly from extensive private reading carried on with very little direct help or guidance from a teacher. In the course of this independent silent reading he will be widening his experience far beyond the scope of that which he has either seen, talked about, or heard talked about; and in consequence he will at the same time be continually widening his vocabulary. He needs therefore not only to be able to understand familiar words when they are used in a new or unfamiliar sense; he needs also to be able to deal in his reading with words (often quite long words, at that) which are wholly unfamiliar to him, though we must not of course expect him to cope with too many of these at any one time.

We are now ready to return (at last) to the first-year grammar school class with whom the chapter opened. We can see now that some of these twelve-year-old boys are already securely launched upon the fourth stage of reading progress. Their reading is competent and fluent enough to meet the demands that will henceforth be made upon it by lessons and homework in many of the different secondary school subjects, and they can (and do) read books such as *Jim Davis* on their own with sufficient understanding to give real enjoyment. Others, however, are still lagging behind in varying degrees, largely because their previous environment, both at home and at school, has

[1] N.S.S.E. (1925), Chapter III. See also N.S.S.E. (1937), Chapter IV.

not supplied the opportunity and motive for sufficient practice. They are not yet ready therefore to enter upon the stage of independent silent reading with confidence or with a good prospect of attaining real mastery of the medium; and it is clear that the over-riding task of the English teacher is to bring these boys to the point where they *are* thus ready. His first objective must in fact be to ensure that *all* members of his class are both able and willing to go away and read, let us say, *Treasure Island* (in the original and not in a 'comic strip' version) 'under their own steam'.

Although the immediate goal for these pupils is the ability to undertake silent reading effectively, it remains true that the approach to this goal must be through practice in reading aloud. The teacher is compelled to concentrate on reading aloud at this stage because only thus can he obtain close contact with that process of 're-thinking the ideas on the printed page' which constitutes the essence of the reading-act, and thereby gain the power to affect and influence it. We must insist, however, that the traditional type of lesson in which the book is 'read around the class', each individual pupil reading aloud a few paragraphs at a time, is far from satisfactory — for two reasons. In the first place, the amount of practice it affords is woefully inadequate. Even for the pupil who is most in need of practice there will seldom be time to read more than a couple of paragraphs a week; if the class is large his turn is more likely to come round once a fortnight. From this point of view alone such lessons can be justified only as a means of testing and not as a method of teaching. Secondly (and this is even more important), this type of lesson is distressingly inimical to interest in what is being read. The frequent interruptions prevent any sense of continuous development in the story, and the very mixed level of reading achievement (some of it inevitably halting, toneless, and uncomprehending) excludes any real feeling of involvement on the part of the listening audience. Most teachers will be aware of the danger of thus producing an apathetic or even hostile attitude towards the book in question — and also, it may be, towards reading in general. What is less often recognised is the extent to which the reading assignment itself is at the same time made more difficult. In fact, however, a growing involvement in the developing pattern of meaning does much to smooth the way for all of us whenever we read continuous material of any kind. As we enter into the story or the argument of what we read, we become increasingly aware of the author's drift, of what he is *likely* to be saying next; the context of what we have read so far builds up its own pattern of expectations, in the light of which we are able, as we read on, to narrow down the range of possible interpretations of what comes next, to leap to the right alternative where alternatives offer, to supply the probable or necessary meaning of words, phrases or constructions which would be obscure to us if we encountered them in isolation. The context itself is thus a powerful aid in all reading, and children (at this stage in particular) need to be encouraged to take from it all the help they possibly can. The wise teacher therefore is concerned to foster interest at all costs, and he can do this in the first place by organising the reading in ways which establish the context as firmly as possible, at the same time building up in the class as a whole the sense of being 'inside the story'.

When planning the first-form lessons with this aim in mind the teacher has three well-tried procedures at his disposal.

Firstly, the teacher himself may read aloud while the class follow in their books. If he reads reasonably well (and it goes without saying that every teacher of English *must* train himself to read well), this mode of reading will do fuller justice to the material than is possible in any other way, and it is therefore particularly valuable as a 'lead-in' at the beginning of a lesson or when embarking on a new book. It may also be the only satisfactory way of dealing with the occasional passage or chapter which, for one reason or another, is really above the class's capabilities; the chapter in *The Wind in the Willows* entitled 'Dulce Domum' comes to mind as an obvious example. Quite apart from its beneficial effect on interest, however, this procedure does more for the pupils than is sometimes realised. As they follow the line of print with the eye while simultaneously listening to the voice of a good reader converting the print to meaningful sound, they are participating in the act of reading at only one remove. The reader's grouping of words, phrases and clauses, the instinctive modulations of his voice, the patterns of intonation, stress and rhythm which he imposes on the words, all provide a guide and model for that interpretation of the thought behind the print which the pupil has to learn to accomplish for himself; thus the 're-thinking' which is indicated by the sound of the voice reading aloud begins gradually to be transferred to the pupil's silent reading of the printed word.

Secondly, those sections of the story in which dialogue occurs can be given a dramatised or semi-dramatised reading in which different pupils read the parts of the various characters, while yet another pupil acts as narrator. It is not usually appropriate to carry the dramatisation very far at this stage, since the readers will probably need to concentrate all their attention on the words; but it is often helpful to have the readers out in front of the class where their voices will be heard more easily and where their grouping (roughly according to the requirements of the situation in the story) can make identification easier and suggest some of the relationships between the characters. It will in any case be necessary to train the readers to omit the recurring 'he said' and 'she replied' which can so easily become both distracting and ludicrous; and the role of the narrator will call for a fluent reader with a fair amount of mental agility. Once these difficulties have been overcome, this method of reading has the advantage not only of bringing the scene alive but also of supplying a strong motive for each reader to give his words their true value – to interpret them with understanding and to combine and shape them in the way which brings out their full meaning.[1] In addition, the bits of dialogue are usually fairly short and relatively simple and idiomatic in their construction, so that they are likely to be suitable material for the more inexperienced readers to try their skill on.

Thirdly, some passages may be read in unison by groups of children, or even by the class as a whole. This has the advantage of providing practice for many more children; on the other hand, it can sometimes have an adverse effect upon interest, particularly if the groups are large and the resultant reading tends to degenerate into a monotonous singsong. The best results are usually obtained with groups of about five or six; it is not too difficult for a group of this size to keep in step with each other, and at the same time each individual feels that his own voice is making a necessary and significant contribution to the total volume of sound. (The purely mechanical difficulty of 'keeping together' can also be reduced if the group stand close together in a small semicircle, at the side or front of the classroom; the teacher may sometimes find it helpful to join in reading alongside the children until the group begin to establish their own tempo.) The full value of this method becomes apparent when the

[1] One instance from *Lorna Doone*. John Ridd is impudently pleading for a chance to ride the highwayman's horse: 'Only trust me with her, and I will not over-ride her,' to which Faggis replies, 'For that I will go bail, my son. She is like to over-ride thee.' This last sentence calls for a dual stress (on both 'she' and 'thee'); at this level, grasp of meaning is intimately bound up with grasp of 'the way it should be said'. The virtue of the dramatised reading is that it brings the issue out into the open and gives the pupil both the opportunity and the incentive to get it right.

teacher knows his class well enough to arrange the groups so that each contains a mixed level of reading ability: the lead given by the more competent readers can then help the weaker members of the group to surmount difficulties which they would stumble over on their own, and can enable them to gain a good deal in confidence and fluency under cover of the co-operative effort. For the less able reader, reading in unison is in fact a useful intermediate stage between following in the book while someone else reads and the more exacting responsibility of reading aloud on his own. It is seldom advisable, however, to keep on with this method of reading for very long at a stretch; and it is important to confine its use to material which is really suited to it. Just which kind of prose passage *is* suitable is not at all easy to determine—at any rate in the abstract; as a rough guide I would suggest experimenting in the first instance with passages in which the children's interest and enjoyment seem likely to be at their most intense and in which the sentences are neither unduly long nor unduly complicated in structure.

It should be evident that each of these three procedures has its own characteristic merits and advantages, and the judicious teacher will therefore try to ring the changes on them as much as possible. He will often, in fact, want to incorporate all three within the same lesson, though naturally bearing in mind that different kinds of material lend themselves to different methods of reading. In any case in planning a lesson of this kind, a main aim must be to ensure that the reading brings out and enhances the meaning of what is read; this means, for one thing, that the pauses in continuity which occur when changing over from one reader or one method of reading to another should be kept to a minimum, and that when they are inevitable we should make sure that they fall at a natural break in the narrative.

As an instance of the kind of lesson-plan which these principles would lead us to adopt, we may turn again to Chapter IX of *Jim Davis*. Here the teacher might read the first two paragraphs (pages 85–86) to get the lesson started with a swing, after which the next four pages can be read 'in character' by three boys selected and detailed beforehand to read the speech of Jim, Marah and Extry, assisted by another boy acting as 'narrator'. This should give a largely uninterrupted reading as far as page 90. The brief episode (pages 90–92) of the signing and witnessing of smugglers' articles might then be given a more thorough-going dramatisation, with the

35

smugglers in front of the class suiting their actions to the words; after which the chapter's three final paragraphs could be read in unison by one of the groups. (They are not perhaps so obviously suitable for group reading as some parts of the two succeeding chapters which deal with the fight at sea, but they will probably serve the purpose adequately, all the same.)

I have already stressed that an overriding aim in reading-lessons at this stage must be to foster an attentive absorption in the content of what is read. This is done in the first instance by organising the reading-aloud in a way which realises as vividly as possible the experience embodied in the printed words while at the same time giving as many pupils as possible the kind of reading practice which they need. Can the teacher do more than this? I am convinced that he both can and should—by a limited amount of questioning of a kind which leads the children further 'inside the story'. The questions need to be strictly limited in number, since frequent interruptions can easily impede the flow of the narrative and prevent it from developing a cumulative hold upon the pupils' imagination. They must be confined also to central issues ('the important elements of meaning in their essential relations') and should never dwell upon detail which has only marginal significance for a grasp of the story as a whole. Such questions are properly conceived not as tests of understanding, but as aids to understanding; they are designed to draw attention to important aspects of meaning which may have been overlooked or misunderstood, and thereby to help the pupils build up for themselves a fuller and more vivid imaginative re-creation of the author's experience. Since they are to be valued not as a backward glance over what has already been read but rather as an aid to the fuller understanding of what is yet to be read, the proper place for them is usually at selected points during the reading of a chapter rather than at the end of it.

To illustrate the kind of question which can be useful in this way we may turn again to the same chapter from *Jim Davis*. We might interrupt the conversation between Jim and Marah at the top of page 89 to ask why Jim has now become so dangerous to the smugglers, and, following on from this, why Marah 'couldn't let him go even if he wanted to'. The answers to these questions, so long as they are suitably backed up by reference to the nature of the secret Jim has discovered and the ways in which Marah fears he might be induced to give it away, should bring out the situation clearly enough, as well as indicating Marah's position of limited authority among the smugglers. It might also be worth while to give a firmer shape to the impressions the class should have gained of the character of Marah and his apparently mixed attitude towards the boy; and this could be achieved by asking (preferably during the pause occasioned by a change in the method of reading at the end of Marah's private conversation with Jim) whether they think Marah was sincere when he said (p. 87), 'I'm going to talk to you like a father.' Apart from these questions there is little in this chapter of central importance to the story which a first-form should not be able to take in sufficiently for themselves — and there is no point whatever in asking questions merely for the sake of asking them.

It will be noticed that while the questions I have recommended do require the class to look again at the exact meaning of some important sentences or phrases, they are not concerned primarily with the meaning of difficult words. It is true that a reader's ability to grasp the meaning of a passage as a whole depends on his ability to attach meaning to the individual words in it; but this should not mislead us into thinking that he needs to know the precise meaning of every word before he can understand the passage satisfactorily. In reality the main way in which we all learn to understand new words is by meeting them in a context of use. We hear the new word used for the first time in conversation, or we see it in the course of our reading, in company with a number of other words to which we can already attach meaning. From the sense of these surrounding words and from the occasion on which they are spoken, or from their position in the story or the argument in the case of a piece of written English, we are able to form an impression of the meaning to be attached to the new word. Of course, the first time we encounter the word, perhaps the first few times even, our impression of its meaning may be vague and imprecise. Only after we have heard or seen a word used a number of times can we feel at all certain of the exact shade of meaning it has on any particular occasion. The point is, however, that we can and do learn the meaning of a great many new words in the course of our reading simply by taking notice of the clues or pointers to their meaning which are contained in the context; and this habit of reasoning from the context is the mode of attack upon unfamiliar words which the twelve-year-old pupil needs above all to develop in the phase of wide reading upon which he is just entering. Moreover the process is most characteristically one of *gradual* differentiation of meaning—a movement through stages of loosely-defined vagueness towards an increasing exactness and precision. Take for instance the word 'frigate' in the opening sentence of our chapter from *Jim Davis*: 'The inner room was much larger than the prison chamber; it was not littered with boxes, but clean and open like a frigate's lower deck.' The pupils to whom this is a completely new word may well need to be shown how to pronounce it (since it is one of those words, so frequent in English, in regard to which 'phonic training' doesn't help much); but as far as its meaning is concerned he should have no difficulty in inferring from the sentence itself that a frigate is a particular type of ship, probably a fairly large one since it has more than one deck. And surely this is all he needs to know, as far as this immediate use of the word goes. Is it really worth stopping the lesson (almost before it has got started) to send the class to their pocket dictionaries to learn that a frigate is 'A large type of fast sailing-ship used in war before introduction of steam; next in size to ships of the line, carrying about 25 to 50 guns; corresponding in type and function to modern cruiser'? The information has its value and interest, undoubtedly, but are these relevant to our present purpose of reading *Jim Davis* with understanding and enjoyment? I believe we may state as a general, indeed an invariable, principle that during reading-lessons in the early stages of the secondary school the teacher should *never* ask a question upon the meaning of an individual word *unless* that meaning is essential to a grasp of the total pattern of meaning of the passage in which it occurs. Otherwise such questions can all too easily get in the way of the main aim of the lesson, which must be to establish as firmly as possible the pattern of the context as a whole so that this in turn may serve as a framework and support to facilitate the interpretation of subsequent difficult words. Of course the experienced teacher will know well enough how to avoid the more extreme forms which such distraction *might* take; he won't, for instance, allow a question upon the meaning of 'frigate' to develop into a lengthy dissertation (complete with blackboard diagrams in different-coloured chalks) upon the shape, size and rig of different types of sailing-ship. And if he is at all qualified to teach English, his questioning will reflect his awareness that what we are concerned with is in any case the meaning of the word in its own particular context, here and now, and not with the pursuit of that abstract and usually unreal figment which we may term 'the dictionary meaning'. All the same he may often need to be on his guard against a misplaced conscientiousness in his dealings with individual words – misplaced because the degree of definiteness and exactitude which he is tempted to insist upon is not appropriate to the stage of linguistic development which the children are at.

For I must emphasise that I have no wish to belittle the importance of exact and sensitive response to details and shades of meaning as an *ultimate* objective of reading progress. Such precision belongs, however, to a comparatively late stage in the development of the individual pupil. And so far as the meaning of any particular word is concerned, it also belongs properly to a comparatively late stage in his acquaintance with it and not to the first time of meeting it.

I am not suggesting either that the dictionary has no part to play in this; to give them training in the intelligent use of a dictionary is indeed one of the ways in which we can help secondary school children to get along successfully 'on their own' in reading. But the right way to use a dictionary is not to fly to its aid every time one encounters a new word. (How many adults, how many English teachers even, would do this themselves? In any case a dictionary consulted in this way is only too often likely to be either unhelpful or positively misleading.) When we meet an unfamiliar word (or, for that matter, a familiar word used with an unfamiliar connotation) the proper course is to use all the possible clues that can be gleaned both from the context and (by analogy with other known words) from the shape and form of the word itself, in order to deduce the probable meaning in this instance. Only when we have done this (and even then only if we still have cause to feel uncertain) should we turn to a dictionary for confirmation of our deductions. The English teacher has a responsibility for helping his pupils to form sound habits of this kind, and he needs to be aware of the true nature of this responsibility from the beginning.

(ii)

Given the right kind of help and encouragement, most boys and girls should have entered upon the stage of 'wide reading to extend and enrich experience' well before the end of the first year in the grammar school or of the second year in the secondary modern school. Once this has been achieved, their independent silent reading outside school hours becomes much the most important factor in their reading progress – and also, indeed, in the growth of their command of language in general.

The reading habits and tastes of children around these ages have been extensively studied, particularly in the United States, although unfortunately none of the large-scale surveys are at all recent.[1] To bring the picture up to date we have to fill it out with information taken from a number of local studies of relatively small groups of children which may or may not be representative.[2] This gap is perhaps less serious than it at first sounds, since on the most important issues there is a notable congruence in the findings of the many inquiries conducted at varying dates in different parts of the English-speaking world. Thus Jordan, for instance, found that although the most popular authors change from one decade to the next, the characteristic features of their books remain much the same; and subsequent studies seem to have confirmed this.

On some important issues, however, the evidence remains far too fragmentary. In the first place, how extensive is children's leisure-time reading in the nineteen-sixties? Is it true that the advent of television has reduced it alarmingly? All earlier surveys have found children reading a great deal between the ages of ten and fifteen — far more, in most cases, than they will read at any subsequent period of their lives. Jenkinson, in 1940, recorded grammar school boys as reading on average between sixty and seventy books a year, while grammar school girls read between seventy and eighty — all this in addition to their reading of newspapers, magazines and comics. His sample of senior elementary school children was unfortunately a biased one, containing far too high a proportion of A stream pupils; within this sample he recorded boys as reading an average of fifty books a year, and girls an average of sixty. There can be no doubt that children today are reading very much less than this; the only question is how much less. There is reason to think that grammar school pupils have been those least seriously affected, and it is likely that in their case we should not be far out if we reduced Jenkinson's figures by about one-fifth. The trend in the secondary modern school is much more difficult to pin down, since the amount read by these pupils seems to vary enormously from one area to another and from one school to another. It is still possible to find the secondary modern with a well-stocked library and a tradition of taking seriously the

[1] See for the United States, Terman and Lima (1925), Washburne and Vogel (1926), Jordan (1926), and Lazar (1937); for Great Britain, Jenkinson (1940); and for New Zealand, Scott (1947).

[2] I have drawn in particular upon: Black and Schofield (1958); Stewart (1960); Percival (1963); Butts (1963); and Lawrence (1964).

encouragement of out-of-school reading, where the A stream read between thirty and forty books a year and the B stream between twenty and thirty; there are other schools where the teachers would find it difficult to point to a single pupil who reads as much as this. In fact, despite the improved standards of reading ability documented in the Newsom Report, it seems clear that there is a substantial minority of secondary school children who never put this ability to any use of their own outside school hours. For the most part these non-readers belong to families of 'addicted viewers' in which it is habitual to spend upwards of twenty hours a week with the television set tuned in to the I.T.V. programme; according to Abrams (1961) this group constitutes about one-third of all families possessing a television set.

But although the main cause of the decline in children's reading over the past fifteen or twenty years has undoubtedly been the introduction of commercial television in 1955, followed by the rapid advent of the television set into almost every home, other social changes over the same period have also contributed. Thus there are some indications that children's reading now falls off markedly in amount around the age of thirteen or fourteen – the very age at which boys and girls tend to diverge from the family pattern of viewing and indeed to watch less television than at earlier ages. The relevant factor here may well be the large proportion of spare time which young adolescents now devote to gregarious social activities – a change accentuated artificially by the current teen-age cult, but associated also with the long-term trend towards earlier sexual maturity. Perhaps, too, the early-maturing fourteen-year-old finds it less easy nowadays to come upon books which match his (or her) continuing emotional immaturity while at the same time satisfying the evident wish to feel grown-up. More positively, on the other hand, we can note a number of changes which must surely have worked to keep the decline in check – the vastly improved provision by school and public libraries, the increased availability of well-produced and plentifully-illustrated informational books written in easy language, the abundance of cheap paper-back editions.

When these uncertainties have been allowed for, we can conveniently present the present state of our knowledge in the form of four imaginary 'profiles' – composite portraits which are based not merely on personal observation but also for the most part on well-authenticated research evidence.

Let us take first the case of John Smith, a boy of average ability who is in the 'A' stream of a small but well-run secondary modern school. Although there is a television set in the living room at home, and although he spends an hour and a half or more sitting in front of it every evening, he manages nevertheless to do a good deal of reading in his leisure time. Throughout his school career he buys at least one 'comic' every week, and sees several others which are passed round among his friends. But he also reads a very considerable number of books—on an average about three a month over the period of four years he spends in the secondary school. Most of these books he borrows from the school library or from the junior section of the local public library, for he possesses few books of his own. The over-whelmingly greater proportion of them are works of fiction; most of them are stories written specially for children, and not many of them are by authors whom his English teacher at school has ever heard of. If this teacher were to sample a few of these books himself (as he certainly ought to do), he would find that, although the titles and authors are different, the type of story they contain is very similar, in most respects, to those which he himself read at the same age. Even in terms of topic and setting, many of the popular books of today are not so very different from those which were in vogue twenty-five or thirty years ago. Thus at the age of twelve John Smith spent a good deal of his time reading stories about boys of his own age, and their exploits either at school or during school holidays. For the next couple of years he occupied himself mainly with adventure stories of various kinds—stories about pirates and smugglers, about explorers in remote and savage parts of Africa or South America, or about sheriffs, cowboys and frontiersmen. At one stage during these years his reading was drawn very largely from the Biggles series; at another time his visits to the public library were taken up with searching the shelves for stories about space travel. Later, as he drew near to the end of his school career, his interests turned more towards crime and detective stories, and he was also affected by the current craze for the more sensational kind of 'real adventure' story about the Second World War, many examples of which he could see prominently dis-played, in cheap paper-backed editions, in a nearby newsagent's shop. Though these were not strictly fiction (or at any rate not avowedly so) John clearly read them very much as though they were. At the same age, however, he also began for the first time to read a significant proportion of books which could only be classed as 'non-fiction'; most of these were technical in nature, and many of them had to do with his own particular hobby or special interest, which happened to be motor-cycles and motor-cycle racing. When he left school and started work at the age of fifteen-and-a-half, his reading dwindled almost to nothing. At present he still borrows a book occasionally from the public library during the winter months; but already many of his friends at work never read a line of print outside the *Daily Mirror, Reveille* and the *T.V. World.*

John's cousin George is a pupil at the local grammar school. He reads more than John (in spite of television he has read an average of about fifty books a year for the past five years), but the books he favours are very similar indeed. He reads a little more non-fiction than John, but not very much. The stories and novels he enjoys include rather more by authors whose names mean something to his English teacher (he has been enthusiastic at different times about Arthur Ransome, Stevenson, Buchan, Rider Haggard, Conan Doyle and H. G. Wells); but his reading is extremely variable in quality, and he is just as likely to be found absorbed in an undistinguished and ephemeral boys' book which his teacher would condemn roundly as 'trash'. In general George has been attracted to very much the same type of story as John, but at an earlier age: so that he was already reading at twelve many of the books which were popular with his less gifted cousin at thirteen or thirteen-and-a-half. Now that he is sixteen George too is reading much less than in the past; in his case this seems to be due mainly to the increased amount of time he has to spend on homework during the G.C.E. year.

John's sister Joan also goes to a secondary modern school. She reads a good deal more than her brother; in fact, in amount (though not in quality) her reading does not fall so very far short of her cousin's. Whereas neither of the boys would ever condescend to read a book written specially for girls, Joan has at various times read quite a number of adventure stories intended mainly for boys, though she has always been inclined to prefer those which offer not only excitement but also a certain amount of romantic and sentimental interest as well. When she first entered the secondary school her taste ran towards stories about children of her own age, and for a time she showed an insatiable appetite for Enid Blyton's 'Five' series. At about this age she was also much drawn towards stories about animals, especially those about horses or dogs. Later, in addition to joining with her brother in reading about pirates and smugglers, spies and airmen, she would seek out less violent but by no means uneventful stories dealing with home and family life. She has always been more ready than either of the boys to return again to her favourite books, and she has reread *Little Women* three or four times. Now that she is approaching the end of her school career, she has turned to fiction that is more adult in theme though not always, it must be admitted, particularly adult in treatment. Love stories and romantic novels now claim a good deal of her attention, and she has a standing weekly order with her newsagent for two 'love-comics', *Valentine* and *Mirabelle*. She also reads a certain number of girls' career novels, even though she has no serious expectation of ever herself taking up the occupation of air hostess, veterinary surgeon, physiotherapist, or whatever it may be.

Joan has an elder sister, Marjorie, who went to the local girls' high school. She has always read even more extensively than either her sister or her cousin, averaging some sixty books a year between the ages of ten and fifteen. The development of her tastes at different ages followed a pattern similar to that which we have observed in Joan, but was usually a year or more in advance of it. She read more boys' books than Joan, and she showed some liking for historical novels. When her interests turned, at the age of fourteen or fifteen, towards more adult topics she showed a readiness to become absorbed in some of the 'classics' of English fiction (Charlotte Brontë, Dickens and Hardy, for instance) – particularly if the novel in question had recently been adapted in a radio, television or film version. She also read at this age a certain amount of adult fiction by contemporary 'middlebrow' novelists, and a number of detective stories. Non-fiction has not at any time formed a significant proportion of the reading of either of the girls.

What then are the characteristics of the books which really appeal to these children? What qualities do they, in common with other children of the same age-range, look for (even, one might say, insist upon) in the reading they choose for themselves when adult pressure or dictation is absent? The various experts who have made a serious attempt to study children's reading-preferences at first hand give answers to these questions which are remarkably consistent in their main outlines. The most popular books are invariably fiction. They contain plenty of fast-moving action and are marked by vivid dramatic presentation. The story is told in a straightforward way, and its progress is not held up by long paragraphs of description of scenes or characters or by detailed analysis of feelings and motives. Instead, the characters are established incidentally in the course of recounting what they do or say. (It is significant that the commonest adverse comments upon an unpopular book are 'too much description', 'not enough action' or 'not enough conversation'.) The characters themselves are presented in terms of a clear-cut and conventional 'black-and-white' morality, the sympathetic ones being unequivocally 'good' while the unsympathetic are unmistakably 'bad'. This is not to deny that the hero or heroine may have some faults, usually of a minor kind, or that there may be an occasional character (Long John Silver, for instance) who excites mixed and ambivalent feelings; but such complexities need to be the exception rather than the rule. The hero or heroine is normally a young person, not very far removed in age from the readers themselves. Any moralising is implicit rather than obtrusive, but the moral atmosphere in general is simple and straightforward, avoiding anything which might disturb the young reader's conventionally-accepted views of right and wrong. It is perhaps as a corollary of this that a happy ending, in which virtue is finally triumphant, seems to be almost indispensable.

What leads children to seek out and prefer books which satisfy these conditions? Here, naturally, we move on to more doubtful ground. Even so, it seems fairly clear that a major motive (probably one should really say *the* major motive) is the desire to obtain vicarious imaginative satisfaction of a wish-fulfilment kind – satisfaction primarily, that is, of wishes and impulses that are denied outlet in current day-to-day living. As Terman and Lima put it: 'The child does not read, as the adult does, for an hour's entertainment or instruction; he reads himself by a process of empathy, into the book, and finds there a satisfying fulfilment of his subconscious wishes.'[1] Children achieve this satisfaction by identifying themselves with a hero or heroine and thereby enjoying his or her adventures, dangers and triumphs at second hand. This is clearly why they require a story to have as its centre of interest a young person whom they can easily see as a slightly idealised version of themselves. Thus girls of fifteen or sixteen (but not as a rule boys) take readily enough to *Pride and Prejudice* because they find no difficulty in 'stepping

---

[1] Terman and Lima (1925), page 17. It is worth quoting the strikingly similar formulation arrived at independently by Rankin (1944): 'The findings suggest that children who select these books often do so because they are able to identify themselves with the characters and thus vicariously live a life that might conceivably lie ahead of them.' See also Whitehead (1956).

into the shoes' (as it were) of Elizabeth Bennet, and 'living' the events of the novel in her person. *Silas Marner*, on the other hand, makes a much less direct appeal to them, even though it is no less generously provided with incident; the events are seen through the eyes of a number of different characters in turn, there is no single centre of identification, and adolescent readers usually need a considerable amount of help from a teacher before they can begin to appreciate what it has to offer them.

Of course it is not suggested that children are unique in bringing to their reading a demand for this kind of imaginative gratification. There is a great deal of adult reading-material (thrillers, westerns, detective stories, love stories and so on) which it seems natural to think of primarily in terms of 'substitute-living'; and there can be little doubt that (as was implied in the reference above to *Pride and Prejudice*) wish-fulfilment represents one strand in the complex appeal of even the greatest works of literature. What is claimed is that in children this motive is so strikingly preponderant as to reduce all other motives to a distinctly subsidiary role. Not that this necessarily means that other types of satisfaction which can be derived from reading are wholly unimportant to them. So long as this overriding demand for wish-fulfilment via identification has been satisfactorily met, they are perfectly willing, for instance, to absorb a certain amount of information from their reading as well; indeed they rather welcome it, as the success in recent years of the career-novel surely goes to show. But unless the field of knowledge is one in which an exceptionally strong curiosity has been aroused (a self-chosen hobby, for example), it seems that the emotional and imaginative satisfaction must be there as a kind of bait. Otherwise the child prefers to satisfy his curiosity through other media than that of reading.

By now some readers may well be muttering to themselves: 'If *this* is all that children get out of their favourite books, what real value can they be said to have for them? Surely education had better either ignore or discourage an interest in reading which is no more than a pretext for day-dreaming?' Such a reaction, though understandable, seems to me mistaken. In the first place reading of whatever kind, so long as it results in enjoyment, does at least form a basis on which more mature tastes may develop later on. For this reason alone the far-sighted teacher will not be unduly discouraged by (or discouraging about) the apparent triviality of much of his pupils' reading, so long as they show real zest for it. He will recall the robust common sense of Dr. Johnson's pronouncement: 'I would let [a boy] at first read *any* English book which happens to engage his attention; because you have done a great deal when you have brought a boy to have entertainment from a book. He'll get better books afterwards.' In the second place we should not underestimate the importance to children's psychic health of the emotional and imaginative satisfactions they obtain from their reading, even when that reading seems to the adult to be of such poor quality as to have little possible educational value. Some years ago a distinguished psychoanalyst[1] with a special interest in children's problems wrote an interesting essay in which she analysed the themes of some of the most popular children's books and discussed their probable significance in the mental life of their young readers. She concluded that the favourite stories at different ages reflected the particular phantasies and emotional conflicts which most preoccupy children at that stage of development, and that the instinctual gratification they supply has the function of helping the child to deal with these inner conflicts and achieve a resolution of them. Thus, to take one limited instance, simplification of moral issues accompanied by idealisation of hero and heroine, though distastefully 'unrealistic' from the adult point of view, seems to be needed by children at certain stages as a means of assisting them to maintain faith in ideals of conduct which they are finding difficult to live up to in real life. The adult should recognise that his own judgment may be irrelevant; what is in question is the value of the book to the child who reads it at a particular point in his own individual development, and this is not nearly so easy to assess as teachers sometimes assume. Moreover it would be misleading to give the impression that this value is necessarily confined to that of a psychological stabiliser—a prop which helps the child preserve his emotional balance as he treads the uneven path from infancy to maturity. This, our third and last point, is in some ways the most important. There is good ground for believing that the main motive for reading in childhood is indeed a search for emotional satisfaction of a compensatory kind; and much of what children like to read may fairly be judged to give them little more than this. But under conditions where a wide variety of reading-material is readily available to them, they also read much that clearly

[1] Friedlaender (1942). A shortened version of the same essay appeared in *New Era*, Vol. 39, April 1958.

does something more. The additional benefit which thus accrues to them is not to be thought of merely in terms of increased knowledge and information, though it may often include that. It is rather an extension of the capacity for experience, an enlargement and refinement of that imaginative sympathy through which we gain an increased grasp of the realities of human living and a deeper insight into the ways in which human beings (including ourselves) think and feel and behave and affect one another. As teachers we are rightly concerned to foster this element in our children's reading, realising that the quality of the imaginative experience we derive from our books has a close bearing upon the quality of experience we are capable of in our everyday living. D. H. Lawrence's penetrating comment is peculiarly relevant here: 'It is the way our sympathy flows and recoils that really determines our lives. And here lies the vast importance of the novel properly handled. It can inform and lead into new places the flow of our sympathetic consciousness, and it can lead our sympathy away in recoil from things gone dead.' The only caveat needed is a renewed insistence that the experience and sympathetic consciousness that we have to concern ourselves with is that of the child; any judgments we as adults make in this field will be valid only insofar as we have made a serious attempt to enter into the more chaotic and unstructured world of the young reader, shedding for the time being our own width of reference, maturity of perception, and awareness of subtle shades of feeling.

We may sum up the main line of our argument so far in the following quotation from W. J. Scott:

> . . . books perform two important functions in the lives of boys and girls: they help them to grow up by giving them imaginative experience, even if distorted, of the adult world and preparing them for participation in it; and they compensate them for the difficulties of growing up by creating for them a fantasy world in which life can be lived more pleasantly and easily than is usual in the real one. [Scott (1947), p. 60.]

The teacher or librarian who has the responsibility of choosing or recommending books for children needs to give full weight to these functions, and to recognise that each is important. Over and above this, he needs to read for himself some of the most popular books, and to spend time discussing them with children he knows really well. If he does so, it will be borne in upon him not only that the two functions mentioned by Scott are in most children's books very closely intertwined, but also that they may, in different books, be mixed together in very different proportions. At the ten- to twelve-year-old level, for instance, we may take, on the one hand, Enid Blyton's 'Five' series, in which the compensatory element is offered in almost undiluted form. Here the emphasis is on incident; the reader is whisked through an unbroken sequence of 'exciting' events, the interrelations between which are indicated only in a perfunctory way, with little concern for plausibility save on the most superficial level. The adult personae are the merest counters; and the children who are the main protagonists are differentiated from each other only by name, sex, and the tag of some attributed idiosyncrasy which (repeated *ad nauseam*) is the nearest this writer ever gets to 'characterisation'. Nor is there any serious attempt to give imaginative life to the indispensable stock apparatus of caves, secret passages, dungeons, treasure chests and the like; each is there merely as a pretext for the next item in the kaleidoscopic flux of 'adventures'. Over against these we may set Arthur Ransome's 'Swallows and Amazons' series, also highly popular with intelligent (middle-class) children of about the same age. Here too wish-fulfilment is the main determinant of narrative pattern; parents and adults are ingeniously got out of the way, so that the children may sail, camp and explore on their own, remaining childlike in their enjoyment of holiday adventures but meeting them with precocious expertise and responsibility. But the adventures are provided without recourse to the stock conventions of melodrama; they emerge with logic and consistency from an imagined situation, and each fresh development is prepared for in ways which reward the attentiveness of the reader instead of discouraging it. The operations of fishing or camping or sailing are presented with a wealth of concrete but clearly-visualised detail; any map which figures in the story is actually there, within the book itself, to be pored over and interpreted; if the children put their messages into a secret code, the reader is able to study and follow the code's workings, and even perhaps use it for himself. Consequently 'adventure' here is more than merely the excitement of 'having things happen'; its satisfactions are felt to be bound up with the fascination of grappling with the real intricacies of things and processes. More important still, the characters themselves are delineated in terms which, though simplified, are perceptive and just; the children, for instance, may be for the most part 'types' (and somewhat idealised at that), but their typicality is recognisably and observably that of children at a particular stage of growth, and their feelings and reactions have an imagined validity which is the fruit of genuine, if limited, insight and sympathy. Thus, even in the process of indulging his need for fantasy-living, the young reader is at the same time enlarging his horizons and consolidating his grasp upon reality.

As a further illustration of the kind of difference we are concerned with, we may place side by side two extracts, each from a book which is well liked by boys of twelve to fourteen. The first has as its setting the Second World War:

As he spoke his left hand moved towards the bomb release. With the other he straightened the aircraft until it was gliding on a direct course for the U-boat.

'Look out!' shouted G... suddenly, in a voice shrill with alarm, as nearly a score of men dashed out from places in which they had evidently been hiding.

B... did not answer. He flicked the throttle wide open and held on his course. The engines roared and the machine gathered speed.

An instant later the flak came up. And it came in such quantity and with such accuracy that G... was startled and amazed.

'Those fellows have had plenty of practice,' said B... through his teeth. His expression did not change nor did his eyes leave the mark.

G... held his breath. The aircraft still had a quarter of a mile to go and it was rocking through a hail of tracer shells and machine-gun bullets. It was hit, not once but several times. G... could hear metal ripping through wood and fabric. It seemed like suicide to go on, but he knew it was no use saying anything; knew that nothing would cause B... to abandon his attack while he still had a wing to keep the machine airborne. He felt the machine bounce slightly as the depth-charges left their racks, and was shifting his position to watch their downward track when an explosion nearly turned the machine on its back. It plunged wildly as it recovered, but even so he thought they were down. Then, with fabric streaming from the port wing, B... was taking evading action, taking it desperately.

'Did I get her?' he snapped, the object of the attack still paramount in his mind.

G... looked down but could see nothing clearly for smoke. He noted, however, that the smoke came from the position where the submarine had been. 'I don't know,' he told B.... 'If you didn't hit her it was a pretty close miss.'

Still pursued by fire the aircraft was down to a hundred feet, racing over the sea with the island slipping away astern.

'There's nothing more we can do here. I'm going flat out for home,' declared B... tersely.

*　　*　　*

B... glanced at the petrol gauge on the instrument panel. 'We shan't get home,' he answered calmly. 'Call A... on the radio and ask him to come out to meet us. Tell him to stand by to pick us up when we hit the drink.'

'Do you think we shall last as long as that—I mean till he gets here?' asked G... anxiously.

'Frankly, no,' returned B... evenly. He altered course slightly.

'What are you doing?' queried G....

'Making for those icebergs. There should be slack water under the lee of them. We shall stand a better chance there than on the open sea. Tell A... what we're doing. Give him the position of the island too. Tell him the sub is there, and my orders are that he carries on if he fails to find us in twelve hours.'

. . . G... went off to the radio compartment. One glance was enough. The instrument was a shell-shattered wreck, damaged beyond all hope of repair. He went back to B..., relieved that the aircraft was still running fairly smoothly. 'No use,' he reported tersely. 'The transmitter looks like a cat's breakfast.'

B...'s jaws clamped a little tighter. 'I doubt if it would have helped us much even if it had been in order.'

'How—why?' asked G... sharply, not liking the expression on B...'s face.

'Take a look outside.'

G... looked out through a smashed side window, and understood. Grey mist was closing in all round. There was no horizon.

'The wind's swinging round to the north,' said B... quietly. 'I was afraid of it. It's been inclined that way all day. The fog's getting worse, and it's getting worse fast. We should just have time to reach the 'bergs.'

It would have been easy to choose a popular boys' book of much shoddier quality than this, and there is clearly a certain kind of competence at work here, on its own level. But interest and tensions are maintained almost entirely by an unrelenting accumulation of incident; there is no dwelling on any single item in the sequence, and little attempt at any genuinely realised immediacy of presentation. The generalised imprecision of 'nearly a score of men dashed out from places in which they had evidently been hiding' reveals how little the author feels he needs to worry about details so long as the narrative is kept going at a cracking pace. Technical terms are used freely but unspecifically, their function being more to impart atmosphere than to define any particular happening; 'taking evasive action, and taking it desperately', for instance, evokes in its context no precise image of an actual operation, merely a generalised sense of urgency and danger. This exclusive reliance on fast-moving external action naturally leaves no room for any development of the emotional quality of the situation described. As far as human motives, thoughts and sensations are concerned, the writer is content to ring the changes upon a singularly limited repertoire of conventional stereotypes. G...'s 'alarm' and 'anxiety' serve merely as a foil for the superhuman singlemindedness and imperturbability of B ... whose jaws remain clamped tight throughout and who invariably replies 'calmly', 'evenly' or (when things are at their very blackest) 'quietly'. The tension and mental stress which would be inseparable from such an experience in real life are wholly absent, and the characters are presented as the merest silhouettes with no interior life whatever.

The second extract is set in eighteenth-century England; the two characters, one of them wounded in the leg, are making their escape up a cliff-face by a sheep-track known as 'the Zigzag':

In a minute I knew from E...'s steps that he had left the turf and was upon the chalk. Now I do not believe that there were half a dozen men beside in England who would have ventured up that path, even alive and untrammelled, and not a man in all the world to do it with a full-grown lad in his arms. Yet E... made no bones of it, nor spoke a single word; only he went very slowly, and I felt him scuffle with his foot as he set it forward, to make sure he was putting it down firm.

I said nothing, not wishing to distract him from his terrible task, and held my breath, when I could, so that I might lie quieter in his arms. Thus he went on for a time that seemed without end, and yet was really but a minute or two; and by degrees I felt the wind, that we could scarce perceive at all on the undercliff, blow fresher and cold on the cliff-side. And then the path grew steeper and steeper, and E... went slower and slower, till at last he spoke:

'J..., I am going to stop; but open not thy eyes till I have set thee down and bid thee.'

I did as bidden, and he lowered me gently, setting me on all-fours upon the path; and speaking again:

'The path is too narrow here for me to carry thee, and thou must creep round this corner on thy hands and knees. But have a care to keep thy outer hand near to the inner, and the balance of thy body to the cliff, for there is no room to dance hornpipes here. And hold thy eyes fixed on the chalk-wall, looking neither down nor seaward.'

'Twas well he told me what to do, and well I did it; for when I opened my eyes, even without moving them from the cliff-side, I saw that the ledge was little more than a foot wide, and that ever so little a lean of the body would dash me on the rocks below. So I crept on, but spent much time that was so precious in travelling those ten yards to take me round the first elbow of the path; for my foot was heavy and gave me fierce pain to drag, though I had tried to mask it from E.... And he, forgetting what I suffered, cried out, 'Quicken thy pace, lad, if thou canst, the time is short.' Now so frail is man's temper, that though he was doing more than any ever did to save another's life, and was all I had to trust to in the world; yet because he forgot my pain and bade me quicken, my choler rose, and I nearly gave him back an angry word, but thought better of it and kept it in.

Then he told me to stop, for that the way grew wider and he would pick me up again. But here was another difficulty, for the path was still so narrow and the cliff-wall so close that he could not take me up in his arms. So I lay flat on my face, and he stepped over me, setting his foot between my shoulders to do it; and then, while he knelt down upon the path, I climbed up from behind him, putting my arms round his neck; and so he bore me 'pickaback'. I shut my eyes firm again, and thus we moved along another spell, mounting still and feeling the wind still freshening.

At length he said that we were come to the last turn of the path, and he must set me down once more. So down upon his knees and hands he went, and I slid off behind, on to the ledge. Both were on all-fours now; E... first and I following. But as I crept along, I relaxed care for a moment, and my eyes wandered from the cliff-side and looked down. And far below I saw the blue sea twinkling like a dazzling mirror, and the gulls wheeling about the sheer chalk wall, and then I thought of that bloated carcass of a sheep that had fallen from this very spot perhaps, and in an instant felt a sickening qualm and swimming of the brain, and knew that I was giddy and must fall.

Then I called out to E..., and he, guessing what had come over me cries to turn upon my side, and press my belly to the cliff. And how he did in such a narrow strait I know not; but he turned round, and lying down himself, thrust his hand firmly in my back, pressing me closer to the cliff. Yet it was none too soon, for if he had not held me tight, I should have flung myself down in sheer despair to get quit of that dreadful sickness.

'Keep thine eyes shut, J...,' he said, 'and count up numbers loud to me, that I may know thou art not turning faint.' So I gave out, 'One, two, three,' and while I went on counting, heard him repeating to himself, though his words seemed thin and far off: 'We must have taken ten minutes to get here, and in five more they will be on the under-cliff; and if we ever reach the top, who knows but they have left a guard! No, no, they will not leave a guard, for not a man knows of the Zigzag; and, if they knew, they would not guess that we should try it. We have but fifty yards to go to win, and now this cursed giddy fit has come upon the child, and he will fall and drag me with him; or they will see us from below, and pick us off like sitting guillemots against the cliff-face.'

So he talked to himself, and all the while I would have given a world to pluck up heart and creep on farther; yet could not, for the deadly sweating fear that had hold of me. Thus I lay with my face to the cliff, and E... pushing firmly in my back; and the thing that frightened me most was that there was nothing at all for the hand to take hold of, for had there been a piece of string, or even a thread of cotton, stretched along to give a semblance of support, I think I could have done it; but there was only the cliff-wall, sheer and white, against that narrowest way, with never cranny to put a finger into. The wind was blowing in fresh puffs, and though I did not open my eyes, I knew that it was moving the little tufts of bent grass, and the chiding cries of the gulls seemed to invite me to be done with fear and pain and broken leg, and fling myself off on to the rocks below.

Then E... spoke. 'J...,' he said, 'there is no time to play the woman; another minute of this and we are lost. Pluck up thy courage, keep thy eyes to the cliff, and forward.'

Yet I could not, but answered: 'I cannot, I cannot; if I open my eyes, or move hand or foot, I shall fall on the rocks below.'

He waited a second, and then said: 'Nay, move thou must, and 'tis better to risk falling now, than fall for certain with another bullet in thee later on.' And with that he shifted his hand from my back and fixed it in my coat-collar, moving backwards himself, and setting to drag me after him.

Now, I was so besotted with fright that I would not budge an inch, fearing to fall over if I opened my eyes. And he, for all he was so strong, could not pull a helpless lump backwards up the path. So he gave it up, leaving go hold on me with a groan, and at that moment there rose from the under-cliff below a sound of voices and shouting.

'Zounds, they are down already!' cried E..., 'and have found M...'s body; it is all up; another minute and they will see us.'

But so strange is the force of mind on body, and the power of a greater to master a lesser fear, that when I heard those voices from below, all fright of falling left me in a moment, and I could open my eyes without a trace of giddiness. So I began to move forward again on hands and knees. And E..., seeing me, thought for a moment I had gone mad, and was dragging myself over the cliff; but then saw how it was, and moved backwards himself before me, saying in a low voice, 'Brave lad! Once creep round this turn, and I will pick thee up again. There is but fifty yards to go, and we shall foil these devils yet!'

The excitement here is a matter of entering into the experience of the narrator in his hazardous situation, an experience which has been realised with vivid immediacy both in the external world of action and in the internal world of feeling. The physical reality of the ascent is presented in enough detail for us to follow and visualise its progress stage by stage, and its impact on the boy's consciousness comes alive for us in, for instance, E...'s scuffling movement with his foot or the changing feel of the wind. The human relations, too, are portrayed with a due awareness of complexities, as in the irritable resentment which arises between the two characters but is kept in check by their mutual forbearance. Moreover, courage is not conceived of as mere insensibility: the fear which has to be overcome is given its full weight, and there is realism and insight in the way the boy's conflict is resolved, though here again recognition of human complexity does not diminish our respect for the bravery shown. We cannot doubt that the young reader who satisfies his need for vicarious adventure within the pages of this book will also (to quote W. J. Scott again) 'return from his imaginative journey with some addition to his understanding of men's motives and behaviour, some education of his emotions'.[1]

I have included a discussion of these particular examples because it seemed desirable to illustrate in some detail the kind of criteria which the adult can properly apply to children's books when he tries to estimate their value to the boys and girls who read and enjoy them. It seems clear to me that the right course for the teacher is to recognise the child's legitimate need for wish-fulfilment and fantasy-living in his reading, but to encourage him whenever possible to find this vicarious satisfaction in books which offer at the same time some forward movement in range and quality of imaginative experience. The best means of achieving this will be considered at length in the next section of this chapter. For the moment it will be enough to stress that, given the right kind of influence from school and teacher, there is no need for children to stagnate among the repetitive vapidity of Blyton or the standardised thrills of Biggles. Experience shows that, under tactful and judicious guidance, they can be led to enjoy and ultimately to prefer books of a progressively higher quality.

[1] The extracts discussed in the preceding pages are drawn from *Biggles' Second Case* by W. E. Johns (Hodder & Stoughton, pp. 74–78) and *Moonfleet* by J. Meade Falkner (Arnold, pp. 109–114).

At the same time the teacher must be warned not to expect too much from his efforts. His own aim is to lead the child on from the book which offers the most immediate and easy enjoyment towards that which, at the cost of a somewhat greater effort of attention, pays a much higher dividend in satisfaction. Fortunately he can count on support in this from the powerful forces towards growth which exist within the child's own make-up. But there are also, in the culture of our own society, powerful forces in the world outside the school which pull continually in the opposite direction. Comics and commercials, headlines and hoardings — these typify the influences which are at work all the time bludgeoning or beguiling our children into eschewing mental and spiritual effort and accepting the satisfaction which is easy, immediate and ready-to-hand. Popular reading has become, in the present century, an integral part of what may be termed the entertainment industry — an industry run on mass lines whose outstanding characteristic is the compulsion to find a mass audience for its wares. This compulsion derives largely from certain technical and economic aspects of the communication-media which the industry seeks to exploit. A modern newspaper, a cinema film or a television programme is fantastically expensive to produce; each requires the investment of a very large sum of capital, whose recoupment (at a profit) is possible only in terms of a mass audience, an audience, that is to say, numbered not in thousands but in millions. In the case of the newspaper or television programme which has been harnessed to the advertising needs of modern mass-production industry, dependence upon advertising revenue gives a still further impetus to this drive towards a maximum audience. But the same impulsion is observably present elsewhere, even without this additional turn of the screw.

Why should this search for a mass audience necessarily lead to a levelling-down of quality? We may quote in answer the following succinct statement of the position in the case of television; it has in reality a much wider application:

For creating large audience pride of place must go not to the enjoyability of a programme but to the universality of its appeal. This may seem a subtle distinction, but it is immensely important. To get a maximum audience a television programme must appeal to everyone at once, even if this means appealing keenly to no one. It must play down to the lowest common factor in us all, treating us as units in a mass, without personality, without individuality. That is why so many commercial programmes are so utterly without character of any kind. Long experience shows that the perfect formula for a commercial broadcast is variety plus sex, plus crime. This is the kind of programme which fewest of us will switch off, even if none of us really enjoys it. This is the direction in which, perhaps after an initial period of good intentions, British commercial television will inevitably drift.[1]

This process of 'playing down to the lowest common factor in us all' is at work to some degree in all popular entertainment, popular journalism and popular fiction. Clearly it is flatly counter to all the English teacher's efforts. It affects the child indirectly by creating an environment in which it seems the natural thing to take one's pleasures passively, expending the minimum of effort upon them – to 'have the wireless on', for instance, without ever really listening to it, or to watch a television serial at the same time as one eats one's supper. And it also impinges upon the child more directly because it shapes the entertainment and the reading-material which is aimed specifically at his custom. Its effect is doubly objectionable here because in children the capacity for imaginative response changes and develops so rapidly as they grow older. Yet the majority of children's television programmes aim at a heterogeneous audience aged anywhere between six and fourteen. Children's comics attempt to attract as wide an audience as possible over an age-range of some four or five years. (Children's books, it is true, can still on the whole afford to address themselves to a narrower age-grouping – but in many cases they only succeed in competing with the comic by aping its less desirable characteristics.) It is clear that, where children are concerned, the pursuit of a mass audience must usually mean that the greater part of that audience will be responding at a level far below their real capacity. Thus it comes about that some children are content to move in their reading from Noddy through Beano and the Famous Five to their final haven of *Mirabelle* – a progression which is marked by a certain change in subject-matter but no real development in imaginative quality or emotional maturity.

It is idle to blame the children themselves for this state of affairs. The responsibility rests upon the adult community, for it is adults who control and produce the reading-material and entertainment programmes in question. As teachers of English we may sometimes be led to question the assumption that, in this field, children's welfare can safely be left to the free play of the profit motive. We

[1] Mayhew (1952).

find ourselves compelled to expend much of our energy in a ceaseless struggle *against* the mainstream of contemporary 'mass-civilisation', and we may be forgiven if we are sometimes a little discouraged. But we are not altogether despondent, for we know that children have a natural resilience of spirit which makes it possible for us to achieve a great deal despite the disproportionate odds.

(iii)

The traditional way of dealing with English prose in the grammar school is to issue at the beginning of each term a 'set' of thirty-five copies of some prose work which will then be 'read in class' at the rate of one lesson a week over a period of twelve or thirteen weeks. A few decades ago it would have been easy enough to guess what the set would consist of. For the first year, Kingsley's *Heroes*, *Robinson Crusoe* or *Gulliver's Travels* (the latter suitably abridged); for the middle school, a selection of essays by Goldsmith or Addison, Kinglake's *Eothen*, Stevenson's *Travels with a Donkey*, perhaps a novel by Scott, Thackeray or Dickens. One's guess could not go very wide of the mark, since the whole teaching-procedure was based on fairly clear-cut assumptions. There were certain works of English literature which every educated adult should be acquainted with; before leaving school, the pupil ought to have read and studied these books, to have had their beauties pointed out to him, and to be able to remember something about them. As Professor Gordon (1947) put it: 'The nineteenth century believed that only good literature should be read in school. But by "good" they really meant "good" for an educated and cultured adult. So we have a legacy of English classics to be read in school, many of them never to be read again.'

Some remnants of the 'legacy' are no doubt still to be found in school stockrooms, gathering a fresh layer of dust each year; but they can seldom be observed in active class-room use, having been re-placed by fresh sets of books which may have less merit as literature but are, on the whole, more likely to appeal to the average thirteen- or fourteen-year-old. The change is certainly not to be regretted; A. J. Jenkinson was perfectly right to point out the dangers of a situation in which, from the pupil's point of view, there is a yawning gulf between 'what I have to read in school' (in other words, 'literature') and 'what I really enjoy reading'. On the other hand, the teacher under the old dispensation had at least the advantage of knowing just what he was trying to do; nowadays we stick to the tradition of the single class-reader without apparently feeling very sure of its purpose. The wide variety in choice of book is itself a reflection of this uncertainty of aim. Here is one grammar school which has chosen for its second form *The Otterbury Incident*, another where the choice has lighted on *Prester John*, a third which has plumped for *David Copperfield* (complete and unabridged). Or again we may find one third form supplied with *Pilgrim's Progress*, another with *The Invisible Man*, another with *Silas Marner*, yet another with *Three Men in a Boat*. In the secondary modern school, where there has always been more diversity of practice than in the grammar school, the range is even wider. And though there is certainly a tendency these days to choose fiction (a commendable attempt to meet the class's taste halfway) the trend is by no means invariable: the volume of essays is not wholly dead, though it has survived by becoming 'Lighter' or 'Modern' and pinning its faith on Robert Lynd and J. B. Priestley rather than Addison and Steele. There are also many schools where, if a class is issued with a prose-book at all, it is no more than a dreary-looking collection of extracts, the passages themselves being too short to generate any real interest or involvement, and the whole being made even more forbidding by an appended apparatus of vocabulary exercises and so-called 'comprehension questions'.

What are these class-readers supposed to be for? To establish the reading-habit? To introduce the pupils to writers whom they might not otherwise read? To ensure that they read some good books at least? To provide practice in reading-aloud? To serve as material for linguistic exercises? It would seldom be easy to extract a clear answer, and many teachers would probably say that they try to combine a little of each of these aims at different times.

It would seem that the one clear gain in all this is the new awareness that, for anything worthwhile to be achieved, the reading-material we present to a class must be such that they will be interested in it and will enjoy reading it. But this recognition in itself raises new problems.

If the book is one the children really enjoy, is it not also likely to be one which they could just as well read on their own? If it is a novel, would it not be more natural for them to read it on their own anyway, since most modern novels are so obviously intended for solitary, silent reading? Does a novel gain anything by being read aloud in forty-minute sections at weekly intervals? (Would the teacher himself care to read *War and Peace* on a similar instalment plan?) What line is one to take if the book succeeds so well in arousing interest that some of the class take to reading ahead in it on their own? (I have seen it seriously suggested that the right course is to gather in the books at the end of each lesson and impound them in a securely padlocked cupboard for the intervening seven days!) Since any class of thirty to forty pupils is made up of individuals who vary greatly in intelligence, reading ability and emotional maturity, is it in any case possible to find a single book which is well suited to all of them? And even if a few such books can be found, how much impact will be made by the three or four books read in class in the course of the year as compared with that of the thirty, forty, or fifty which the child chooses for himself and reads on his own?

My contention is that these problems cannot really be solved in terms of the single class-reader, and that during the second, third and fourth years of the secondary school course the *main* focus of the teacher's efforts in regard to prose should be shifted away from read-ing done during lesson-time, and on to the voluntary self-initiated reading carried on outside school hours. By this time boys and girls have normally reached the fourth of the stages listed by W. S. Gray: the stage, that is, of wide independent silent reading. This wide reading is indispensable as the basic means whereby children at this age acquire and extend their command of language in all its aspects. Just as in earlier years the accumulated experience of listening to other people speaking enabled the child to acquire his intuitive grasp of the patterns of speech, so now for the older child the accumulated experience of reading builds up gradually an intuitive sense of the patterns and structures of the written language. Through it comes increased vocabulary, the ability to spell, to punctuate, the ability to write. As we have already seen, it is immensely important, too, in enabling children at this stage to satisfy certain fundamental needs in their current emotional and imaginative life. And given the right kind of opportunity and the right kind of encouragement, it can lead on ultimately to reading of a much higher quality and thus form the foundation of an enduring taste for literature. All in all it is essential to see this out-of-school reading as a natural tendency towards growth which the English teacher can enlist as a most powerful ally; and there can be no more important task than that of influencing its direction so that it may lead on to more mature forms of reading-experience.

As a first step he must ensure that there are plenty of suitable books ready to hand for his pupils to choose from; for there is clear evidence that availability exerts more influence on the quality of children's reading than any other single factor. In most localities nowadays the public library has a children's section which is well stocked with both fiction and non-fiction, and if there are any pupils who do not make use of it they should be encouraged to do so. The teacher himself would do well to become acquainted with its resources; if these seem to him seriously deficient in any way, something may be gained by a friendly approach to the children's librarian on the basis that children's reading is a problem of mutual concern. Even more important in some ways (and certainly more accessible to influence from the English teacher) is the school library. A weekly library period for each form can ensure that all pupils become familiar with what this has to offer them. Some of these periods can usefully be devoted to instruction in the techniques of using a library;[1] but most of them should be set aside for browsing freely among the shelves, particularly in cases where not all the members of the form are avid readers already. The main objective is that the children should borrow, and finish reading at home, books which they have first sampled during the library period. In addition to books bearing upon school subjects such as history and geography, and upon hobbies or other specialised interests of childhood, there should be a generous provision of fiction of the kind which really appeals to children. So long as this factor of 'appeal' is given full weight, there is usually no need for the school librarian to pitch his standards unduly low, for experience shows that to stock a children's library with books of good quality tends to increase the number of books borrowed rather than to reduce it.[2]

Some teachers try to influence their pupils' choice of books by issuing lists of recommended library reading for each form or year; under certain circumstances these may have some effect, but it is not uncommon to find that they are largely ignored by the children for whom they are intended. We have to reckon with the fact that children at this stage want to be independent in their choice of reading-material and like to feel that in this area of their lives at least they can keep control in their own hands. It is indeed one of the attractions of books, as contrasted with other comparable media such

[1] For suggestions about this kind of work see Stott (1947), Chapter 5.
[2] See White (1946), page 12.

as films or television, that the reader can enter into the experience more intimately and make it his own in a more directly personal way. Instead of being limited to a small number of standardised possibilities the reader can select from a great variety of books to suit his own mood and his own individuality; the book can be picked up, skipped, or laid down just as he feels inclined. Consequently the boy or girl is inclined to resist any encroachment upon these prerogatives, especially if it comes from an adult. For this reason it is better to work by means of frank and uninhibited class discussion rather than by recommendation or persuasion from the teacher. If a lesson-period is regularly set aside for this (once a fortnight will usually be quite enough) a few children can be asked each time to bring along a book which they have read recently and to interest the rest of the class in it, either by reading an exciting extract from it, by retelling some of the events, or by explaining what they found of particular appeal in it. At first (and perhaps for a long time) the teacher may find that the books thus recommended are disappointingly poor in quality—but he must tolerate this, without expressing his own disapproval or attempting to interpose any kind of censorship. In time, if he is patient, he will see the natural forces of growth begin to assert themselves. The book which successfully communicates a distinctive imaginative experience evokes a more positive reaction than the 'run-of-the-mill' commercial product, and is likely to seem more worth exhibiting and reading from. The more intelligent and mature children in the form are usually those who read most, and who are therefore most ready to bring along books and join in discussion of them. There comes the time when one of the standardised 'series' books which have hitherto been universally popular meets with an adverse comment from some—it is thought to be 'silly', 'soppy', 'always the same', 'too impossible', or 'boring'. Heated argument may follow, but a step forward has been taken, and this expression of opinion by compeers, however inarticulately formulated, counts for far more with the rest of the form than anything the teacher could have said.

I have stressed that in these periods the teacher needs to keep himself in the background. His role is to establish the forum in which the children's own differing tastes and opinions can find expression and interact on one another; he has to ensure that each child has the opportunity to contribute, and that as many as possible actually do so. Further than this his own influence, if it comes into the open at all, should be exerted positively rather than negatively. He will remain silent when the authors discussed are ones of whom he knows either nothing or nothing to their credit; on the other hand, when a boy is recommending Wells or Ray Bradbury, Sherlock Holmes or Father Brown, he may show an interest and knowledgeability which is not in evidence at other times. And when he knows his form well enough he may on occasion risk a suggestion of his own: 'If you like A, why not try also B?' But he had better be sure of his ground. A recommendation which proves to be ill-judged will take a long time to live down, and it is all too easy in this matter of taste for the adult to provoke an attitude of resistance and counter-suggestibility.

Ideally, the work in connection with library reading should be supplemented by provision for each class of a mixed set of 'home-readers'. In recent years many English teachers have experimented with their own form of 'home-reading' scheme, and have found that there is much to be said for spending a scanty book-allowance in this way rather than on a complete set of a single 'class-reader'. For the cost of forty copies of *Kidnapped* we can have, say, five copies each of eight different titles, which should make it quite possible to cater for the different levels of taste and ability within the average form. The books are intended mainly for reading 'out-of-school', though at the beginning of the term some lesson-time may be given over to silent reading to ensure that everyone makes a good start, and that the book is given a fair chance to 'take hold'. Each boy or girl is free to choose for himself within the limits of what is available, but is expected to read at least one of the titles during the term or half-year. It is an advantage to have about half a dozen copies of each title, since this makes possible a certain amount of group work and discussion in lesson time once a few children have finished reading any given book. The groups may write book reviews for the class-room wall display; they may prepare a dramatised version of an exciting or amusing episode, and then act it in front of the rest of the form; or they may script and record (on the tape-recorder) a programme similar perhaps to the old sound radio series 'May We Recommend', designed to attract further readers to the book. As a result of activities such as this, it will be found that most of the class will read (or at the very least attempt) more than one of the titles (a system of exchanges can be made to work fairly smoothly so long as the books have been well selected); and some pupils can usually be induced to read each of the eight books in the course of the term.

Through a scheme of this kind the teacher's influence is brought to bear in a positive way which at the same time avoids any oppressive sense of dictation. The books chosen will be of slightly higher quality than those which the children would choose for themselves from the library, but otherwise not obviously different in kind. There should then be no need either for moral pressure from the teacher in order to 'get the book finished' or for periodic tests to check that the book has in fact been read. Such tests are in any case undesirable, since they almost inevitably focus on inessential or irrelevant aspects of the reading experience, and distort unjustifiably the attitude with which the child approaches a work of literature. We don't after all read *Middlemarch* or *The Rainbow* in order that we may be able to remember the names of the characters or the events of the plot, and it is hard to see why we should treat children's fictional reading as though its main end were the residue of factual information it leaves behind. A children's story, like an adult novel, should be read for the sake of the emotional and imaginative satisfaction it brings; this is the only motive for reading it which the wise teacher will think it worth his while to foster.

The list of suggested books which follows is in no sense exhaustive, and it is confined to ones which are (or have lately been) available in fairly cheap editions. Naturally, the grading of titles is intended only as a very rough guide, since tastes and circumstances differ so very widely from neighbourhood to neighbourhood and from school to school.

The following symbols have been used to indicate publishers:

A   Edward Arnold
AU   Allen & Unwin (Windsor Selections from English Literature)
C   Collins (New School Classics *or* Laurel & Gold Series)
CU   Cambridge University Press
CW   Chatto & Windus (Queen's Classics *or* Beaver Books)
D   Dent (Literature of Yesterday *or* King's Treasuries of English Literature)
Ha   Harrap (English Classics *or* Modern English Series)
He   Heinemann (New Windmill Series)
Hu   Hutchinson (Unicorn Books)
L   Longmans (Heritage of Literature Series)
Ma   Macmillan

Me Methuen (Modern Classics *or* Venture Library)

Mu Murray (Albemarle Library *or* School Library of Famous Books)

N Nelson (Teaching of English Series *or* School Classics)

O Oxford University Press (Oxford Children's Library *or* World's Classics)

P Penguin, Puffin or Peacock Books

Pe Pergamon Press (Athena Books)

U University of London Press (Pilot Books)

Some Books suitable for use as Home-Readers

FIRST YEAR

Secondary Modern Streams

Finn Family Moomintroll (Jansson). P.

Black Beauty (Sewell). C·D·N·P· U.

Poo Lorn of the Elephants (Campbell). U.

Emil and the Detectives (Kastner). N·P.

The Box of Delights (Masefield). He·P.

Thimble Summer (Enright). He·P.

Chang (Morse). N.

The Family from One-End Street (Garnett). He·P.

Jim Davis (Masefield). L.

Little House in the Big Woods (Wilder). P.

Ballet Shoes (Streatfeild). D·P.

Minnow on the Say (Pearce). O.

The Wind in the Willows (Grahame). Me.

Swallows and Amazons (Ransome). P.

Jan (Barrington). L.

Robin Hood (Green). P.

Flood Warning (Berna). He·P.

Grammar Streams

Chang (Morse). D.

The Family from One-End Street (Garnett). He·P.

Jim Davis (Masefield). L.

Ballet Shoes (Streatfeild). D·P.

Swallows and Amazons (Ransome). P.

Jan (Barrington). L.

Bran the Bronze Smith (Reason). D.

Coco the Clown (Poliakoff). D.

The Secret Garden (Burnett). He·P.

Captain of Dragoons (Welch). AU.

The Country Child (Uttley). N.

Treasure Island (Stevenson).

The Prince and the Pauper (Twain). CW.

The World Upside Down (Mayne). O.

Theras (Snedeker). D.

Tom Sawyer (Twain).

Children of the New Forest (Marryatt). C·N.

Tarka the Otter (Williamson). L·P.

Nada the Lily (Haggard). D.

SECOND YEAR

Secondary Modern Streams

Bran the Bronze-Smith (Reason). D.

The Wheel on the School (de Jong). He·P.

Captain of Dragoons (Welch). AU.

Little Women (Alcott).

No Boats on Bannermere (Trease). He.

Avalanche (van der Loeff). P.

The Secret Garden (Burnett). He·P.

Theras (Snedeker). D.

Treasure Island (Stevenson).

She Shall Have Music (Barne). D.

Tom Sawyer (Twain).

Children of the New Forest (Marryatt). C·N.

The Radium Woman (Doorly). He.

The Bonnie Pit Laddie (Grice). O.

The Goalkeeper's Revenge (Naughton). He·P.

Nada the Lily (Haggard). D.

The Boy Who Was Afraid (Sperry). He.

The Cave (Church). He.

Grammar Streams

The Otterbury Incident (Day Lewis). He.

The Radium Woman (Doorly). He.

The Microbe Man (Doorly). He.

The Boy Who Was Afraid (Sperry). He.

The Lost World (Doyle). Mu.

White Fang (London). He·N.

King Solomon's Mines (Haggard).

Moonfleet (Falkner). A·P.

The Splendid Journey (Morrow). He.

Allan Quatermain (Haggard). C·N·U.

Sherlock Holmes Stories (Doyle). Mu·O·P.

The Invisible Man (Wells). C.

The Silver Sword (Serraillier). He·P.

Prester John (Buchan). N.

The Light in the Forest (Richter). Me.

The Prisoner of Zenda (Hope). D.

THIRD YEAR

Secondary Modern Streams

The Otterbury Incident (Day Lewis). He·P.

King Solomon's Mines (Haggard).

The Silver Sword (Serraillier). He·P.

Grammar Streams

Sea Hunters (Robb). L.

The Call of the Wild (London). He·L.

Short Stories (Wells). N·P.

Bird of Dawning (Masefield). He·P.

READING AND LITERATURE

Secondary Modern Streams

Danger Rock (Armstrong). D.
White Fang (London). He·N.
The Lost World (Doyle). Mu.
Sea Hunters (Robb). L.
Prester John (Buchan). N.
Sherlock Holmes Stories (Doyle). Mu·O·P.
The Invisible Man (Wells). C.
Allan Quatermain (Haggard). C·N·U.
Three Singles to Adventure (Durrell). He.
The Light in the Forest (Richter). Me.
The First Men in the Moon (Wells). C.
The War of the Worlds (Wells). He·P.
The Pearl (Steinbeck). He.
First Blood (Schaefer). He.
Bealby (Wells). Me.
Dr. Syn (Thorndyke). Hu.
The Call of the Wild (London). He·L.

Grammar Streams

The Pearl (Steinbeck). He.
The Wooden Horse (Williams). C.
The Colditz Story (Reid). U.
First Blood (Schaefer). He.
Bealby (Wells). Me.
Fifteen Stories (Jacobs). Me.
Three Men in a Boat (Jerome). D.
Zoo Quest to Guiana (Attenborough). U.
Cider with Rosie (Lee). CW.
Sailing Alone Around the World (Slocum). Me.
The Diary of Ann Frank. Hu.
The Canyon (Schaefer). He.
Jane Eyre (Brontë).
The Honey-Siege (Buhet). CW.
Smith (Garfield). P.
Johnny Tremain (Forbes). P.

FOURTH YEAR

Secondary Modern Streams

The Honey-Siege (Buhet). CW.
The Wooden Horse (Williams). C.
Short Stories (Wells). N·P.
Aspects of Science Fiction (ed. Doherty). Mu.
Zoo Quest to Guiana (Attenborough). U.
The Red Pony (Steinbeck). He.
Man Meets Dog (Lorenz). Pan.

Grammar Streams

The Treasure of the Sierra Madre (Traven). Hu.
Maidens' Trip (Smith). P.
Spanish Gold (Birmingham). Me.
Tell Freedom (Abraham). AU.
The Red Pony (Steinbeck). He.
The Day of the Triffids (Wyndham). Hu.
King Solomon's Ring (Lorenz). Pan.

Secondary Modern Streams

Maidens' Trip (Smith). P.

The Treasure of the Sierra Madre (Traven). Hu.

Tell Freedom (Abrahams). AU.

Three Men in a Boat (Jerome). D.

Ring of Bright Water (Maxwell). D.

The Colditz Story (Reid). U.

The Diary of Ann Frank. Hu.

In Hazard (Hughes). CW.

Brother to the Ox (Kitchen). D.

The Day of the Triffids (Wyndham). Hu.

The Hanging Tree (Johnson). Hu.

Animal Farm (Orwell). L·P.

The Kon-Tiki Expedition (Heyerdahl). AU.

A Pattern of Islands (Grimble). Murray, complete edn.

Man-Eaters of Kumaon (Corbett). O·P.

Jane Eyre (Brontë).

Lady-in-Chief (Woodham-Smith). Me.

A Kestrel for a Knave (Hines). Pe.

Grammar Streams

A Pattern of Islands (Grimble). Murray, complete edn.

The Kon-Tiki Expedition (Heyerdahl). AU.

In Hazard (Hughes). CW.

Three Men on the Bummel (Jerome). D.

The Autobiography of a Super-Tramp (Davies). AU.

Kipps (Wells). C.

Brother to the Ox (Kitchen). D.

No Picnic on Mount Kenya (Benuzzi). L.

Man-Eaters of Kumaon (Corbett). O·P.

Lois the Witch (Gaskell). Me.

The Getting of Wisdom (Richardson). He.

The Old Man and the Sea (Hemingway). Cape.

The Member of the Wedding (McCullers). P.

The Rover (Conrad). N.

Tono-Bungay (Wells). C.

Memoirs of a Fox-Hunting Man (Sassoon). Faber.

The Bridge of San Luis Rey (Wilder). L.

A Tale of Two Cities (Dickens).

The Trumpet-Major (Hardy). Ma.

The stress which I have laid so far in this section upon the pupil's independent silent reading has been deliberate; I am aware, however, that there are many good teachers in whom it will provoke a certain sense of disquiet. One such teacher observes:

I have tried this business of encouraging children's private reading, over a number of years, and I agree that your scheme has much to be said for it. But it has one limitation which you seem in danger of forgetting.

It can lead children to read more extensively, but it cannot help them to get more from what they do read. The reading of my present fourth form is voracious, but it is also distressingly inaccurate. They skim through whole chapters paying heed only to the story; they skip sentences or paragraphs which they find difficult to understand; and if we read a passage together in class my questioning usually reveals that they have gathered only the most hazy and imprecise notion of what the author is actually saying. Surely throughout the secondary school we need to train our pupils to read effectively as well as encourage them to read extensively. And I don't see how this can be done except by reading together and talking about books or extracts, a copy of which is there in front of each member of the class, for him to refer back to when necessary.

There is good sense in this reminder that the teacher's aim is necessarily a dual one: on the one hand, to develop strong and enduring interests in reading — motives for reading which will persist after the boy or girl leaves school; on the other hand, to improve the efficiency of the reading-process itself — to foster the reader's ability to 'take what is there' and to re-create, as fully and as sensitively as possible, the experience which lies behind the words on the page. Nor can we assume that this ability is bound to develop of its own accord as an inevitable by-product of wide reading; experience and experiment on both sides of the Atlantic have shown that even the most practised and highly-educated readers often misunderstand what they read to a surprising extent. We must recognise that 'to realise and live again an author's experience is a difficult feat'.

What kind of training will help? It is true that the essential element is co-operative class-room effort in which the pupil is led, under the guidance of the teacher, to look again at some part of what he has just read, to check his own interpretation of its meaning against that of other readers, and to attend more closely to aspects of meaning which he may previously have overlooked or taken in only in a distorted form. Such work necessarily involves dwelling upon the details of the passage read — upon particular words and phrases, in fact; but it must be made clear that what we have in mind requires not attention to the individual words or phrases as 'things-in-themselves' but rather to their function as vehicles of communication, to the contribution they make in their own particular context to the meaning of the whole. Our aim is to establish the habit of attentive awareness as an integral part of the act of reading; and this awareness ought to extend ultimately beyond the bare skeleton of factual meaning to the less obvious undertones, implications, suggestions, and shades of feeling which are carried by the particular selection and organisation of words which the writer has chosen to use.

All the same, it must be remembered that to read with full understanding is an ideal which is seldom if ever attained even by the educated adult; as far as children are concerned, it is a goal which we have to lead them towards gradually. Moreover we must never fall into the error of regarding the work we do in the class-room as an end in itself. The habit of increasing attentivity which we try to foster will become valuable only if it is transferred to the silent reading which our children do on their own; and this carry-over is unlikely to take place unless certain conditions are fulfilled.

In my view the most important of these conditions is that any passage we select for attention in the class-room must make a powerful initial impact on the children when they first read it; it must excite in them a degree of interest or curiosity which makes them *want* to go further into it. It is equally important that the results of such further acquaintance should be unmistakably rewarding, so that the children themselves feel that the closer attention they have given to the text has increased the enjoyment and satisfaction they have gained from it. Clearly this requires in the first place that the passage must be one which does not yield up its full richness of meaning on a single reading; it must have some depth and some quality to it. It means also that the teacher must use tact and discretion in deciding how far to pursue his quest for fuller understanding; it is futile, and may be disastrous, to attempt to 'squeeze the orange dry'—to persist in trying to extract the last ounce of detailed meaning from a class which has already become bored and restless. The teacher's treatment of the passage must in fact be selective; he has to make up his mind beforehand which aspects of meaning are the most important ones for his own class to grasp. What is more, he must be able to recognise the point at which further discussion becomes nugatory, and be prepared to stop there. Experience teaches one that, in this respect, much depends on the passage itself; the more absorbingly interesting it is to the class, the more exhaustive is the treatment which it can safely bear. But the highest degree of selectivity will in general be needed with the younger and with the less able forms. As a class moves upwards through the school it should be possible to exact from them an increasingly close and prolonged attention to what the words are saying.

It may be thought that what I am recommending now is a series of 'comprehension lessons' of the kind which the tired teacher can nowadays find neatly pre-packaged for him in innumerable books of graded comprehension exercises. This is not the case. Books of this kind owe their existence to a different set of considerations. They are modelled (whether consciously or not) upon the comprehension section of the O Level G.C.E. English Language paper, and are a manifestation of the mistaken belief that the right way to prepare pupils for an examination is to ensure that for many years beforehand they practise answering questions which are as nearly as possible identical in form with those which they will encounter 'on the day'. As far as my present argument goes, the questions provided in these books may or may not be sound as *tests*; the point is that as a technique for teaching children to read with understanding they are wholly misconceived, since, even where they do not wander off into linguistic or grammatical irrelevancies, they almost invariably follow a stereotyped pattern which ignores the specific qualities of meaning inherent in the particular piece of writing, and instead concentrates mainly on calling for 'equivalents' to arbitrarily selected words and phrases considered in isolation from the context as a whole.[1]

More fundamental (and irremediable), however, than the unsatisfactoriness of the appended questions is the unsatisfactoriness of the extracts themselves. Despite claims to the contrary, these are seldom satisfactorily graded either for appeal or for difficulty. Worse still, they are almost invariably either too short or too incomplete. Read in their original setting in the books from which they have been torn they might perhaps have more to offer; presented as they are in inglorious and fragmentary isolation the reading of them is bound to be a tantalising and depressing experience instead of an enjoyable and satisfying one. I know of no volume of passages or extracts for junior or middle forms which I would care to use, in any sustained way, as material for training in attentive reading; and I find it difficult to envisage a volume of this kind which would meet the real needs of pupils of this age. I believe that the kind of class-room work which we have seen to be necessary is much better carried out incidentally in the course of reading a 'real book'; and for this reason it

[1] Morris (1963) attributes the persistent vogue for 'quiz-techniques' in 'teaching' comprehension to the influence of the American psychologist E. L. Thorndike and his work, dating from 1917, on 'reading as reasoning' and 'readability control'. However, it seems unlikely that in Great Britain, at least, Thorndike's influence can have been a decisive or even a major factor.

seems advisable that, *in addition to* their home-reading scheme, each class should be provided with at least one 'class-reader' every year — a continuous prose work, that is, some parts of which are read together and 'worked on' communally in the class-room.

Under such conditions the passages selected by the teacher for more detailed consideration are encountered by the children in their natural setting and context. Since interest is cumulative, they excite a readier and warmer response than is possible with a series of discrete extracts where the class has to 'start from cold', as it were, at the beginning of each lesson. And the injunction (always implicit in these lessons) to 'look again more closely at the meaning' seems more purposeful, less of an arbitrarily imposed exercise; so that the habits of attentivity formed by such training stand a better chance of being transferred to out-of-school reading.

At the same time the need will always be with us to supply some motive for such work over and above that of docile compliance with class-room ritual or the teacher's whim; and much of the teacher's ingenuity and expertise has to go into devising acceptable incentives for this more careful attention to meanings and to the words through which the meanings are conveyed. Among such devices (one might almost call them 'dodges') the activity which will suggest itself most frequently is undoubtedly that of dramatisation. It has many advantages; in a dramatised reading of a suitable episode the desire to 'bring it alive' leads on naturally to reference back to the text to discover exactly what is happening, how the conversation is to be spoken, what actions, gestures and expressions accompany it, what the characters are like, and so on. With younger forms, too, one often comes across brief episodes where the judicious use of mime can do much to evoke a fuller imaginative realisation of feelings, events and actions. But it is important to avoid a too exclusive reliance upon the dramatic method since it loses much of its virtue if it comes to be thought of as an invariable routine, and in any case one often wants to deal with material which is not well suited to it. A few of the possible alternatives are listed briefly below:[1]

(i) *Adaptation as part of a radio serial:* This is, of course, a variant on the dramatic method; but it has the advantage that it can sometimes be applied to episodes which would be recalcitrant to dramatisation under normal class-room conditions. The authentic atmosphere of Jacob Marley's ghost, for instance, can be more

[1] Further useful devices are described in Walsh (1965), Chapter 7.

readily evoked by means of the voice alone than by a dramatised reading in which the visible presence of the actor clanking his chains might come perilously near to the ludicrous. In fact, Dickens's novels, much of whose quality resides in the rich ebullience of their verbal texture, are often well served by this treatment; the inevitable emphasis upon the writer's words gives the method virtues as well as limitations. If a tape-recorder can be used to record and play back the final version of the episode, this gives a helpful reality to the conditions imposed by broadcasting as a medium.

(ii) *Discussion of how an episode might be filmed:* This is probably best suited to a second or third year form. An example might be the episode in *Moonfleet* when the diamond merchant cheats John Trenchard and Elzevir Block by pretending that the gem they have brought to him is only paste. The class are given ten to fifteen minutes to read the relevant pages over to themselves silently, at the end of which they will be called upon to give their own ideas of exactly what would be seen upon the screen in a film adaptation which did its best to be faithful to the original. Besides providing occasion for a check upon the accuracy of differing interpretations, the subsequent discussion can lead to a heightened awareness of the differing potentialities of the two media.

(iii) *Making maps, diagrams or illustrations:* These should be used with caution, and confined strictly to cases where the activity has the clearly-defined function of focusing attention upon some significant aspect of the writer's meaning; it is an abdication of the English teacher's responsibility to set children to drawing or painting an illustration merely for the sake of giving them something to do. There are, of course, a number of books in which a map of the terrain is already provided: *Treasure Island*, *Prester John*, *Bevis*, for instance. Even so, the reader of *Bevis* is led to a closer understanding of the difficulties encountered by Bevis and Mark on their sailing-boat's first expeditions if he draws his own maps showing the routes they followed and the direction of the wind. And in the same book drawing a diagram of the home-made anchor is a natural and helpful way of coming to grips with the exact nature of the mechanism described.

(iv) *Composition exercises:* The kind of composition work I have in mind is to be thought of not as an end in itself but rather as a means of securing a closer and more sensitive reading of some part of the book on which it is based. A class reading *Robinson Crusoe* might,

73

for instance, be asked to reconstruct the entry which Crusoe would have made in his Journal (if he hadn't run out of ink by then) on the day when he first encountered Friday. Events which the novelist has pictured through the eyes of one character may be worth retelling from a different 'angle of view'; a form reading *Lorna Doone* might be required to reproduce orally the account of John Ridd's ride which was given later that evening by Faggis, the highwayman and owner of the mare. Sometimes an opportunity may be offered by a letter which is referred to in the novel but not actually printed. Thus in Chapter XIII of *Pride and Prejudice* Mr. Bennet mentions to his family for the first time the reply that he has written to Mr. Collins' portentously friendly overture; a fourth form called upon to write this reply will need to master the precise relationship between the two correspondents, to understand the 'odd mixture of quick parts, sarcastic humour, reserve and caprice' that make up Mr. Bennet's character, and to deduce not only the general import of his letter but also the tone and spirit in which it would be written.

Such composition exercises justify themselves if they act as an incentive for the children to look again at the text and to seek out and notice the significance of details which passed them by at a first reading. There is also a place at times for the composition which is more loosely related to the text, demanding not so much a detailed reference-back to it, as a thorough imaginative entry into its spirit and intention. Thus a first form after reading *The Wind in the Willows* may be asked to imagine a sequel in which Mr. Toad buys an aeroplane; and a third form may invent new Just-So Stories or go on from reading *The Invisible Man* to write their own story with the title of 'The Invisible Schoolboy'.

(v) When reading a book with older forms we may come upon an issue which can profitably be turned into a debate. Which of the two Loveday brothers, John or Bob, deserves to gain more of the sympathies of the reader of *The Trumpet-Major*? In *A Tale of Two Cities* is Monsieur Defarge or Madame Defarge the more detestable villain? Or if the book is *The History of Mr. Polly*, the argument may be concerned with the exact causes of Mr. Polly's indigestion, and the order of their importance. Whatever the issue, the class will be given time for silent reading to gather evidence in support of their own viewpoint, for it will be insisted in the debate that no opinion can carry much weight unless it is backed up with 'chapter and verse'.

Invaluable though these teaching devices can be, there should come a time (probably in their third or fourth year) when the class no longer jibs at 'working over' a passage through questions and discussion, even though no 'incentive' has been thought up to make the procedure palatable. Naturally the passages the teacher chooses for this detailed study will present difficulties which the young reader could not negotiate for himself; they should also be ones which have some central significance in the book as a whole, for it would be wasteful to expend too much effort on pages which, however difficult, have only marginal importance.

As an example of a 'key passage' of this kind (one which almost chooses itself for extended study if one is reading the story with, say, a fourth form) we may take the episode of the fight with the fire in Conrad's *Youth*:

We tried. We battened down everything, and still she smoked. The smoke kept coming out through imperceptible crevices; it forced itself through bulkheads and covers; it oozed here and there and everywhere in slender threads, in an invisible film, in an incomprehensible manner. It made its way into the cabin, into the forecastle; it poisoned the sheltered places on the deck, it could be sniffed as high as the mainyard. It was clear that if the smoke came out the air came in. This was disheartening. This combustion refused to be stifled.

We resolved to try water, and took the hatches off. Enormous volumes of smoke, whitish, yellowish, thick, greasy, misty, choking, ascended as high as the trucks. All hands cleared out aft. Then the poisonous cloud blew away, and we went back to work in a smoke that was no thicker now than that of an ordinary factory chimney.

We rigged the force-pump, got the hose along, and by-and-by it burst. Well, it was as old as the ship—a prehistoric hose, and past repair. Then we pumped with the feeble head-pump, drew water with buckets, and in this way managed in time to pour lots of Indian Ocean into the main hatch. The bright stream flashed in sunshine, fell into a layer of white crawling smoke, and vanished on the black surface of coal. Steam ascended mingling with the smoke. We poured salt water as into a barrel without a bottom. It was our fate to pump in that ship, to pump out of her, to pump into her; and after keeping water out of her to save ourselves from being drowned, we frantically poured water into her to save ourselves from being burnt.

And she crawled on, do or die, in the serene weather. The sky was a miracle of purity, a miracle of azure. The sea was polished, was blue, was pellucid, was sparkling like a precious stone, extending on all sides, all round to the horizon—as if the whole terrestrial globe had been one jewel, one colossal sapphire, a single gem fashioned into a planet. And on the lustre of the great calm waters the Judea glided imperceptibly, enveloped in languid and unclean vapours, in a lazy cloud that drifted to leeward, light and slow; a pestiferous cloud defiling the splendour of sea and sky.

All this time of course we saw no fire. The cargo smouldered at the bottom somewhere. Once Mahon, as we were working side by side, said to me with a queer smile: 'Now, if she only would spring a tidy leak—like that time when we first left the Channel—it would put a stopper on this fire. Wouldn't it?' I remarked irrelevantly, 'Do you remember the rats?'

We fought the fire and sailed the ship too as carefully as though nothing had been the matter. The steward cooked and attended on us. Of the other twelve men, eight worked while four rested. Everyone took his turn, captain included. There was equality, and if not exactly fraternity, then a deal of good feeling. Sometimes a man, as he dashed a bucketful of water down the hatchway, would yell out, 'Hurrah for Bankok!' and the rest laughed. But generally we were taciturn and serious—and thirsty. Oh! how thirsty! And we had to be careful with the water. Strict allowance. The ship smoked, the sun blazed . . . Pass the bottle.

We tried everything. We even made an attempt to dig down to the fire. No good, of course. No man could remain more than a minute below. Mahon, who went first, fainted there, and the man who went to fetch him out did likewise. We lugged them out on deck. Then I leaped down to show how easily it could be done. They had learned wisdom by that time, and contented themselves by fishing for me with a chain-hook tied to a broom-handle, I believe. I did not offer to go and fetch up my shovel, which was left down below.

Things began to look bad. We put the long-boat into the water. The second boat was ready to swing out. We had also another, a 14-foot thing, on davits aft, where it was quite safe.

Then, behold, the smoke suddenly decreased. We redoubled our efforts to flood the bottom of the ship. In two days there was no smoke at all. Everybody was on the broad grin. This was on a Friday. On Saturday no work, but sailing the ship, of course, was done. The men washed their clothes and their faces for the first time in a fortnight, and had a special dinner given them. They spoke of spontaneous combustion with contempt, and implied they were the boys to put out combustions. Somehow we all felt as though we each had inherited a large fortune. But a beastly smell of burning hung about the ship. Captain Beard had hollow eyes and sunken cheeks. I had never noticed so much before how twisted and bowed he was. He and Mahon prowled soberly about hatches and ventilators, sniffing. It struck me suddenly poor Mahon was a very, very old chap. As to me, I was as pleased and proud as though I had helped to win a great naval battle. O! Youth!

The night was fine. In the morning a homeward-bound ship passed us hull down—the first we had seen for months; but we were nearing the land at last, Java Head being about 190 miles off, and nearly due north.

Next day it was my watch on deck from eight to twelve. At breakfast the captain observed, 'It's wonderful how that smell hangs about the cabin.' About ten, the mate being on the poop, I stepped down on the main-deck for a moment. The carpenter's bench stood abaft the mainmast: I leaned against it sucking at my pipe, and the carpenter, a young chap, came to talk to me. He remarked, 'I think we have done very well, haven't we?' and then I perceived with annoyance the fool was trying to tilt the bench. I said curtly, 'Don't, Chips,' and immediately became aware of a queer sensation, of an absurd delusion—I seemed somehow to be in the air. I heard all round me like a pent-up breath released—as if a thousand giants simultaneously had said Phoo!—and felt a dull concussion which made my ribs ache suddenly. No doubt about it—I was in the air, and my body was describing a short parabola. But short as it was, I had the time to think several thoughts in, as far as I can remember, the following order: 'This can't be the carpenter—What is it?—Some accident—Submarine volcano?—Coals, gas!—By jove! we are being blown up—Everybody's dead—I am falling into the after-hatch—I see fire in it.'

The coal-dust suspended in the air of the hold had glowed dull-red at the moment of the explosion. In the twinkling of an eye, in an infinitesimal fraction of a second since the first tilt of the bench, I was sprawling full length on the cargo. I picked myself up and scrambled out. It was quick like a rebound. The deck was a wilderness of smashed timber, lying cross-wise like trees in a wood after a hurricane; an immense curtain of solid rags waved gently before me—it was the mainsail blown to strips. I thought, The masts will be toppling over directly; and to get out of the way bolted on all-fours towards the poop-ladder. The first person I saw was Mahon, with eyes like saucers, his mouth open, and the long white hair standing straight on end round his head like a silver halo. He was just about to go down when the sight of the main-deck stirring, heaving up, and changing into splinters before his eyes, petrified him on the top step. I stared at him in unbelief, and he stared at me with a queer kind of shocked curiosity. I did not know that I had no hair, no eyebrows, no eyelashes, that my young moustache was burnt off, that my face was black, one cheek laid open, my nose cut, and my chin bleeding. I had lost my cap, one of my slippers, and my shirt was torn to rags. Of all this I was not aware. I was amazed to see the ship still afloat, the poop-deck whole—and, most of all, to see anybody alive. Also the peace of the sky and the serenity of the sea were distinctly surprising. I suppose I expected to see them convulsed with horror. . . . Pass the bottle.

The explosion is the culminating point in the long series of mishaps which have overtaken the *Judea* on what proves to be her final voyage; as such it occupies a central place in the tale. What we shall want our fourth form to take from the passage is above all an appreciation of the extraordinary vividness with which the explosion itself is rendered. This vividness comes largely from the precision with which Conrad has realised and presented Marlow's own sensations in the few brief moments immediately before, during and after the explosion; but these two final paragraphs depend for their full effect upon the reader's awareness of what has been unobtrusively indicated about the state of mind of Marlow (and of the other members of the crew) during the earlier stages of the struggle against the fire. In selecting, for a fourth form, from the superb complexity of realised experience offered by the passage we are led therefore to concentrate our questioning around the reactions and feelings of the human participants in the incident.

We start by reading the extract through aloud without interruption of any kind (and it will usually be as well for the teacher himself to undertake this reading). Next we turn back to the beginning and work forward again with accompanying questions and discussion, taking a paragraph or two at a time; each section will thus be read again by the class, but this may be done either silently by the class as a whole, or aloud by a pupil, as immediate convenience dictates. We may open with a simple question of a factual kind. 'What methods did the crew use in their attempts to put out the fire?' (Three methods are actually mentioned; the sentence 'We tried everything,' might imply others which remain unstated.) 'How did they feel while they were making these different attempts?' (This should lead at first to notice of the words 'disheartening', 'frantically', 'taciturn and serious—and thirsty', and, after the futile attempt to dig down to the fire, the sentence 'Things began to look bad'. The note of 'disheartening', it will be observed, is taken up again in Mahon's wry regret for the 'tidy leak' which had given them so much trouble earlier in the voyage, and in Marlow's reference, only seemingly irrelevant, to the rats; that this leads us outside the confines of the extract itself is merely an example of the fact that in any novel of real quality the texture of meaning locally is inevitably and inseparably bound up with the complex interweaving of experience which makes up the unity of the work as a whole. At this point the paragraph commencing 'We fought the fire and sailed the ship too . . .' will bear fairly detailed examination for the evidence it affords of the men's sense of their dangerous plight and the mood in which they faced it.) ' "Then, behold, the smoke suddenly decreased." How did the men feel now? And the Captain? Mahon? Marlow himself?' (Here it should be possible to elicit the covert contrast between the unchecked elation of the crew and of Marlow, and the more sober and cautious reactions of the elderly captain and mate—'It struck me suddenly poor Mahon was a very very old chap.' The same contrast may be noted in the penultimate paragraph between the remarks of the carpenter and the captain.)

We should now be ready to attack the two final paragraphs. 'Where is Marlow when the explosion begins and what, exactly, is he doing? At what point does he realise what is actually happening? Why is he so slow to realise this? What does he at first think is happening? What words or phrases show his reluctance to recognise the fact of the explosion? ("queer", "absurd delusion", "seemed". "No doubt about it—") Do you see a relationship between this reluctance and the two rather fantastic similes in the sentence beginning, "I heard all round me . . ."? Can you find, among the other explanations which occur to him, one which seems almost equally fantastic and far-fetched?'

Then, moving on to the last paragraph of all: 'How long did all this take? Where did Marlow find himself at the end of it? "It was quick like a rebound"—why? What did he see? Which words bring out his reaction to what he saw? Which bring out that of Mahon?'

At this point we ought if possible to read the whole passage aloud once more, so that the class's parting experience may be a unified one which incorporates within it the details and interconnections, unnoticed at the first reading, which the class-room questioning and discussion have brought to light.

No doubt to many English teachers a lesson of the kind I have just tried to outline represents their standard practice and therefore will seem scarcely worth detailed exemplification. There may be others, however, whose conception of a 'prose study' lesson would be somewhat different; and it is perhaps worth drawing attention to one or two of the possibilities which my own lesson would deliberately exclude. In the first place there is no attempt (even at this fourth-year stage) to elucidate at all exhaustively the *full* meaning of the passage. Many details have been left completely unmentioned, and some of these (the contrast, for instance, between the *Judea* and the 'sea and sky' which surrounds her) would have a certain importance in any completely satisfactory reading of the extract. A number of difficult words, too, remain unexplained, and while the meaning of many of these will be fairly evident from the context, there may be others (pellucid, for instance) about which most of the form will have gathered only a very hazy notion indeed. There need be no taboo on referring to such points, of course. If any members of the class choose to mention or ask about them they will be discussed and explained. But the lesson as shaped and directed by the teacher will be focused around the passage's central structure of meaning, and will confine itself rigorously to the words and details which bear closely on this. Secondly, there is no attempt to deal with the writer's 'style' or 'technique'. We do not, for instance, think it appropriate or worth while to point out to the class the variations of sentence-structure which occur at the climax of this passage; nor, in reading the companion story, *Gaspar Ruiz*, would we be concerned to draw attention to the art with which Conrad employs shifts in the time-sequence or alterations in the mode of narration. Our aim in these lessons is not that our pupils should be able to point to and name the 'methods' the writer has used in order to gain his 'effects'; what we are really out to do is to ensure that they experience these effects as fully as possible. Admittedly the distinction between the two aims may sometimes be a fine one. Again I am not trying to set up a taboo; the short disjointed sentences at the end of the penultimate paragraph of our *Youth* extract might well excite spontaneous comment from a bright form, and there would be no need to evade such discussion. My concern is simply to suggest the proper direction for the teacher's emphases. Unfortunately, knowledge about 'how the writer gains his effects' is all too often spurious (at any rate at the level of simplification which would bring it within the scope of the fifteen- or sixteen-year-old pupil). Nor is it (even when securely based) of any real help in achieving that full realisation and re-creation of experience which is what we mean by 'reading'. What we surely want above all is that our pupils should be able to make a thoroughgoing imaginative entry into the experience of the novel or story — that they should be 'inside' the story while reading, and at the same time that the experience of the story which they thus create for themselves should be controlled, firmly and sensitively, by the actual words the writer has used. To invite attention to the writer's technique is, on the contrary, to ask the pupil to stand aside from this act of imaginative penetration, and, thus led outside the experience, to contemplate it from without as a deliberately constructed artefact. At best this can only be a distraction from the real business in hand; and to many pupils it will offer, with its accompanying sense of something definite and clear-cut which can readily be 'learned', a beguiling and deceptive substitute for the difficult art which they still have to master — that of responding, fully, sensitively and accurately, to what they read.[1]

Have I too readily assumed that the books we use as 'class-readers' will be fiction? Certainly there is no compelling reason why they should necessarily be so; and the training we provide in 'reading with understanding' ought to cover a wide range of different kinds of prose, informative and expository as well as imaginative and creative. But in practice we do find that the complete books which are most worth reading together with classes between the ages of eleven and sixteen are, with a few notable exceptions, works of fiction. The books which meet our needs as 'class-readers' will differ from the 'home-readers' mainly in demanding (and repaying) a rather greater degree of attention and effort; the satisfactions which they offer to the young reader in the end ought to be very much the same in kind, but more, rather than less, intense in quality. Since part of our aim is to enable our pupils to take in a novel as a unified experience, there are distinct advantages to the book which is of no more than moderate length and has (unlike, say, some of the more rambling and discursive of Dickens' novels) a perceptible unity of organisation. A large proportion of the book can then be read together in class (it will seldom be either possible or desirable to read it all in this way); and the reading and discussion does not need to be spread over such an unduly long period of time that the readers have forgotten the beginning of the book before they reach the end of it. Short stories, too, have the advantage of fitting conveniently into the time-table made up of forty-minute lesson-periods; and some useful collections

[1] The categories of technical criticism of fiction—theme, character, plot, climax, dénouement, setting, atmosphere, etc.—are in any case only abstractions from that total experience of a novel which the reader gains by responding to its words. So long as their true nature is kept clearly in mind, these terms have a certain usefulness in advanced critical discussion as a convenient shorthand by means of which different readers can exchange notes, as it were, about particular aspects of their own response. To the teacher himself they may be useful in giving an intellectual structure to his own response, in charting for him a map, so to speak, which will help him to guide his pupils through the imaginative experience of the novel without losing his bearings. To the pupil who is still learning how to read a novel, however, the map can never be a means of gaining the experience; that can come only from exposure to the words themselves. See C. H. Rickword, 'A Note on Fiction', reprinted in *Towards Standards of Criticism* (Wishart).

of these have begun to appear in school editions during the past few years.

Of course, circumstances may arise in which a long novel is the only possible choice; and in this case, although the disadvantages are real, they are seldom insurmountable if a determined and planned attack is made on them. Since the greater part of the book will clearly have to be read outside lesson-time, the first task is to lead the class into the story, in a way which engenders enough interest to make them want to go on with it. This can usually be achieved by a rapid reading-together (aloud) of the first chapter or two, the teacher probably doing the bulk of the reading, and perhaps skipping some of the lengthier scene-setting if this is not wholly indispensable. From this point onwards the class will be set a target for each week or fortnight's reading, due notice being given that in a specified future lesson a certain chapter will be read together and that by then they will be expected to have read up to that point on their own. Choosing sections which are to be dealt with in class may not be altogether straightforward; usually we shall want to take the episodes which are most important for an understanding of the plot or structure of the book as a whole, but these will need to be spread out to some extent over the length of the book, and sometimes it may be advisable to select a chapter of rather less central significance either because it would be too difficult for the children to negotiate successfully on their own, or because enjoyment of it is particularly likely to be enhanced by a communal reading. Treatment in class should at any rate be such as to add something (in vividness of experience or depth of understanding) which most of the pupils could not get from reading the same pages by themselves. It is desirable, too, to aim at some variety of activity in these lessons from week to week, ringing the changes upon the possible methods of treatment (dramatised reading, miming, radio version, silent reading followed by discussion, composition-work, diagram-making, etc.) according to the particular requirements of the material in hand.

I shall conclude this section with a short list of books (including some of 'conte' or 'nouvelle' length, but not excluding longer novels) which have been found suitable for class-reading at different stages. There is, inevitably, some overlap with the list suggested earlier for home reading. The same symbols are used to indicate publishers; in a few cases (indicated by an asterisk) the use of an abridged version is recommended:

Some Books suitable for use as Class-Readers

FIRST YEAR

Secondary Modern Streams

Jim Davis (Masefield). L.
The Prince and the Pauper (Twain).
  CW.
Treasure Island (Stevenson).
The Adventures of Tom Sawyer
  (Twain).

Grammar Streams

Martin Hyde (Masefield). L.
Treasure Island (Stevenson).
The Boy Who Was Afraid (Sperry).
  He.
A Christmas Carol (Dickens).
A Country Child (Uttley). N.
The Rose and the Ring (Thackeray).
  D·N.
The Adventures of Tom Sawyer
  (Twain).

SECOND YEAR

Secondary Modern Streams

The Boy Who Was Afraid (Sperry).
  He.
Martin Hyde (Masefield). L.
A Christmas Carol (Dickens).
The Splendid Journey (Morrow).
  He.
The First Men in the Moon (Wells).
  C.

Grammar Streams

Moonfleet (Falkner). A·P.
White Fang (London). He·N.
The Call of the Wild (London).
  He·L.
The Light in the Forest (Richter).
  Me.

THIRD YEAR

Secondary Modern Streams

The Call of the Wild (London).
  He·L.
White Fang (London). He·N.
King Solomon's Mines (Haggard).
Prester John (Buchan). N.
The Prisoner of Zenda (Hope). D.
The Invisible Man (Wells). C.
Moonfleet (Falkner). A·P.

Grammar Streams

Short Stories (Wells). N·P.
The Pearl (Steinbeck). He.
Six Stories (Twain). CW.
Off-Beat (ed. Whitehead). CW.
The Day of the Triffids (Wyndham).
  Hu.
The Chrysalids (Wyndham). Hu.
*Moby Dick (Melville). CW.

83

Secondary Modern Streams
The Silver Sword (Serraillier).
He·P.
The Light in the Forest (Richter).
Me.

FOURTH YEAR

Secondary Modern Streams

The Pearl (Steinbeck). He.

Three Men in a Boat (Jerome). D.

The Kon-Tiki Expedition (Heyerdahl). AU.

A Pattern of Islands (Grimble).
Murray, complete edn.

Six Stories (Twain). CW.

Off-Beat (ed. Whitehead). CW.

The Day of the Triffids (Wyndham).
Hu.

The Red Pony (Steinbeck). He.

The Canyon (Schaefer). He.

The Chrysalids (Wyndham). Hu.

People and Diamonds (ed. Holbrook). CU.

The Getting of Wisdom (Richardson). He.

Grammar Streams

The Red Pony (Steinbeck). He.

Life on the Mississippi (Twain).
CW.

Honey in the Horn (Davis). Hu.

Jane Eyre (Bronte).

Youth and Gaspar Ruiz (Conrad).
D.

Typhoon (Conrad). D·He.

A Tale of Two Cities (Dickens).

Huckleberry Finn (Twain).

People and Diamonds (ed. Holbrook). CU.

The Getting of Wisdom (Richardson). He.

Twentieth Century Short Stories
(ed. Barnes and Egford). Ha.

Mainstream, Book I
(ed. Whitehead). CW.

Lark Rise (Thompson). O.

(iv)

As already pointed out, we have come increasingly during the present century to think of reading not merely as a perceptual skill but rather as an active taking of meaning from the written or printed symbols — a 'thought-getting' process. More recently still we have realised that our conception of reading needs to be extended even further. No one can be said to have fully mastered the art of reading until he is able not only to take in the meaning of what he reads but also to assess its worth. To consider how much credence we can give to what we read, to estimate its value for us, to decide how much importance to attach to it—are we not bound to admit that 'reading' in its fullest sense must necessarily include these elements within it? To the four stages in the process of learning to read which we have already described (pp. 30–31) we ought in fact to add a fifth —that in which the reader begins to examine critically what he reads and to form, in regard to it, judgments of relative value. As the Second Report on Reading of the American N.S.S.E. put it: '. . . any conception of reading is inadequate which fails to include reflection, critical evaluation, and the clarification of meaning.' [N.S.S.E. (1937), p. 26.]

The need to develop (ultimately) in our pupils this ability to react critically to what they read is perhaps obvious enough to require little arguing. Some ability to discriminate, to select intelligently among the multiplicity of alternatives which offer, is clearly indispensable if our reading is to add anything significant to our capacity for living; to put the case at its very lowest, the reader who lacks this will inevitably, in any civilisation at any period, waste an unconscionably large proportion of his time. At the level of the individual life alone this is a serious matter, for the quality of our experience in general is profoundly influenced by the quality of our reading. In a democratic society which continually demands from its citizens that they exercise their powers of decision in a responsible way, taking into account all the relevant information, and assessing the merits of rival arguments with a balanced judgment, our concern must necessarily take on an added dimension.

Yet the disturbing fact is that in the Western world of the mid-twentieth century this power of discrimination has become more difficult of attainment than ever. Never before has there been such a strident multitude of siren voices beckoning us away from the pursuit of true judgment, by playing ruthlessly and insistently upon our complacency, cupidity, social timidity, frustrations, prejudices, irrational fears, prurience, and mental laziness. And this 'trading on the range of human infirmities' (Veblen) starts early. From the moment they acquire language, our children are assailed day in and day out by advertising slogans—from the television set, on cereal packets, on hoardings, in comics. At adolescence they are singled out as targets for psychological manipulation by manufacturers of soft drinks, clothes, confectionery, popular entertainments, all single-mindedly intent on wheedling from them in the immediate present their current spending-money and on securing in the future their lifelong allegiance to a brand-name. These commercial pressures diffuse their aura and influence into a host of social and cultural attitudes, as newspapers, magazines and television serials covertly but wholeheartedly endorse the hierarchy of goals enshrined by the copywriters. The urge towards social conformity, the need to wear the 'in-look' and to go along with those who 'set today's trends' becomes an imperative value seldom questioned. The insistent emphasis, in advertisements, upon 'newness' is reinforced by unremitting publicity for this week's Top Ten, this month's best-seller, this season's hair-style or television-idol; in this mental climate it is understandable that some young people need persuading to open any book written more than ten years ago, so convinced are they that it is bound to be 'square'. Moreover, underlying the ethos of the entertainment industry is an assumption even more pregnant with consequences for the educator: the assumption that what we all need in our leisure hours is *distraction*, an effortless, painless (and pleasureless) time-killing which demands of us no more than glancing at illustrations, scanning headlines, or gazing in mild stupefaction at a flickering screen for the span of thirteen minutes which separates one commercial from the next. In this context the levelling-down implicit in the quest for mass-audience leads inevitably to that trivialisation which is the hall-mark of all popular newspapers and television programmes today—a trivialisation in which serious issues can be presented only in irrelevantly personalised terms and in which the scale of values is so inverted that few protest when Sunday papers pay huge sums to regale their readers with the sadistic or salacious reminiscences of convicted murderers and prostitutes. In an environment such as this the future adult, in his own interests both as citizen and as individual, desperately needs to be equipped with some degree of critical awareness. If he is to retain any capacity for a humane existence, any integrity as a person, any individuality even, he needs to acquire some power of resistance against these debasing and dehumanising pressures.

All the same, it is easier to perceive the need than to know how to meet it. I do not mean merely that the teacher engaged in such work will have to call upon all his reserves of tact if he is to avoid alienating many of his pupils—particularly those who are ready to see his cautionary warnings as either a gratuitous display of social superiority or a veiled attack upon the values and standards of their own homes. Nor am I thinking solely of the difficulty which is crucial for all attempts to train critical awareness—the hard fact that it is only the method of judging that can be learnt, not the judgments themselves. Certainly we must never forget that the pupil's own genuine, independent and first-hand judgment is the only one that really counts; nothing much is gained by *knowing* that the *Daily Citizen* is a more trustworthy and responsible paper than the *Daily Pin-Up* if you still prefer to spend your breakfast-time with the *Pin-Up*.

No, our central problem is an even more recalcitrant one. The plain fact is that at present the overwhelming majority of our children leave school before they are mature enough to profit from this type of training. Ironically enough it is precisely those who will suffer most through lack of it who are most certain to leave too early to receive it.

I have no doubt at all that the later years of adolescence form the most fruitful period for this introduction to critical reading. At earlier stages it is seldom profitable to raise questions of value (overtly at any rate) partly because the adult and childish standpoint are too far apart to offer much common ground, and partly because children's own values and judgments are in any case shifting and changing so rapidly as they grow up. But at sixteen or seventeen the boy or girl is beginning to settle down into a more stable pattern of personality; he is willing, and often eager, to discuss with a sympathetic adult the standards which are to determine his future choices of conduct and living. And his experience, though still inadequate to sustain the fierceness with which he will sometimes adopt and defend particular opinions, is nevertheless wide enough to make it worth while to discuss at some length the possible or justifiable grounds for such opinions.

But this development cannot be forced. If we attempt critical work too early we run a dual risk. In the first place the pupils' ability to 'read with understanding' may still be too undeveloped to provide a secure basis for attempts at evaluation. Clearly the power to take what is there in the given piece of writing, to grasp the writer's intention and to give to the words embodying that intention the response which they properly evoke, is an indispensable prerequisite for this new stage. However superficially 'correct' it may seem, a value-judgment which lacks such a basis is worse than useless, harmful indeed in its tendency to encourage a slap-happy and cocksure opinionatedness which will stand in the way of genuine future progress. And in the second place there is the danger of developing an attitude which is merely negative and destructive—a cynical know-ingness about the bad which is unmatched by any positive attachment to the good. This can easily arise if pupils are led to embark on critical work before they have gained a wide enough experience of reading which is both of high quality and really satisfying to them personally. To 'see through' the shoddy or dishonest appeals of 'Admass' is not enough in itself—and may be little more than a fashionable pose or a smart intellectual exercise. Only a firm awareness and appreciation of what good writing has to offer can supply the standards of comparison which entitle us to condemn the cheaply inferior, and enable us to resist, in the long run, its omnipresent blandishments.

Even so, provided we adopt certain safeguards, there is some elementary critical work which can reasonably be attempted from about the fourth year onwards with most grammar school forms and with some of the abler ones in secondary modern schools. It will be best to confine ourselves, to begin with, to everyday reading material of a fairly simple kind—advertisements, official notices, extracts from newspapers and periodicals. With such material, difficulties of understanding can be kept to a minimum, and there is little danger of producing a generalised suspicion of the printed word which might 'put them off' reading of this kind altogether. (If we were to subject works of literature, and especially poetry, to direct critical attack at this stage, this danger could not be so readily discounted.) There must be as little didactic pressure from the teacher as possible; the emphasis will be upon free and frank discussion in which the children learn to formulate and justify to each other their own reactions and opinions. We put before them pieces of writing with different intentions and varying levels of achievement, asking them in each case to decide for themselves what effect the writer has set out to produce, and on what kind of reader. The question proposed is not merely 'How far has the writer accomplished what he set out to do?'; the pupils are expected also to consider to what extent the different intentions are in themselves valuable, commendable, or reputable.

We may, for instance, bring along a mixed batch of advertisements. Which of these provide information? Which seek to persuade by appealing to emotion or prejudice? Which feelings in us do they play upon? What kind of reader is likely to react in the way the copywriter has clearly counted on? The class may then be set to work (perhaps in small groups) to collect examples of the different types of appeal (sex, fear, cupidity, snobbery, conformism, etc.) commonly used in advertising; later they may go on to concoct between them parodies of the kind of advertisement that might be used to launch a new brand of soap powder, toothpaste or breakfast cereal. On another occasion we collect together in the class-room the same day's issue of as many different newspapers as possible. We compare the headlines in the different papers; we examine the amount of space given to particular items of the day's news, and also the amount of space devoted to different types of 'news' (political, international, crime, sport, 'human interest', sex) and 'features' (background to the news, cartoons, competitions, gossip and chit-chat, editorial comment, readers' letters, hobbies, fashion, entertainment); we compare the treatment of some particular event in different papers, looking for evidence of bias in the way the facts are selected and arranged, noting the extent to which fact and opinion are kept separate, observing the trivialising effect which may come from presenting a serious issue in terms of personalised 'human interest', or from 'angling' it to exploit some unimportant but eye-catching side-issue; we notice also any differences in the language that is used – length of sentences and paragraphs, number of 'cross-heads', range of vocabulary, predominance of emotionally-toned words, and so on – and we try to account for the differences we find. Inevitably discussion of this kind cannot be confined solely to the qualities of the exhibits actually in front of the class; it is bound to lead outwards to consideration of wider issues, and to become, in effect, a rudimentary sociological inquiry into the modern newspaper industry, its readership, its economic structure and its dependence upon advertising revenue, its relationship to other media of mass communication, and its merits and demerits as a means of moulding public opinion. Provided the teacher is aware of the possibility of bias in himself and careful to keep any prejudices of his own well under control, this is no bad thing; it demonstrates the relevance of English studies to the problems of contemporary living in a way which most adolescent pupils find refreshing and salutary.[1]

[1] For more detailed suggestions about class-room work with newspapers, see Wilkinson (1956) and Andrews (1958). Valuable background material for the teacher, covering press, advertising, and popular reading in general, will be found in Angell (1933); Leavis and Thompson (1933); Thompson (1939), (1943) and (1965); and Williams (1962). In addition, Hall and Whannel (1964) suggest lines of approach which would be particularly useful with older pupils, though their emphases and detailed judgments are sometimes highly questionable.

In addition to this explicitly critical work it must be remembered that the English teacher will often, even during the years of compulsory schooling, be engaged in activities which, in less direct ways, prepare his pupils to bring their powers of judgment to bear upon their reading. The questioning, for instance, which trains them to read accurately is at the same time unobtrusively training them to select the important elements of meaning in what they read. In the middle school the complementary disciplines of note-making and summarising will also require the ability to discriminate between the essential and the inessentials, and to recognise how far particular details support an argument or contribute to a line of thought; so long as this task is not allowed to degenerate into the merely mechanical exercise of 'reducing' each and every précis-passage to 'a third of its original length', it will call, moreover, for some nascent capacity for assessment, some sense of which passage is packed with closely organised meaning and which is mostly empty rhetoric or elegant trifling. Rather similar from this point of view is the way our pupils learn, more by example than precept, how to give the appropriate degree of attention to different types and levels of reading-matter. (Perhaps training of this kind, over-systematised though it may be in many American courses of 'reading instruction', is rather too much neglected in English schools; to know how to skip and when to skip is, after all, an indispensable attribute of the mature reader.)

Moreover, questions of relative value will always be there in the background of good English teaching at any stage, guiding the teacher in his choice of the reading-material he presents to his pupils, or in the suggestions he makes designed to lead them on from the book they enjoy to the better book which they can learn to enjoy even more. True, in the years of compulsory schooling, they will usually be present in the consciousness of the teacher rather than in that of the children; but in their absence there can be no certain and lasting progress. And, when all is said and done, it is this positive experience of worthwhile reading, this discovery of the deep satisfactions offered by good books and above all by works of imaginative literature, which is the most important preliminary to any kind of critical work. We are led back again to the central task of all English teaching—the need to ensure that all children gain the widest possible acquaintance with forms of experience in language which are of finer quality than those to which they are exposed in the home and the street. This experience of speech and writing which is good in its own way and at its own level (or, if not always exactly that, at the very least honest and decent) will be valuable in its own right. For the minority whose education lasts long enough it will be the essential foundation upon which the capacity for judgment and discrimination can later be built. We must trust, too, that for some at any rate of the others it may eventually provide standards of comparison which will enable them at times to see through and reject the cheap, the slipshod and the debilitating.

Chapter 3

THE TEACHING OF POETRY

Memory

One had a lovely face,
And two or three had charm,
But charm and face were in vain
Because the mountain grass
Cannot but keep the form
Where the mountain hare has lain.

SOME of my readers will no doubt either recognise this poem or be able to attribute it to its proper author. Thus identified, it will, for them, fall immediately into place in a certain context, historical, social or literary — an intricate network of associations left behind in part by their past experience of poems of the same period or by the same writer, and in part by their reading of works of criticism, literary history, or scholarly exegesis. They should perhaps remember that when a poem is presented to a class in school there is seldom any such already-existent context available for the boy or girl to fit it into; each poem has to make its way on its own merits, as a thing-in-itself.

Others, to whom the poem is unfamiliar, may feel more than anything that it seems just a little irrelevant. 'What has this to do with me — let alone with the lesson I have to take with 4c tomorrow?' (To be found slightly irrelevant is, one might suggest, the most common fate of poetry in the modern world; will not precisely this, in all probability, overtake 'The Lotus-Eaters' or Keats' 'Ode to Autumn' when tomorrow afternoon 4c dutifully open their poetry books at the appointed page?)

Others again (it may be only a few) will find as they read the poem that it engages with some deeply-felt experience, stirring levels of being which the commerce of day-to-day life rarely disturbs, and bringing with it a sense of illumination and of what Coleridge called 'a more than usual state of emotion with more than usual order'. And surely it is just this interaction, on a more than superficial level, between poem and reader that we should be concerned with when we deal with poetry in school; what matters in our poetry lessons is the occasion when, for someone at least, reading a poem is felt to be important in a personal sense, a significant mode of experience, impinging upon the life within and radically affecting it. This is clearly something different from taking a poem as material for study, whether linguistic, historical, aesthetic, biographical, psychological, or what-have-you. It is not even a matter of understanding the poem, for understanding, however full and exact, can remain an achievement of the intellect only, cold, external, and detached. Nor is what we are after quite the same, really, as 'enjoying' the poem. Some element of enjoyment or satisfaction must enter, no doubt, into the response proper to any work of art, but it is easy enough to imagine a reading of a poem with a class (Noyes' 'Highwayman' perhaps, or Masefield's 'Spanish Waters') which would be enjoyable in much the same way as a switchback ride, and about as valuable. And it could hardly be said that enjoyment is quite the word for our own experience of, for instance, *King Lear*, or of Hopkins' sonnet, 'I wake and feel the fell of dark'; play and poem engage us deeply and intensely, but in a way that verges on the painful, at times almost on the unbearable.

Does this sound a little too portentous? If anyone should doubt, cynically, whether this kind of 'interaction' can ever occur in poetry lessons in the main body of the secondary school, I can only suggest that the sceptic takes along to a second or third form copies of D. H. Lawrence's 'Snake' and reads it aloud to them as well as he is able. I have never known this to fail; they may not exactly 'like' it, but the hush of attention attests that they are held, arrested, transfixed by it.

But, of course, this is only one poem; we know that in the ordinary hurly-burly of the class-room such occasions come all too rarely, and this despite the inextinguishable missionary zeal which most teachers bring to their endeavours with poetry. Before we can go further we ought to consider why it is that, in a branch of English teaching which enlists so much honest, well-intended and often well-judged effort, the outcome of it all is so frequently rather discouraging. And we might start by trying to look at the problem from the point of view of the children themselves. What are the obstacles which stand in the way of their realising how much the reading of poetry has to offer them as a living form of experience?

First of all comes the obvious point that, with extraordinarily few exceptions, children never read poetry, *except* in the class-room. In this, of course, they are far from being unique. (They are perhaps not even dissimilar from the majority of teachers.) Their abstinence is only a symptom of the singularly low esteem in which poetry is held in contemporary society at large. Of all the different types of book which they might, in favoured cases, find on the bookshelves in their home, the volume of poetry is surely the most improbable. The chance of their ever having heard poems read aloud on television or radio (apart from school programmes) is so remote as to be virtually negligible. This relegation of poetry to the utmost periphery of normal human activity has become so much a part of the accepted fabric of our own society that we may find it hard to realise that there have been phases of English culture which were utterly different in this respect—times when hearing poetry spoken or sung (ballads, madrigals, folksongs, lute-songs, the poetry of the Bible or the liturgy) formed part of the background in which all children grew up. Nowadays the average child's out-of-school contacts with anything even dimly resembling poetry are astonishingly scanty. He will have had a wealth of nursery rhymes recited to him in infancy; that tradition, though it may now be in decline, is still, fortunately, a living one. Apart from this, what? The 'lyrics' from current popular songs; the incantatory jingles blared forth as the accompaniment to TV commercials; vapidly benevolent rhymes on the inside of Christmas or birthday cards; the halting couplets which caption the monotonous adventures of Rupert Bear; the flat little poems in Annuals about animals or fairies—and that is all. How can the taste for poetry flower if it has to grow from a soil such as this? In dealing with prose we can at any rate count on our pupils (in most cases) gaining for themselves a wide acquaintance with stories which have some distant kinship with the books we put before them in school; the stories they read for themselves may often be of indifferent quality, but they do form a starting-point from which advance is possible. We shall find no basis of this kind for what we try to do in poetry lessons.

In these circumstances the first task of the teacher is to supply as far as he can the deficiencies of the environment; before he can get very far in teaching poems, he must somehow persuade his children to acquire that wide experience of the poetic mode which they signally lack. They must be induced to read a great deal of poetry (good or bad) which really appeals to them; for only out of this can arise the sense that to read poetry is both natural and enjoyable. So long as what they are reading has some of the life of genuine poetry (and is not merely synthetic or mass-produced verse-mongering), its quality is not, to begin with, of prime importance. A stress upon enjoyment seems to me fully justified at this initial stage, although by itself it would certainly not be enough later on.

In these days a certain amount along these lines will probably have been accomplished in the junior school. In the earlier years of the secondary school, however, the teacher will be well advised to devote a good deal of the time available for poetry not so much to 'teaching' particular poems as to creating and fostering a background of poetic experience. We need to have on hand in the class-room not merely the allotted 'set' of poetry anthologies, but also as wide a range as possible of different volumes of poems (single copies will do). Most of these will be copies of other anthologies designed especially for children (the stockroom cupboard will often yield a useful nucleus of discarded or incomplete sets, or specimen copies), but it is useful also to have some volumes of individual poets (Lear, Carroll, de la Mare, D. H. Lawrence, Stevenson, Masefield, Belloc's *Cautionary Tales*, Eliot's *Practical Cats*) and of course some collections of ballads. With these resources on tap the class will spend a great deal of their time compiling their own anthologies, in a special exercise book or loose-leaf folder; they will be encouraged to follow their own tastes with little prompting from the teacher, scouring the sources available to find poems they really like, copying out their choices neatly, and illustrating and embellishing them if they wish, so that at the end of the year the compilation which results may be both an expression of individuality and a source of pride. It would be a mistake for the teacher to exercise any censorship on grounds of quality. If some children bring along from home or elsewhere poems or pseudo-poems of little merit (culled perhaps from an annual or from an antiquated children's encyclopedia) these are to be admitted without comment; but, in fact, if plenty of good and suitable poetry is available, it will be found that children often show surprising enterprise and maturity in their selection from it.

Out of this work can arise the occasional 'Poetry Programme' (the tape-recorder can be used for this) or 'Poetry-Speaking Festival'. Each child may be asked to present a favourite poem to the rest of the class, either reading it aloud as a means of sharing enjoyment, or learning it by heart beforehand; or, alternatively, a group of children may be set the task of preparing a programme of spoken poetry to

95

last, say, twenty minutes, in which case some of the speaking may be done chorally if they so desire. Some activity of this kind is essential if we are to preserve a due awareness of the all-important sensuous qualities of sound and rhythm which can be lost if poetry is read by the eye alone. It is useful also to play from time to time gramophone records of spoken poetry, especially if recordings can be found of poems which children have already chosen for their anthologies. Besides providing a standard of poetry-speaking which may (sometimes, though not necessarily) be higher than that which the teacher can set himself, these can help to confirm the children's sense that reading poetry is an activity which has some place in the world outside the class-room and which some adults (other than teachers) do at times concern themselves with. There is similar benefit to be had from giving the children opportunity and encouragement to make up poems of their own; whatever the merit of the creative work they produce at this age, to dabble in the medium on their own account does certainly foster the acceptance of poetry as something which is neither esoteric nor precious, but a normal and natural facet of human life.

The activities I have mentioned so far are concerned to provide a background of poetic experience; I hope it will be agreed that they are indispensable, and must not on any pretext whatsoever be squeezed out of the time-table in either the grammar, technical or modern school. At the same time more than this is needed if children are to make real progress in their capacity to read poetry; they must be confronted from time to time with poems which the teacher has chosen to read and discuss with them in order to extend the range and depth of their poetic response. At this point we come closer to the heart of the problem. Let us try again to look at it from the standpoint of the children, taking as our focus a particular example —a well-known anthology piece which children often meet in exactly this way at the age of eleven or twelve.

The Eagle

He clasps the crag with crooked hands;
Close to the sun in lonely lands,
Ringed with the azure world, he stands.

The wrinkled sea beneath him crawls;
He watches from his mountain walls,
And like a thunderbolt, he falls.

Can we by an effort of empathy enter into the reactions of our eleven-year-old class when they are faced with this for the first time? Though the poem clearly has a topic likely to arouse a lively interest in many of them, a certain aura of obscurity may well enshroud the point and purpose of its treatment here. It is difficult to assimilate it to anything they are accustomed to meet outside the pages of their school poetry anthology. It doesn't give information about eagles, as might a school textbook, or an encyclopedia; nor does it tell a story, in the manner of the books they borrow from the library. Yet it is evidently difficult; when the teacher has read it to the class, that is not the end of the matter. More is expected, though the exact nature of this 'more' may not be easily graspable. In these circumstances it may be not unnatural for the children to feel that the difficulty ought to reside in something that the teacher could explain if he would, very much as the science teacher explains a difficult point in science or mathematics. Certainly it is hard to learn that to read and respond to a poem is something that one can only do for oneself, a matter essentially of what I have called 'interaction'.

Does 'difficulty' perhaps seem an inappropriate word to use about Tennyson's 'Eagle'? Nevertheless, poetry in general has its difficulty, just as this particular poem may have for the eleven-year-old; it demands of the reader a kind and degree of effort not usually exacted by prose. We must not, of course, exaggerate the differentiation implied here between poetry and prose; certainly I have no wish to endorse the nineteenth-century heresy of some underlying ethereal substance peculiar to true poetry, a vein of true poetic gold to be identified infallibly by the divining-rod of ecstatic physiological reaction. There can be no clear-cut dividing-line between them; poetry and prose are more alike in their mode of operation than they are different, so that most of the teaching-principles already elaborated in regard to prose will apply, suitably modified, to the teaching of poetry as well. Nevertheless, there is one distinction which appears to be generally valid: poetry is, characteristically, more compressed than prose, the organisation of the words is more closely knit, the verbal texture denser. It is this quality (unmistakably related to the greater importance in poetry of imagery and metaphor) that makes possible the concentration of a whole world of meaning into a relatively short lyric poem.

We, of course, are aware (in a way that children cannot be) that this concentration is not a matter of words only; it represents and expresses a complex organisation of experience. Our experience of poetry has implanted in us a recognition that it is concerned most typically with embodying and communicating in words an individual human being's concrete sensuous experience, together with an interpretation of its universal human significance. To attain through the words to a re-creation of this delicate and complex spiritual organisation can never be easy. What may make it all the more difficult for children is the fact that the re-structuring and readjustment which is called for is often one of attitudes and feelings; whereas it is well known that at certain stages of adolescence boys and girls become shy of any expression of strong feeling. They are made uneasy by it and tend to fight their uneasiness by adopting a jeering defensive stance. As a further manifestation of this resistance to emotional involvement they may be inclined also, in their enforced encounters with poetry, to be always on the look-out for something definite, clear-cut and safe to hold on to; they may restrict their attention to the narrative or factual content of the poem, busy themselves with acquiring background information, biographical or historical, or take refuge in the technicalities of rhyme scheme, metre, or poetical 'devices'. (I remember picking up once, in a fifth form I had taken over at short notice, a poetry anthology in which almost every line of every page had had pencilled in one or other of the cabalistic symbols 'met' or 'sim'. Were these eccentric marginalia the residue of some thoroughly bad poetry teaching, or did they represent rather the pupil's own powerful impulsion to retreat from anything so disturbing as actually reading the poems as such?)

In face of this determined hostility to poetry (which shows itself most frequently or most openly in boys' schools) it may sometimes be better to give up the struggle for a time, and I should respect the judgment of any conscientious and experienced teacher who concluded, with some given third or fourth form, that he could use the weekly poetry lesson more profitably in developing a heightened response to imaginative prose as a prelude to a renewed assault on poetry later on. Nevertheless, I believe that, even though they may recoil from it and seek to evade it, boys and girls of this age do in reality need the opportunity afforded by poetry to come to terms with their feelings within the control and discipline of an objectified social medium, and that in the long run it will usually prove worthwhile to persevere. The reluctance must certainly not be exacerbated, however, by an unwise choice of poems — a choice based for instance upon adult standards of poetic value, upon an attempt to cover the ground historically, or upon a conviction that there are certain poems which all children ought to have read before leaving school. Throughout the poetry course we should be looking first and foremost for poems which can make contact, in an intimate way, with the child's most vital experience and interests. This is partly a matter of overt topic, for the poem's initial impact must stir some strong feeling of curiosity or expectancy if the effort to explore it further is to be willingly made. It is no less important, however, that the poetic experience the topic gives rise to should be within, or nearly within, the child's emotional range; a poem with the overt topic of, say, childhood, the animal kingdom, war, or even space-travel will not meet our purpose if the web of feeling constructed around it is an essentially adult one. It will be clear that this requirement rules out at once a very large proportion of the major poetry which has been written in English, since so much of this is in fact concerned with mature adult emotions connected with religious belief, sexual love, or man's relationship to nature. School anthologies in the past (those whose genealogy reads 'By *The Oxford Book of English Verse* out of *Palgrave's Golden Treasury*') were often chock-full of poems which disqualified themselves for this very reason. In 1923, however, Walter de la Mare published a highly original anthology *Come Hither* which drew from a number of hitherto neglected areas (traditional rhymes, folksong, satire, comic and nonsense verse among others), and vastly enlarged our conception of what poetry might have to offer children. In 1935 W. H. Auden and John Garrett made use of these discoveries in their lively if somewhat amorphous school anthology *The Poet's Tongue*, and in the last two decades the trail they blazed has been followed by a number of editors with collections which cater for children's tastes in an enterprising and realistic manner; these are often attractively produced and sometimes fairly well graded.[1] At present, however, it is noticeable that some editors in their concern to find poems which will appeal to children do not give enough weight to poetic quality as such—an aberration which can be studied, for instance, in a disconcertingly uneven

---

[1] Worth examining for school use at secondary level are: *This Day and Age*, ed. S. Hewett (Arnold); *Iron, Honey and Gold* (4 books), ed. D. Holbrook (C.U.P.); *The Rhyming River* (4 books), ed. J. Reeves (Heinemann); *Rhyme and Reason*, ed. E. Robinson (U.L.P.); *The Key of the Kingdom* (4 books) and *Rhyme and Reason*, ed. D. Thompson and R. O'Malley (Chatto & Windus); *Poetry and Song* (4 books), ed. J. Gibson (Macmillan); *The Golden Bird* (4 books), ed. F. Whitehead (Oliver and Boyd); *Voices* (3 books), ed. G. Summerfield (Penguin).

'anthology of tough verse' offered recently under the title *Billy the Kid*. The poems we are looking for need not perhaps be good by exacting adult standards, but they should be 'good of their kind'; they must be such as to extend and refine, in some degree, the child's capacity for experience. The poem which is merely flabby or sentimental (or pseudo-tough) may sometimes have a place in the child's self-made anthology, but it can never repay or justify the time given to it in a class reading or discussion.

Let us assume, however, that the poem to be presented to the class has been wisely chosen, and that the teacher's aim for his lesson is justly conceived. Only the incurably optimistic would deny that there are still many pitfalls to guard against.

In the first place (I suggest) we are liable to go astray by underestimating the difficulty of reading poetry. We may allow ourselves to behave in the class-room as though a poem can be taken in and understood at a single reading, after which we (or the children) are ready to talk about it, or about our reactions to it critically. 'Do you like it?' we might ask. 'What is there about it which appeals to you?' 'What *sort* of poem is it?' Yet in fact few poems are so translucent that they can be more vaguely or dimly apprehended after a single reading, or even after a couple of readings. (At this point the reader might turn again to the short poem 'Memory' quoted above (page 92) and consider whether even now he feels ready, for his part, to answer questions of this kind about it.) We need to recognise that poetry as a rule takes time to yield up its meaning, and that premature attempts to categorise or to formulate opinions about it can only get in the way of this process.

On the other hand, even if we accept the fact that poetry is difficult, we may still go astray by mistaking the nature of the difficulty. Many teachers seem, indeed, to feel that poetry because of its difficulty calls for a devious, gingerly approach. Before we dare come to the poem itself, the right atmosphere for it must somehow be created—perhaps by a little pep-talk, perhaps by telling the class how they ought to feel when the poem is read, perhaps by supplying some information about the poet who wrote it. Now it is unlikely that 'atmosphere' induced by extraneous means can ever be of the 'right' kind; since our objective is the atmosphere which the poem's own words create for us, anything else is bound to give us a false start. Certainly biographical information cannot in the nature of things be what our pupils need. I have tried conscientiously to bring to mind any knowledge about Tennyson which might conceivably help towards an understanding of 'The Eagle', and the only fact which seems to have even the slightest relevance is his shortsightedness—a characteristic which according to Mr. Harold Nicolson may have had an influence on his perception and description of natural phenomena in general. It is in any case the hall-mark of the true poem (as of any other work of art) that it has somehow detached itself from the particular local circumstances of its creation and achieved a permanent objective and public significance; this 'timeless' quality is at once what makes it worth our attention and what we must help our pupils to attend to.

More plausible is the feeling that what we need to launch our poems may be some preliminary background information about its topic. 'Have you ever seen an eagle?' the teacher might think it incumbent on him to ask. 'What did it look like?' And so on. And if the children's responses are meagre and disappointing perhaps there is somewhere a coloured plate, a lantern-slide, a film-strip, that can be found to do the trick? It cannot be denied that the prior experience the children bring to a poem will have some effect on what they make of it; yet there can be no doubt that this approach, too, is misconceived. It is, after all, *Tennyson's* eagle that the reader is called upon to visualise—the highly specific image called forth by the poet's words in the poet's order; and this will not be at all the same as either the bored and disconsolate creature which Jones once saw behind the bars in a zoo, or the gaudy outline staring forth from an illustration in a natural history book. It is all too easy for the teacher to bring into the forefront of attention the personal idiosyncratic reminiscence (what I. A. Richards has termed the 'mnemonic irrelevance'), and so obstruct the development of that objective and shareable experience which awaits the reader within the poem itself.

This is not, of course, to contend that background information can never be relevant or helpful to the understanding of a poem. I remember a West Indian friend once mentioning to me the baffled incomprehension with which he had read, in his own country, T. S. Eliot's lines:

> Weeping, weeping multitudes
> Droop in a hundred A.B.C.s.

To someone who had never seen a London teashop the words offered no foothold whatsoever. Where some such needed element of experience is found to be missing, the teacher will obviously do his best to supply it as concisely and expeditiously as he can. The trouble is, though, that a verbal footnote can seldom be an adequate substitute for the first-hand knowledge which the poem is quite likely to assume and depend upon; consequently if we find ourselves called upon at all frequently to supply background information in the course of our poetry lessons, there is no doubt that we ought to review very carefully our choice of poems. The real point to keep in mind is that generally speaking the proper starting-point for our poetry appreciation lesson can never be outside the poem itself.

There is one further misconception of the nature of poetic difficulty which deserves examination because it is so widespread. Poetry (the teacher reasons in this case) is hard to understand, so that it would surely be well to smooth the way by picking out the difficult or unfamiliar words beforehand; if the pupils have been 'taught' the meaning of these words already, all will be plain sailing when they come to them in the poem itself. True, the somewhat arid atmosphere of a vocabulary lesson (words chalked on the board in lists, and a laborious thumbing of dictionaries) may not be quite what one would choose as a lead-in to the joyous experience of poetry; and I have heard of teachers who thought it worthwhile to circumvent this snag by anticipating in Friday's vocabulary lesson the obscurities foreseen in next Tuesday's poem. But, alas, both the conscientious effort and the ingenuity are misplaced. The characteristic difficulty of poetry is seldom (if ever) a matter of difficult words; seldom (if ever) is the obscurity of a kind which could be dispersed by a dictionary exercise. In Tennyson's 'The Eagle' for instance, there are no individual words which offer difficulty as such; with the possible exception of 'azure' (and even this is, surely, deducible from the context?) all the words are ones which the average first-former would be perfectly familiar with. And yet the poem has its difficulties —difficulties which are in essence a matter of assembling the appropriate associations to well-known words and excluding the inappropriate, or perceiving the relationship, *in their context*, between words which are familiar in themselves but here are conjoined in unfamiliar ways. (Why is the word 'hands' used to refer to the eagle's claws? How can the sea be said to 'crawl' or to be 'wrinkled'?)

It should be clear that in reading poetry the meanings we are concerned with are not those which the words carry in ordinary prose discourse, and may not be ones which could easily be extracted from a dictionary. In prose as well as in poetry it is, of course, invariably the context which defines the precise shade of meaning which is to attach to any given word; but in the case of poetry, with its more closely woven verbal texture, this influence from the context is both more intimate and more highly specific. (As a further example we might take the use of the word 'form' in the poem 'Memory'. The image of the mountain hare requires us to include in our response to this word the special, almost technical, sense of a 'lair' — a place where a hare couches; and the delicate play between this specialised meaning and the more general one is crucial for our 'taking' of the poem's meaning as a whole.) Should this argument from general critical and linguistic principles fail to carry complete conviction, we can, as it happens, turn for support to an experimental study carried out in America of children's mental processes when reading poetry.[1] This provides almost irresistible evidence for the conclusion that the difficulties children encounter in reading poetry relate not to individual difficult words but rather to the organisation of the words and the relationships which exist between them. Sometimes the difficulties arise from unfamiliar syntactical constructions (the inversions or contractions which are common in poetry but rare in prose); more often it is the poet's highly metaphorical use of language which proves the stumbling-block.

In any event we should be able to see by now that when we go astray in our poetry lessons it is because we are in one way or another evading the main issue. What we have to do above all is to let the poem make its own impact, so that the words can do their own work. We have in fact to find ways of arranging that there shall be, on the part of the pupils, an attentive exposure to the poet's words in the poet's order. To read the poem aloud, perhaps more than once, is in itself a useful initial step towards this end. If the reading is done with understanding and feeling (and it will normally be necessary for the teacher, with his prior knowledge and preparation, to read at this stage of the lesson), there is a good chance that much of the poem's meaning will be absorbed unconsciously and intuitively. And questions which lead the children to pick out and read aloud again a particular line or particular phrase have some value from the same standpoint.

Beyond this, however, we need to devise ways of helping the pupils

[1] Weekes (1929). See also Kangley (1938).

to give to the words and their meanings the right kind of attentiveness. This is not a matter of 'analysis', and certainly not a matter of discovering or pointing out aspects of the poet's 'technique'. The process is one of drawing attention (usually by questioning) to some of the key points in the meaning of the poem – those focal points or nodes around which the total poetic meaning is organised and concentrated. In searching, during the preparation of the lesson, for these nodes of meaning it will be found that the 'tip' commended by F. R. Leavis to the critic, 'Scrutinise the imagery', holds good for the teacher as well. In 'Memory', for instance, it is the image of the hare and its form which sustains the whole structure of poetic meaning. We are to ponder on both the resemblances and the dissimilarities between the image and the human situation which it defines and illuminates; to explore sensitively and delicately the elements of feeling and attitude which are introduced by the metaphor; to question, too, what it is that is contributed by the fact that it is a *mountain* hare which is invoked. Similarly in 'The Eagle' we shall find ourselves coming close to the heart of the poem if we allow our attention to dwell on such words as 'clasps', 'crooked', 'hands', 'ringed', 'wrinkled', 'crawls', 'walls', and 'like a thunderbolt'. In seeking to persuade our pupils to linger similarly on the relevant imagery, our most natural gambit will be to ask questions in the form 'Why this word?':

'Why "clasps"?' ' "Ringed with the azure world" – why "ringed"?' 'Why is the sea "wrinkled"? Why is it said to "crawl"?' 'Why does the eagle fall "like a thunderbolt"?'

Not, be it noted, 'Why does the writer use this word?' – an invitation to futile and irrelevant psychological speculation: nor yet 'Why is this a good word for the writer to use here?' – though this may be in a certain sense implied, to put the question in this way would be to ask in the answer for an evaluative emphasis which the class cannot possibly be ready for at this stage. No, the question as we frame it will be concerned essentially with the exploration of meaning within the context of the poem itself; so that the natural response to the question about the sea will be that, as seen by the eagle, the waves or breakers are so far beneath him that they look like wrinkles on a smooth surface, and that from this height they appear to move so slowly that they can be said to crawl.

However, although the fruitful question to ask will usually pose itself at first to the teacher in this typical form, it must be recognised that there are numerous other factors at work in the class-room situation which will call for a modification of this pattern. Thus one cannot ask this kind of question more than a few times within a single lesson without inducing in the class a feeling of satiety or boredom; this is particularly evident when one is dealing with younger pupils or with less able streams. With such classes only a very limited amount of this work is possible at any one time; and the teacher has therefore to select his line of questioning rigorously beforehand. There is the danger also that questions of this kind may concentrate attention too much on details, and fail to achieve an adequate sense of the total pattern of meaning which gives them their significance. This danger is obviated to a certain extent if the teacher has ensured that the detailed items he chooses to dwell on are in fact the most significant ones—the nodes or focal points, in fact; but even so the coalescence of the part with the whole may still, at times, be difficult to achieve.

There are, however, two alternative devices which it is often possible to use to circumvent this difficulty; as it happens 'The Eagle' affords a suitable illustration of both. In the first place, if we study the poem carefully enough we shall sometimes be able to find one or two questions of a more generalised kind which make an indirect approach to those very words or images which we have rightly judged to be important. In asking such questions we are typically setting a problem which can only be solved by close reference back to those detailed words or images which we want our pupils to ponder over and dwell on. Thus in the case of 'The Eagle' the questions might be: 'Whereabouts is the eagle? What tells us that he is very high up? How many things can you find mentioned in the poem that show us this?' These are not, it should be noted, *merely* factual questions. In looking for evidence to support their answers the children are led inevitably to the words 'clasps' (and perhaps also 'crooked'), 'close to the sun', 'ringed with the azure world', 'wrinkled' and 'crawls'; yet at the same time these elements are perforce brought together in a unified web of meaning. With some classes the final line also may be brought into the pattern of discovery prompted by these questions. With other classes the simile of the thunderbolt, central and clinching in its significance, will remain unexplored and ungrasped; and for them we shall need to turn to the second of our alternative approaches. We start by saying: 'Now we're going to read this poem aloud. How do you think it ought to be read?' Obviously, to arrive at a satisfactory answer to this must involve noticing precisely what it is that the poem is saying, and, more particularly, the feeling which its words carry. To help our class towards this it may be necessary to break the question down a little and give them certain leads. 'Should our reading be loud or soft?' we might ask. 'Ought we to read it smoothly or with a strong rhythmical beat?' In the case of 'The Eagle', however, we should probably go straight to the key issue. 'Should this poem be read fast or slowly? Should it all be read at the same pace? Should the last line in particular be read at the same pace as the rest? If not, why not?' Immediately we are led to the contrast in movement which is a basic element in the poem's structure, and in discussing just how to read the final line (and trying out our ideas) we cannot fail to find out the full significance of the simile—its implication that, besides falling almost vertically from a great height, with immense weight, speed and force, the eagle is also falling upon its prey with all a thunderbolt's disastrous destructive power. And when the class goes on from its discussion of 'how to read' to an actual reading (perhaps in unison, or perhaps in groups) the poem's meaning will not only be understood intellectually but will also be felt in a more direct and intimate way in the process of sounding out the words.

So far we have succeeded in discussing only the teaching of one brief poem six lines long—material for class-room activity lasting a quarter of an hour or so at the most. I believe it will be found, however, that most of the poems we teach in the secondary school lend themselves in some degree to one or other of the approaches exemplified in this discussion: on the one hand, questioning which directs attention to the imagery of the poem; on the other hand, discussion of how to read the poem in such a way as to bring out fully both its meaning and its feeling. But of course each poem we deal with is a unique entity, with its own highly individual qualities of meaning and form, its own innate reason for being thus and not otherwise. We should beware of any mechanical application of general principles (however sound) which does not accord with or spring from the poem's inner nature; for this reason our first task whenever we teach a poem must be to master its meaning for ourselves as fully as possible, so that we may have clearly present in our consciousness those particular qualities which constitute its true poetic value. Of course we should not make the mistake of supposing that our own personal interpretation of it can ever be complete, impeccable, finally authoritative; indeed one will often find that the pooling of individual responses and reactions which takes place during a class-room discussion does much to modify or fill out the details of one's own reading. But the teacher must be equipped beforehand with an understanding of the poem which is well-founded and just in its main outlines; for only on this basis can he plan the strategy which will bring his class to an equally just appreciation of what the poem has to offer them. Not that the experience they can take from it will necessarily be the same as that of the teacher; since they are still immature human beings, their own grasp of it will usually be incomplete and may often be limited to only a small part of its full meaning. Blake's 'The Tyger' is, I suppose, the classic instance of a poem which can be read with profit on many different levels: while even the brightest of sixth forms is unlikely to exhaust its full complexity, much of its poetic meaning can also be understood and enjoyed, on a more purely intuitive plane, by the average first form. The hall-mark of the good teacher of poetry is his ability, first, to respond sensitively and accurately to the poem he is teaching, and second, to form a just estimate of those aspects of it which will be both within the range of his pupils and valuable to them.

Since so much depends on the particular poem one is dealing with, it will be best to use the limited space remaining in this chapter for the discussion of a few additional examples. There can be no difficulty about finding instances of poems which lend themselves to the approach *via* reading aloud. Many ballads are obviously of this kind, and they often contain within themselves a clear indication of the arrangement between voices, or groups of voices, which would be most appropriate; they may call for two individual speakers (as in 'Edward' or 'Lord Randal'), or for a combination which includes a narrator to act as chorus (as in 'Binnorie' or 'Casey Jones'). The emphasis will fall quite naturally upon the particular shades of feeling which go with the particular instances of incremental repetition or variation, or upon ways in which the voice can convey the mounting tension which accompanies the progressive revelation of situation in, say, 'Edward'.[1]

---

[1] Even now (it seems to me) we don't make nearly enough use in schools of the rich heritage of poetry and music bequeathed to us by the English folk-tradition. For many of our pupils (especially the less gifted ones) the 'literary' tradition of English poetry will always remain slightly alien, something to be approached (if at all) with conscious effort. It is, after all, the product of a self-conscious and sophisticated culture which has been at

various times courtly or aristocratic or middle-class in temper, but has seldom if ever been really at one with the popular culture of the ordinary people. We may try to make its complex artistry more homely or more palatable by choosing modern poems which treat familiar subject-matter (Auden on refugees, Thom Gunn on the leather boys?) or which use a familiar colloquial idiom (Robert Frost, Philip Larkin, Vernon Scannell?); but even in our moments of success we are usually aware of having left some pupils stranded on the other side of a barrier. Folk-poetry, by contrast, constitutes a separate and distinct tradition—one which belongs essentially to the ordinary working-people who created it, and which was, for that very reason, long despised and underrated by the cultivated minority. The best of our folksongs and ballads have been fined down by oral transmission to a spare austerity and impersonality. Their handling of universal human themes is distinguished by a 'mature acceptance of the conditions of human existence' (Bantock, 1962) which puts them at the opposite pole to the compensation-culture of Tin Pan Alley; yet at the same time their simplicity of language and down-to-earth directness of impact makes them readily accessible to all. If, for instance, we play to any middle-school form a recording of that fine American ballad 'Buffalo Skinners' (the only one at present available is that sung by Jack Elliott on Topic 12T105, though the words and tune of a finer version can be found on pages 178-9 of *The Penguin Book of American Folk Songs*), the response is immediate, wholehearted—and unanimous. The verbal and musical idiom is one which adolescents today are prepared to meet halfway, particularly now that the folksong revival has infiltrated, in slightly coarsened form, into the mass media, including television. The frequent repetition and verbal parallelism makes the narrative structure easy to grasp, while (as in so much folk-poetry) the highly-conventionalised metaphors are all the more effective because they are only sparsely used. (Notice the force in its context of the line: 'Our hearts were cased in buffalo hocks, our souls were cased in steel'.) And the characteristic under-statement in the telling of the murder itself underscores the grimness of the story in a way that strikes home to even the most apathetic of fourteen-year-olds.

I have chosen as my example a wholly American ballad because it seems to me that this kind of material will often provide the most thoroughly acceptable starting-point. (In industrialised communities another promising lead-in will be the contemporary factory and mining ballads collected together on such records as *The Iron Muse* (Topic 12T86) or *Steam Whistle Ballads* (Topic 12T104).) No one will pretend that these (or for that matter the similarly useful sea shanties and whaling ballads) represent the highest peak of achievement, but they belong to the authentic tradition, and from them young people can be led by easy stages to an appreciation of the great 'classic' ballads ('Lord Randal,' 'Edward', 'The Wife of Usher's Well', 'The Demon Lover') which have a long history behind them. Scottish teachers will naturally use the native tradition which has been kept alive even into our own day by such fine singers as Jeannie Robertson, but south of the Border it will often be better to approach these through American versions which are easier linguistically and only marginally inferior in quality. It will be realised that when we confine ourselves (as we sometimes must) to the words alone, a good deal is lost; ideally words and melody should be treated as a unity, if folk-song is to gain its full effect. Fortunately there are now many excellent recordings available, some of which are mentioned below. It should be remembered, moreover, that in these days a folk-song club conducted out of school hours may bring to light talent which can be used to good effect in the classroom.

Among the other recordings which will be found particularly useful for this kind of work are: Hedy West *Ballads* (Topic 12T163) and *Old Times and Hard* (Topic 12T117); Jean Ritchie *British Traditional Ballads in the Southern Mountains* (Folkways FA 2301 and 2302); A. L. Lloyd *Leviathan!* (Topic 12T174); A. L. Lloyd and Ewan MacColl *English and Scottish Popular Ballads* (Topic 12T103); the Watersons *A Yorkshire Garland* (Topic 12T167); and the two folk-song records issued in conjunction with *The Golden Bird* anthologies (obtainable from Oliver & Boyd). Indispensable for the teacher are *The Penguin Book of English Folk Songs* ed. A. L. Lloyd and R. Vaughan Williams, and *The Penguin Book of American Folk Songs* ed. Alan Lomax. Recommended also, as background, is *Folk Song in England* by A. L. Lloyd (Lawrence and Wishart or Panther). Another promising approach would be to use Ian Campbell's folk-song anthology for schools *Come Listen* (Ginn) in conjunction with the associated recording by the Ian Campbell Folk Group (Music for Pleasure MFP S 1349).

THE TEACHING OF POETRY

Work of this sort is often particularly successful and valuable with secondary modern classes, since it stresses the direct, intuitive and sensuous apprehension of the poem, rather than a more intellectual and cerebral mode of approach. It is important, however, that it should be seen not as an end in itself, but as an instrument for the discovery and appreciation of poetic meaning. The vacuous 'speech-rhymes' and ambitious 'arrangements' of meretricious verse which are included for choral speaking in some school anthologies seem to me not only useless but potentially harmful. Elaborate and complicated division of a poem into group or solo parts is in any case to be deprecated, since it leads to an undue stress upon the purely technical problems of speaking the verse — entry, attack, keeping together, voice-control. We should aim at an 'arrangement' of the poem which will help to bring out the main divisions in its structure of meaning, and as far as possible the suggestions should be elicited from the children themselves, developing if necessary by a process of trial and error. When first entrusted with this responsibility a class will often be swayed by crude considerations of social justice and want to split up the poem line by line so that every member of the class can have a turn at speaking. Discussion and criticism of the results of their decisions will soon lead them, however, to see the point of the procedure; and at a later stage suitable poems can be handed over to small groups of pupils to work out on their own a method of reading to be presented for the approval of the class as a whole.

W. H. Auden's 'Night Mail' is a good example of the poem which a first or second form will enjoy tackling in some such way, and which at the same time has 'enough in it' to repay the effort exacted. The problem it poses is mainly that of varying the pace and rhythm to suit the different sections; each of these can be treated as a unit and given to a different group for speaking in unison, or the paragraph listing the different types of letter can logically and effectively be broken down further for individual voices, a line or half-line to each. Another poem for the purpose (not perhaps any more difficult in its content, but more difficult to read successfully because its rhythm is more subtle and elusive) is Belloc's 'Tarantella'; this could be attempted by a second or third form. This time there can be no question of dividing the poem into more than two sections; for the key to it is to be found in the contrast between the light, buoyant and dancing rhythm of the first paragraph and the heavy sense of doom in the movement of the second.

It is likely that the poems we choose for lessons with third or fourth forms, being more complex and mature in their thought and feeling, will generally lend themselves in the first instance to an approach by means of questioning rather than by reading aloud. Even so, it should be remembered that a lesson in which the main emphasis has been upon questioning can often be usefully rounded off by some form of group reading. It is certainly desirable that, at the end of any period of time devoted to dwelling upon particular aspects or items of meaning, the class's final experience of the poem should be the unified one provided by a reading-aloud of the whole; and while this reading can often be undertaken either by the teacher or by a single pupil, a group-reading at this stage has the virtue of drawing a larger proportion of the class into an active and direct contact with the poetic experience.

We will conclude by taking a few examples of the different types of issue which may arise when questioning is the chosen approach. Here, first, is a poem of Hardy's which we might take with a first or second form.

A Popular Personage at Home

'I live here; "Wessex" is my name:
I am a dog known rather well:
I guard the house; but how that came
To be my whim I cannot tell.

'With a leap and a heart elate I go
At the end of an hour's expectancy
To take a walk of a mile or so
With the folk I let live here with me.

'Along the path, amid the grass
I sniff, and find out rarest smells
For rolling over as I pass
The open fields towards the dells.

'No doubt I shall always cross this sill,
And turn the corner, and stand steady,
Gazing back for my mistress till
She reaches where I have run already,

'And that this meadow with its brook,
And bulrush, even as it appears
As I plunge by with hasty look,
Will stay the same a thousand years.'

> Thus 'Wessex'. But a dubious ray
> At times informs his steadfast eye,
> Just for a trice, as though to say,
> 'Yet, will this pass, and pass shall I?'

THOMAS HARDY

The appeal which will be made by the topic of this poem can hardly be questioned; at the same time the poetic experience built upon the overt topic (the dog's unawareness of change and mortality, intruded upon, according to the poet's fancy, by an occasional glimmering of perception) is one which the average twelve-year-old will attain to only through judicious guidance and after a certain extension of his capacities and sensibility. The teacher starts by reading the whole poem through aloud. 'Who is speaking in the first five stanzas of this poem? How do we know?' The teacher then reads these stanzas aloud again, and says: 'Now look at these first five stanzas for a minute or two, and see if you can decide what this dog Wessex is like. Can you find one adjective or brief phrase which describes the impression you've formed of him?' This should produce a number of suggestions ('self-centred', 'pompous', 'pleased with life', 'self-satisfied', 'self-important') none of which will be conclusive but in the discussion of which we are led to look for evidence in certain specific words, phrases, or items of behaviour (e.g. 'personage', 'a dog known rather well', 'my whim', 'the folk I let live here with me'). Then we go on to read the final stanza. 'Does this last verse carry on the same impression that we have formed of him so far, or does it introduce some new idea about him? What word in particular shows this? ("dubious") How serious are his doubts? (Do they last for long?) How do you think he would say this last line of the poem? Try to speak it yourself in the way it should be spoken.' Then we conclude by reading the whole poem aloud once more, perhaps giving the words of 'Wessex' to one of the more gifted readers, while the class in unison read the three lines of impersonal narrative.

This poem could perhaps only be taken in a grammar school or with an above-average modern stream. Our next example should, however, go equally well with a second or third form in either type of school.

Morning Express

> Along the wind-swept platform, pinched and white,
> The travellers stand in pools of wintry light,

III

Offering themselves to morn's long, slanting arrows.
The train's due; porters trundle laden barrows.
The train steams in, volleying resplendent clouds
Of sun-blown vapour. Hither and about,
Scared people hurry, storming the doors in crowds.
The officials seem to waken with a shout,
Resolved to hoist and plunder; some to the vans
Leap; others rumble the milk in gleaming cans.

Boys, indolent-eyed, from baskets leaning back,
Question each face; a man with a hammer steals
Stooping from coach to coach; with clang and clack,
Touches and tests, and listens to the wheels.
Guard sounds a warning whistle, points to the clock
With brandished flag, and on his folded flock
Claps the last door: the monster grunts: 'Enough!'
Tightening his load of links with pant and puff.
Under the arch, then forth into blue day,
Glide the processional windows on their way,
And glimpse the stately folk who sit at ease
To view the world like kings taking the seas
In prosperous weather: drifting banners tell
Their progress to the counties; with them goes
The clamour of their journeying; while those
Who sped them stand to wave a last farewell.

SIEGFRIED SASSOON

The teacher will identify this as a purely descriptive piece, clearly
and vividly realised, and consequently attractive on its own level,
but without any deeper significance. It will have its value for our
thirteen-year-old pupils to the extent that they achieve a firm
imaginative visualisation of the details of the scene at each stage in
the sequence of events; but the problem it presents to the teacher is
two-fold. On the one hand he has to use tact and judgment in
deciding which of the details it will be worthwhile to pick out for
special notice by his own class (for the rather loose organisation of
the poem allows him a good deal of latitude here); on the other hand
he has to be careful to avoid 'fragmenting' the poem by spending too
long on any individual item or items. I can see no alternative in this
case to 'going through' the poem selectively, taking the lines in the
order in which they occur, and asking questions about particular
words and images which seem important in building up the scene
as a whole. In planning this part of the lesson we need to think in

terms of both a 'maximum objective' and a 'minimum objective';
preparing first a fairly full sequence of questions which might add
illumination if one had an ideally attentive and responsive class; and
then selecting from these a much briefer list of those which seem all
but indispensable (the discarded questions being kept in mind for
use if circumstances should prove sufficiently favourable). With
many classes the questioning might, I suggest, go something like this:

Where are the travellers standing? What shows us that it is a
cold morning? Why 'pools' of wintry light? What are 'morn's
long slanting arrows'? Why 'trundle'?

What happens when the train is due? What is his 'flock'? Why
'folded flock'? What is the 'monster'? Why 'monster'? Why 'load
of links'? 'Brandished flag'—what sort of movement does that
suggest? What sort of noise is suggested by the word 'trundle'?

What are we told about the 'clouds of vapour'? Why 'volleying'? What sort of movement is suggested by the word 'volleying'?

What other activities go on while the train is still in the station?
What do you suppose the boys are carrying in their baskets? What
is the 'question' they are asking? What is the man with the hammer doing? Why is the word 'steals' used to describe his movements? What does the guard do?

What impression are we given of the travellers now the train
has started? What particular words give that impression? Why is
'glide' a suitable word for the way the 'processional windows' seem
to move? What are the 'drifting banners'? Why 'banners'? What
change comes to the station once the train has gone?

Two subsidiary issues may be mentioned in connection with this.
First the matter of vocabulary. 'Volleying', in line 5, is an example
of a word used with a meaning highly specific to its poetic context; I
cannot see that any amount of vocabulary work dealing with the word
in more customary contexts would be of much help in negotiating it
here. The element of meaning we are required to keep before us is
that of rapid, continuous and forceful utterance of the clouds of
steam. The surest way to get at this is to visualise what steam issuing
from a railway engine actually looks like, and other associations (a
volley from rifles or cannon, a volley at tennis or cricket) have to be
firmly excluded as irrelevant or possibly misleading. 'Brandished' in
line 16 may seem a more doubtful instance; even though it cannot be
regarded as a word that is very important to the poem as a whole,

E

would it not be worthwhile to ensure that all the class have some prior acquaintance with it? In practice, however, it will usually be found that some of the class know the word already, and that most will at any rate have seen a guard waving his flag with a flourish; failing this, the teacher should be able, in the setting provided by the poem, to supply the meaning quickly enough to avoid any distracting hiatus. To attempt to 'teach' this, or any word, in isolation (whether before or during the reading of the poem) seems to me in any case a misunderstanding of the way in which we acquire our store of vocabulary; to meet a new or half-familiar word embedded in the rich and living context of a poem does more to root it within the pupil's mind than a whole sequence of cold-blooded and artificial vocabulary exercises upon it.

Secondly, it may be noted that lines 11 and 12 exemplify the problem of background information: few pupils these days will have had the experience, familiar enough to an older generation, of seeing boys on station platforms selling chocolates or magazines from a shallow wicker basket supported by a strap behind the neck. There is no point in spending much time on the matter in class. A brief explanation from the teacher will remove the difficulty as far as understanding goes; it cannot, however, put the class in a position to appreciate the felicity of the poet's concise description.

To revert to more general issues, it should be said that the questioning suggested above would need curtailing with some forms, even though the interest excited by the subject-matter is likely to sustain this form of activity for a longer period than would be the case with many poems. And although attention will have been directed wherever possible to the suggestive force of the poet's words, it may be conceded that so far a considerable part of the emphasis has necessarily fallen upon the factual content of the poem — upon what might be termed its 'prose meaning'. Before leaving it we shall want to bring into greater prominence the poetic quality of the lines as spoken sound. When we discuss the reading-aloud four sections should suggest themselves, each with a characteristic tempo and atmosphere. The first section (lines 1–4) presenting the expectancy on the platform before the train arrives will be read quietly and at a fairly even pace. The hurry and bustle of the next six lines will require an increase in volume and a more energetic tempo. The next section (lines 11–18) leads steadily and purposefully up to the climax of the train's departure; while the concluding lines need to be read with a smoother rhythmic flow and a gradual diminuendo. We may also ask the class to look for words or lines which are particularly effective in suggesting the sound of the activities they describe ('trundle laden barrows', 'volleying', 'rumble', 'with clang and clack', 'Claps the last door', 'the monster grunts: "Enough!"'/ Tightening his load of links with pant and puff') and to demonstrate how they should be read to bring out this quality to the full. There is scope for a good deal of discussion of this kind, but I would suggest nevertheless that the lesson as a whole (including, perhaps, a couple of complete readings to round it off) probably ought not to be allowed to last for longer than twenty-five to thirty minutes for children of this age.

Next, D. H. Lawrence's 'Bat' — a poem which should appeal to most third or fourth forms, but which has more to it than a cursory reading might suggest. For it would surely be too simple to see it as merely a forceful and wholly unironic expression of the conventional disgust-reaction towards bats. This reaction is indeed expressed with conviction and intensity, even perhaps with a slight degree of wilful exaggeration; but it seems to me that the poem as a whole enacts (unobtrusively but compellingly) the recognition of a certain arbitrariness about such human feelings, and enforces it moreover on a level which makes any overt statement or comment unnecessary.

Bat

At evening, sitting on this terrace,
When the sun from the west, beyond Pisa, beyond
  the mountain of Carrara
Departs, and the world is taken by surprise . . .

When the tired flower of Florence is in gloom
  beneath the glowing
Brown hills surrounding . . .

When under the arches of the Ponte Vecchio
A green light enters against stream, flush from the
  west,
Against the current of obscure Arno . . .

Look up, and you see things flying
Between the day and the night;
Swallows with spools of dark thread sewing the
  shadows together.

A circle swoop, and a quick parabola under the
    bridge arches
Where light pushes through;
A sudden turning upon itself of a thing in the air.
A dip to the water.

And you think:
'The swallows are flying so late!'

Swallows?

Dark air-life looping
Yet missing the pure loop . . .
A twitch, a twitter, an elastic shudder in flight
And serrated wings against the sky,
Like a glove, a black glove thrown up at the light,
And falling back.

Never swallows!
Bats!
The swallows are gone.

At a wavering instant the swallows give way to bats
By the Ponte Vecchio . . .
Changing guard.

Bats, and an uneasy creeping in one's scalp
As the bats swoop overhead!
Flying madly.

Pipistrello!
Black piper on an infinitesimal pipe.
Little lumps that fly in air and have voices
    indefinite, wildly vindictive;

Wings like bits of umbrella.

Bats!

Creatures that hang themselves up like an old rag,
    to sleep;
And disgustingly upside down.
Hanging upside down like rows of disgusting old rags
And grinning in their sleep.
Bats!

In China the bat is symbol of happiness.

Not for me!

The central element in the poem's organisation is clearly the dramatic reversal of feeling which accompanies the realisation that the 'things' which were confidently assumed to be swallows are, in actual fact, bats. This may seem to indicate a 'reading-aloud' approach in the class-room, and certainly the poem is one which gains a good deal from being read aloud; the apparent casualness of the verse-form is rooted in the living idiom of English speech, in a way which gives it both an unforced naturalness and a supple responsiveness to emotional nuance. On the other hand, it is possible for a good deal of the meaning to be missed if we plunge into this form of activity straight away (I have even watched lessons at the end of which most of the class went away believing that the poet looked up and saw *first* swallows, and *then* bats); and it seems advisable, therefore, to give some time at first to explication which will establish the main intellectual and emotional structure of the poem. If we do use questioning we should be prepared, in this case, to be more ruthlessly selective over some parts of the poem than over others. The evocative setting of the scene at the beginning makes a contribution to the whole poem which is by no means negligible for the mature reader; but the associations invoked cannot mean much to the untravelled school-child, who will in any case be impatient to move on to the heart of the poem where the main interest for him lies. I think we should be content for our pupils to take from the opening eight lines little more than an understanding that the time is sunset and the locale Italy where dusk descends with unusual rapidity. 'Where is the writer?' we might ask. 'What time of day is it? Why "taken by surprise"?'

Once we move on to the main body of the poem, the obvious opening question will be: 'When he looks up, what does he see?' Once this point is reached, however, the lesson might develop in a number of different ways, and flexibility needs to be the keynote of whatever plans we make beforehand. The most exact answer to the question would presumably be 'things flying', but we are not very likely to get this. We may get two answers from different sections of the form, 'swallows' and 'bats', in which case the debate can be allowed to develop, disciplined by the demand for evidence from within the poem to support conflicting views, and leading to the further questions: 'At what point in the poem does he first suspect that they may not be swallows? At what point does he become certain that they are bats?' Or we may get only the unanimous answer 'swallows', in which case we can pursue enlightenment at a more leisurely pace, asking first, 'Where are they flying? What is their flight like?' and later, 'What is meant by the question "Swallows?" in line 18? Why does he ask that?' Other questions which may be found useful at some stage in the lesson are: 'What makes him realise that they are not swallows? How did he feel towards them when he thought they were swallows? What are his feelings once he knows that they are bats? Why does he feel this way about them? How long did it take for his feelings to change?' When we go on to discuss and practise a reading-aloud, it will be found that this poem is one that can support a slightly more elaborate form of arrangement for group-speaking, perhaps using two semi-choruses as well as some sections for unison-reading and a few lines for solo voice. But by this stage in the poetry course one would like to be able to divide the class into four groups, and send them off, one into each corner of the room, to spend ten minutes or so preparing their own version for presentation to the rest of the form.

We will take one further example, this time Wilfred Owen's 'The Send-Off', a poem which would be appropriate for a fifth form and might not be too difficult for a good fourth form.

The Send-Off

Down the close darkening lanes they sang their way
To the siding-shed,
And lined the train with faces grimly gay.

Their breasts were stuck all white with wreath and spray
As men's are dead.

Dull porters watched them, and a casual tramp
Stood staring hard
Sorry to miss them from the upland camp.
Then, unmoved, signals nodded, and a lamp
Winked to the guard.

So secretly, like wrongs hushed-up, they went.
They were not ours:
We never heard to which front these were sent.

Nor there if they yet mock what women meant
Who gave them flowers.

Shall they return to beatings of great bells
In wild train-loads?
A few, too few for drums and yells,
May creep back, silent, to still village wells
Up half-known roads.

Some of the key questions, in this case, will be: 'Who was going away, and where to? What were their feelings? What are the "wreath and spray" (line 4)? Who saw them go? What were the feelings of these onlookers? What does the poet mention which underlines the indifference of those who watched? "So secretly" (line 11)—why do you suppose their departure was secret? "Like wrongs hushed-up"—what does the poet suggest by means of this comment? What is the point of the title? Why do you suppose the first and third stanzas are set out in two separate parts?' (So far as I can see, the intention is to set apart the two pairs of lines which refer to the flowers, and to give prominence to them in a way that points their relationship.) 'What kind of return does the writer foresee for these soldiers? Why "creep"? Why "silent"? Why "half-known roads"?' Even at this level in the school some time ought to be given to a final reading-aloud, though it might be felt that any form of group-reading would be at odds with the spirit of this particular poem, and that one or two readings by individuals would be preferable.

I believe that, tackled along these lines, a reading of this poem can be a rewarding experience even for boys and girls who have only the haziest conception of what the 1914–1918 war must have been like; Owen does, after all, demand to be read as literature, not as social history. Nevertheless this is a poem which can gain an added dimension if it is read with some sense of the historical setting in which it was written. A case for 'background' then? But what *kind* of background? Not, I think, anything that could be gleaned from a history lesson, a history book, or a 'briefing' by the teacher. What would be helpful would be to come across the poem in the course of reading other poems by Owen or by some of his contemporaries (Siegfried Sassoon, Robert Nichols, even Isaac Rosenberg with more able classes), and of reading also some prose accounts of the first world war (Sassoon's *Sherston's Progress*, Robert Graves's *Goodbye to All That*, Herbert Read's *In Retreat*, or Barbusse's *Under Fire*). This does suggest the direction in which our poetry teaching ought to develop at this point—towards a grouping-together of the poems read, so that we pursue for a time the work of one writer, or one small group of writers, and are able to notice something of the relationship between particular poems, and also of the relation between the poems and the circumstances which called them into being. It is only by building up gradually in this way a series of nuclei of first-hand poetic experience that we can foster a genuine sense of the historic sequence and tradition of English poetry. The cursory 'historical survey' (one poem from each major poet) cannot do this, any more than a conducted afternoon coach tour can give a sense of the topography of a strange city.

With these older classes we need also to be continually on the look-out for opportunities to build a bridge between their own lives and the world of poetry. If reading poetry seems to offer no more than an elegant diversion or an agreeable pastime, it will certainly be discarded in later adolescence; we have to find ways of showing that it has its relevance to the real world and to their own problems and concerns in living in it. There is no reason why this should come into conflict with our increasing tendency, at this level in the school, to relate the poem to its original setting in the poet's own life or in the life of his time. The only value of this awareness of the merely local or temporal elements is that it can set us free to attend more fully to what there is in the poem of universal and permanent human significance. Thus a consideration of some of those particular features of the first world war which gave rise to Owen's poem can lead us on to discuss to what extent the attitudes and feelings embodied in 'The Send-Off' are appropriate to other more recent wars or to war in general. A sharper focus might be given to the discussion by reading also a poem relating to the second world war (D. J. Enright's 'Monuments of Hiroshima' would be a good choice here); or one might seize the opportunity to read some of those poems of Hardy ('The Man He Killed', 'Channel Firing', or 'Christmas: 1924') which raise issues of the same kind. In a similar way after reading Shelley's 'Ozymandias' we might seek to relate the theme of the poem to more recent instances (Hitler or Mussolini, maybe) of rulers with grandiose ambitions which have left little permanent mark behind them. And there are a number of the later poems of D. H. Lawrence which are often peculiarly worth reading with fifteen- or sixteen-year-olds because they establish in such a direct and unmistakable way the bearing which poetry can have upon choices and decisions which really matter in our daily lives; I am thinking especially of such poems as 'Don'ts', 'We are transmitters —' or 'Things men have made'.

Of course there is the danger in this work that the pupils may come to attend too exclusively to the 'message' or prose content of the poem, and so neglect those all-important aspects of meaning which can only be expressed through the medium of poetry. Certainly we must always be concerned first and foremost to help them to take the poem *as* poem, giving due weight to what is communicated by means of sound, imagery, rhythm and other formal qualities. Nevertheless, in reading poetry as in reading prose there comes a point at which boys and girls need to be encouraged to reflect upon the implications of what they read, to assimilate it into their own consciousness, and to ponder over the value of what it has to say to them personally. And the risks we run in so encouraging them are less obnoxious than the results which flow from that opposite type of emphasis which is still all too prevalent in the teaching of poetry — an emphasis, that is, upon formal and stylistic features (rhyme, metre, figures of speech, onomatopoeia, 'verbal music', and so on) considered either as decorative ornaments merely or as ends in themselves. There can be no place in our poetry-teaching, at any stage, for this sterile pseudo-criticism which concerns itself solely with so-called 'poetic technique'. Genuine criticism ['. . . the training of perception, judgment and analytic skill commonly referred to as "practical criticism" ' (Leavis, 1943)] concerned with the definition and evaluation of the total meaning of the poem, is a different matter, and would be the natural and logical culmination of the tentative pre-critical activity which I have been trying to describe. But as far as poetry is concerned, my own experience and observation strongly suggest that, save with exceptionally keen and able classes, it had better be deferred till the sixth form. Our first responsibility is to add to the meagre numbers of those who care to read poetry in adult life; under present circumstances we shall find our hands too full with this to be able to do all that we would like in training them to read with discrimination.

E*

Chapter 4

DRAMA LESSONS

(i) THE VALUE OF DRAMATIC ACTIVITY

'PLEASE, sir, can we act it?' Eyes light up suddenly; the atmosphere of deferential listlessness gives way to a stir of expectancy; two boys in the back row abandon their surreptitious guerrilla warfare with rulers or compasses; in no time at all a forest of hands is waving in the air. 'Can I be Robin Hood?' 'Can I be Little John?' 'Shall we move the table out of the way, sir?' This is surely the way in which the typical eleven-year-old class responds to any suggestion of classroom acting; and the observant teacher cannot fail to sense that in drama lessons he is tapping sources of energy and enthusiasm which rarely seem to be available in, say, the grammar lesson or the punctuation lesson.

The fact that normal children want to act, and enjoy acting, should be a strong reason for giving dramatic work a place of honour near the very centre of the curriculum; but curiously enough it seems at times to work the other way. True, dramatic activity of some kind is now firmly established in the time-table of almost all primary and most secondary schools—the change since the pioneering days of Caldwell Cook is little short of revolutionary. Yet in the minds of some headmasters and administrators there still lingers the idea that drama is something of luxury, a concession or indulgence which could be relegated without much loss to the dinner-hour, to the end of term (when the 'real' work of examinations is over), or to that restless last period on Friday afternoons. 'Perhaps they do enjoy these charades,' muttered one headmaster censoriously, 'but what are they *learning*?' The practising teacher with his eye upon the children rather than upon the mark-sheets will know well enough that the benefits which accrue from drama lessons are by no means marginal, even if they are not always readily or accurately measurable. Can these intuitions be given the rational and cogent formulation which is needed in order to rout the sceptics?

Certainly some part of what children gain from dramatic activity can be stated clearly enough. Through it they extend the range, fluency and effectiveness of their speech; under the stimulus of an imagined situation words move from their passive 'recognition' vocabulary into active use; as they lose themselves in their roles and so become freed from inhibiting self-consciousness, they learn to move gracefully and easily; they acquire poise and the capacity for expressive gesture and countenance; they learn, too, to work together, for drama cannot exist without co-operation and teamwork. Yet to say all this does no more than scratch the surface. More fundamental, if less clearly demonstrable, is our awareness that, in the successful drama lesson, acting is felt by the children to be a fulfilling and, in some sense, creative activity—one in which the whole personality is involved and through which are expressed significant perceptions and observations drawn from their own living. Dramatic activity of this kind is no childish parlour-game, nor is it a mere technical exercise. It is, on the contrary, a vital imaginative experience; and the value of it goes deep for the child because, essentially, acting is the child's natural way of enlarging his imaginative understanding of other human beings—and therefore his understanding of the nature and conditions of human life itself. The truth of this comes home to us more fully when we have learnt to recognise the essential continuity that exists between the spontaneous imaginative 'play' of early childhood and the 'dramatic play' which provides the basic raw material for our drama lessons. By tracing (even sketchily and imperfectly) the ways in which the one evolves into the other, we can gain a fruitful insight into the value of dramatic activity in childhood and also a renewed conviction of its centrality. For it is well known nowadays that play has an immensely important function in children's lives: it helps them to grow up—or perhaps one should rather say that it is their own way of helping themselves to grow up. Peter Slade's way of putting it is worth quoting for its refreshing clarity: '. . . by observing children and talking to them like human beings, you learn that their life is based on Play, and that is what they like better than anything else. This is not a way of avoiding unpopular duties; it is their way of trying out bits of real life before it comes to them, and living again bits of life they like.'

It was Froebel who first pointed out how much play means in the lives of children, and his pioneer observations led to increasing discussion of play throughout the nineteenth century; yet it is only in the past thirty or forty years that serious and systematic study has begun to place our understanding on a firm basis.[1] Even now we can point to no single unitary explanation of the remarkable variety of activities which we call play, but we are certainly justified in seeing much of it as above all a way of realising wishes in fantasy form. Play, it has been said, is fantasy, woven about real objects. In the light of this let us look at the two functions attributed to it by Peter Slade. First, 'living again bits of life they like'. In very small children it is easy enough to observe play which is straightforward wish-fulfilment of this kind. The three-year-old who has enjoyed the excitement of a train journey will seek over and over again to recapture the delights of the experience, turning chairs in the living-room into railway carriages and enlisting other children or adults as fellow-passengers. There is no very clear dividing-line between this and those forms of play in which the wished-for experience was, originally, that of other people: the small boy playing at being a ticket collector or engine driver; the small girl playing with her dolls, adopting the role of mother, washing them, dressing them or presiding at their tea party; the older child playing at being a cowboy or a Red Indian or a space traveller. As Freud pointed out, all such manifestations are special instances of 'the dominant wish of their time of life—to be grown-up and to be able to do what grown-up people do'. Nor is it any very far cry from this to the case of the seven-year-old who wants to play the events of his favourite story—to be himself Pooh and to draw in others to be Piglet and Christopher Robin. This wish to enact the role of someone you would like to be undoubtedly persists in dramatic activity at later ages, and can often be observed even at the secondary level. ('Can I be Robin Hood?') More liable to be overlooked are the cases where the child's deeper wishes are not the same as the ambitions which are allowed to show themselves in the outer layer of his personality. Sometimes the overly-good child may obtain valuable release and reassurance through playing (at different times) the dragon vis-à-vis St. George, the naughty boy such as Richmal Crompton's William, the crook in a one-act detective play. And I have a vivid memory of some lessons I watched a few years ago with a class of fourteen-year-old girls who were acting *Twelfth Night*. One of the leading spirits in the form, for ill as much as for good, was a lively and irrepressible tomboy whom I would have marked down as a 'natural' for the part of Maria. But the

[1] See Lowenfeld (1935), Walder (1933), Hartley, Frank and Goldenson (1952).

teacher knew her class better than an outsider could. To my surprise she asked this cheerful hoyden if she would like to play Olivia. After only a brief hesitation the girl agreed and entered into the part with great seriousness, assuming a ladylike dignity and grace which was wholly appropriate. It was evident that she had found satisfaction in seizing this opportunity to explore possibilities within herself which in everyday life remained still unrealised.

To sum up thus far, we may say that acting, seen as a development and elaboration of the play-instinct, is a positive outlet for wish-fulfilment, which is available to all children, including those who could not easily obtain comparable satisfactions through reading. It has the advantage, moreover, that the child's fantasy has to express itself through a medium which is social, not solitary, and which enforces its own restraints and provides its own necessary discipline.

There is more to it than this, though. In the first place we cannot fail to notice that it is not only pleasant experiences which provide the raw material for children's imaginative play. Frequently the starting-point may be an experience which was too disturbing to be assimilated immediately. As a typical example we might take a small child's visit to the dentist, which at the time was distressing or even terrifying. For some time this situation will be repeated over and over again in play, until eventually it has been mastered emotionally. To begin with, the representation will take the form of straight-forward repetition, unmodified except perhaps that some of the more painful details are left out. But gradually a transformation takes place. The roles will be transposed, the child himself becoming, in the play version, the dentist or the accompanying parent; the events will be altered so that the episode ends with the victim show-ing heroic boldness instead of cowardly alarm; and so on. The process of gaining mastery over the disagreeable experience is in fact an active and creative one; as Freud puts it, 'Every playing child behaves like a poet in that he creates a world of his own, or, more accurately expressed, he transposes things into his own world accord-ing to an arrangement which is more to his liking.'

As this last quotation implies, play of this kind still draws its energy from the wish-fulfilment motive, but the drive has here been harnessed to an unmistakable constructive purpose. In assimilating through play the unpleasant experience which has already come his way the child is at the same time preparing himself to meet other such experiences in the future—in the case of our specific example, one might say, the next visit to the dentist. We are approaching here the second of the two functions mentioned by Peter Slade: 'trying out bits of real life before it comes to them'. And it seems reasonable to see a parallel between this function of children's play as a preparation for the complexities of adult life and the comparable biological function which has often been pointed out in the play of young animals. Naturally enough it is this forward-looking aspect of imaginative and dramatic play that education interests itself in above all. Here, in the movement towards reality-testing, is something whose value the adult can feel no hesitation about. We should perhaps beware of concentrating on this too exclusively. The small child's spontaneous play shifts rapidly from one level to another, and fulfils a multiplicity of functions; it seems likely that for the older child dramatic activity similarly combines a number of differing satisfactions in varying degrees. But in general we may say that in drama lessons in the secondary school the main task of the teacher is to help the child to move in his acting towards a keener grasp of reality (the reality of human speech, behaviour and emotions) by stimulating livelier and more accurate imagining. In this way we are seeking to utilise an activity which is natural to children, and give it a positive direction and value.

The enrichment of experience which comes to them through acting is central because it proceeds by means of identification. In placing himself temporarily 'inside the skin' of a person other than himself the child is led to step outside the circle of his own ego; he learns to observe and understand the feelings, thoughts and reactions of others, and the learning is peculiarly real to him because it has, in an obvious sense, been 'lived' and not merely guessed at or talked about. If we observe children sensitively and sympathetically we cannot fail to realise that this process of identification lies at the heart of all their intellectual and emotional growth.

(ii) CREATIVE DRAMA

Drama lessons, then, must take the form of acting by the children. This is the all-important activity, and anything else—getting ready to act, considering how we ought to act, discussing and criticising the acting we have already done—should be kept strictly subordinate to it. The material acted may itself be of two kinds: on the one hand drama which the children make up for themselves ('free' or 'creative' or 'improvised' drama); on the other hand, drama which brings to life an already existent dramatic script. We need both in the secondary school, and we should not make the mistake of seeing the one as merely a useful preparation for the other. Perhaps we would be wrong, for that matter, to accept the common assumption that 'free drama' belongs mainly to the first two years of the course, and that from the third year onwards it had better be quietly dropped. We can at any rate take as common ground the rewarding opportunities offered by unscripted drama between the ages of eleven and thirteen; and we had better start now with a few instances of the kind of work which can make the most of these opportunities.

First of all, there is the activity which gives the maximum freedom to the children's own creative impulses, the teacher doing no more than provide the stimulus which will unleash their powers of improvisation. He may perhaps briefly outline a scene or situation (the local market-place on a Saturday afternoon) which the class then 'play out' according to their own lights. There will be no need for an audience since the emphasis is to be on spontaneity and an unself-conscious 'losing oneself' in the chosen role. It will be better, in fact, if every member of the class can find some part to play in what is essentially a crowd scene—though for this to be possible we shall need, as a rule, the use of the school hall. Many of our first-year class may have already experienced lessons of this kind in the junior school, where the physical relaxation and freedom from inner tension which is so necessary will often have been achieved by a preliminary spell of rhythmic movement or movement to music. Teachers who have tried it often say that a suitable gramophone record can be an admirable lead-in to a lesson with a secondary school class as well.

Do some staid imaginations recoil a little from the uninhibited mass activity which this suggests? Won't it simply turn into an unholy bear-garden? Well, certainly the teacher (before he embarks on this activity) has need to be fairly confident of his power to control the forces which he may be letting loose. But the control can be exercised mainly by indirect means—and in particular by taking careful thought beforehand. The scene or situation proposed needs to be one which comes within the first-hand experience of the children, so that the effort of remembering and re-creating its details may enforce its own innate discipline. Subjects for the class as a whole might be a crowded beach on a hot summer day (is the beach sand or shingle?), a large self-service grocery store, a busy shopping pavement with hawkers and street musicians, the end of a seaside pier with anglers and onlookers, a railway station platform. For rather smaller groups (in a large hall three or four of these can be busy in different corners) we might have a barber's shop, a pedestrian crossing, a cinema queue, or a dentist's waiting-room. More exotic subjects (a gipsy encampment, a Red Indian village) *may* have their value at a later stage, if they have been carefully prepared for by either discussion or preliminary research; but they are unsatisfactory for spontaneous improvisation because the children's imagined picture of them is too hazy and inchoate. Lacking firm guidance from within, they either fill in the gaps with clichés derived from film and television, or they cloak their inadequacy with a pretence of clowning ('If I'm doing it incompetently, it's because I'm not really trying'). For related if slightly different reasons we had better avoid situations which draw too heavily upon their capacity to suspend disbelief. I suppose it may be all right to have younger children impersonating trees, birds or candles (though I confess to a certain scepticism about the value of these bizarre transformations); but in the secondary school a distracting sense of the ludicrous attends almost all metamorphoses into non-human shape. There is no need to fight shy of animals which have been humanised in accordance with a well-understood convention (as in Chaucer's *Nun's Priest's Tale* or André Obey's *Noah*); but we are asking for trouble if we allow Sir Gawain to ride a pantomime horse, or a class of twelve-year-olds to crawl around the form-room in the guise of Hamelin's rats. Again it is not, in general, a good idea to ask children to 'act' the role of children. For one thing this cannot bring them any of the extension of imaginative experience which is our main aim. For another, they are usually quite incapable of doing it at all well; since to stand outside oneself, to observe oneself or one's age-peers with detached objectivity, and to embody this observation in the form of acting is a difficult task, calling for a high degree of maturity and even sophistication.

The main way, then, of ensuring a purposeful orderliness in these lessons is to choose the topic wisely, confining ourselves to scenes or situations which, in the material circumstances available, the class can represent with satisfaction to themselves and with a sense of worthwhile achievement. In the earlier stages, too, it may help to eschew speech and stick to mime. Freed from the need to find words and to collaborate closely with others in the interchange which words imply, children can concentrate more fully on getting right their movement, gesture and facial expression. Later on, words can be added gradually. Some teachers recommend at this point the fiction that what we are doing is a crowd scene for a film; at first it is to be 'shot' silent, but in subsequent repetitions the teacher will move round with an imaginary microphone, calling for a brief spell of conversation from each group in turn.[1] Or it can be prearranged that the mimed scene is to culminate in an incident which needs speech — the discovery of an unexploded mine on the beach, or the challenging of a shoplifter in the self-service store.

If this work is to generate a sense of progress we need also lessons, or parts of lessons, in which the emphasis is not so much upon spontaneity as upon the clearer imagining and improved realisation of detail. Children come out in front of the class to mime on their own such actions as untying and opening a parcel, walking across a ploughed field or a pebbly beach, painting a window, or filling and carrying a bucketful of water. Then, working in pairs they mime such actions as washing-up, papering a wall, or pitching a tent; or in small groups they make up and act brief episodes in a hat-shop, outside a telephone booth, in the post office, or on top of a bus. While the teacher needs to keep in view in his own mind the range of skills which need practising, improvement will not come through con-scious application of technique. In the class-room the teacher's role is to build up by judicious questioning and comment a vivid percep-tion of the imagined situation so that the attempt at acting may proceed from the child's own inner experience. (No acting of any value can result from a merely mechanical response to external prompting.) 'What shape and size is the parcel? Is it expected or unexpected? What are you hoping to find inside it? How do you feel when you see what it actually contains?' 'How thick is the mud on the ploughed field? How deep are the furrows?' 'From which direc-tion is the wind pulling against the tent? How strong is it?' 'How long has the woman been inside the telephone booth? Why is the man outside in a hurry? How does he feel at being kept waiting? How might he show his feelings?' In this, as in so much else, generous praise of what is well done is the surest way of fostering growth and progress. When the class are asked to give their own comments, their attention, too, should be directed away from negative fault-finding towards a search for whatever is commendable.

The two types of lesson mentioned so far leave a great deal of

[1] For this suggestion (and also for some of the other ideas in this chapter) I am indebted to E. J. Burton's extremely useful *Drama in Schools* (Herbert Jenkins, 1955).

scope for the children's own creative powers. All that is 'given' is a starting-point, to spark off their imagination—a setting, a situation, an action or occupation, a character. Thereafter they are free to move in a variety of different directions, shaping their material in accord with the prompting of their own inner needs. There is a place also for the third type of lesson in which the outline of a story imposes a firmer control upon the class's imaginative activity: indeed it could be argued that the discipline thus exacted by an already-existent framework represents a step forward which is particularly valuable for the twelve- or thirteen-year-old. There is no shortage of material for these lessons. Ballads, stories from the Bible, from the *Arabian Nights*, from Greek or Norse or Arthurian legends, parables from the New Testament—the discerning teacher will find plenty to choose from. If a suitable version is to hand in books of which all the children have a copy, we can start by reading this aloud together; otherwise it is usually better for the teacher to tell the story in his own words as briefly and simply as possible—a bare skeleton which the children have to clothe with their own actions, movements, characterisation and words. As soon as the essentials have been grasped (with some forms this *may* require a second telling, or a couple of minutes' discussion) we move on to consider how we can act it. 'How many characters shall we want? How many scenes will there be? Where will the first scene take place? Which characters take part in it? How shall we set the stage? Are there any properties we shall need?' The first attempt at acting should follow with a minimum of delay; for the fuller implications and finer details are best discovered in the process of trying it out. In the first 'run-through' it is often advisable to break down the story into a sequence of short, manageable episodes, pausing at the end of each scene for comment on what has been done, and a reminder of what is to come next. If they are not to become constrained and tongue-tied by the demands made upon them, children need to be able to visualise clearly beforehand what is to happen, what the story requires from them in the way of action, speech and characterisation; and while they are young they can only do this successfully in a fairly short burst at a time. Once a first acting-version has been built up in this way, a second attempt can be made without pauses or interruptions; and for this, or for later versions, the cast can be changed to give more members of the class a chance to act. It is seldom desirable to spend more than a single lesson on any one story; what is valuable is the effort of exploring and bringing to life the drama inherent in the narrative, and once this act of imaginative penetration has exhausted its impetus, we gain very little (at this age) by trying to add a further polish to the actual performance. After a while, of course, the class should be ready to take more responsibility for themselves, and they can then be divided into groups, each under a producer, and sent off to corners of the room to prepare and rehearse their own dramatisation of a story for later presentation to the rest of the form. It is remarkable the amount of time and energy children will voluntarily devote to preparing these dramatisations (in the break or the dinner-hour) if the enthusiasm has once taken hold of them.

One word of caution may be in place. In choosing material for this work the teacher needs to cultivate an eye for the dramatic possibilities of the stories he considers — and in particular for those which are within reach of his own pupils under normal class-room conditions. Likely material is often easy enough to recognise — the parable of the Good Samaritan, for instance, the story of the emperor's new clothes, or the exploit of Abu-Hassan and Nouz-Hatoul in the *Arabian Nights*. At other times it may be necessary to look further beneath the surface; a casual reading could easily miss the rich dramatic potential concealed in the ballad of 'Green Broom'. But what must be avoided at all costs is the tale which is either essentially non-dramatic in its mode, or else impossibly difficult. Thus I have more than once seen that fine ballad 'Sir Patrick Spens' recommended for dramatisation — and I can't but see this as singularly wrongheaded. It is true that there are some brief episodes within it which offer the kind of drama we are looking for — the 'reversal' which accompanies Sir Patrick's receipt of the king's message, the (implied) reaction of the court to the news of the shipwreck. But how on earth, we may ask, is the ship's foundering in the storm to be represented in the class-room without destroying the tragic mood demanded by it? Yet the stanzas describing this are among the finest in the poem; to relegate them to occurrence off-stage is to throw away the kernel and keep only the empty husk. In any case, all that is valuable in 'Sir Patrick Spens' is intimately bound up with the actual words of the poem. When dramatising a ballad, we are compelled to let the children leave the text behind and make up their own dialogue, for otherwise no spontaneous life will ever find its way into their acting. But in the case of 'Sir Patrick Spens' to do this is sacrilege.

Of course the same objection will apply to all poems that have any real merit as poetry, and we ought to be very cautious about deciding to dramatise poems of any kind (ballads included). There are, however, a certain number of ballads (the Robin Hood ones, for example) which are no more than narratives done into a jogtrot verse-form which presumably made them easier to remember. Their poetic quality is so slight as to be for all practical purposes negligible and we can dramatise them with a clear conscience. (Admittedly a simplified retelling of the story would often serve just as well.) We shall find other ballads ('Green Broom' is one example) where the dramatic possibilities are real enough, but where it seems a pity to sacrifice the words. In such cases, the use of mime can sometimes help to resolve the difficulty; a mimed version of the story can first be built up independently of the words, and later versions of the mime can then be synchronised with a reading of the poem by the teacher or by other children. Mime itself, however, needs to be used with discretion, since there are distinct limits to the range of incident which it is capable of conveying effectively. As an example of its misuse I quote the humorous ballad 'Get Up and Bar the Door'. I have more than once heard of lessons in which this has been mimed, despite the fact that the whole point of the anecdote depends on the contrast between the self-imposed silence of the 'gudewife' and her husband, kept up throughout all the taunts and indignities which the two highwaymen subject them to, and the ultimate verbal protest through which the husband loses his wager. This is good material for dramatisation by, say, a second form, but if the actors are limited to mime, their task is made impossible.

With first and second forms the value of the three types of lesson so far described can hardly be in doubt; but where, it may be asked, does it all lead to after that? Certainly when self-consciousness sets in during the third or fourth year, this type of dramatic work will often be the first to suffer. If unscripted drama is to continue to justify itself to fourteen- or fifteen-year-olds, they must be able to feel that they are advancing beyond the merely childish level to a new stage of achievement. Some drama specialists have reported encouraging success with an elaboration of mime described as 'dance-drama'; anyone who is inclined to experiment in this direction will find a helpful (if over-rhapsodic) account of work with teen-age classes in Garrard and Wiles (1957). It is more rewarding, to my mind, to move towards some form of group play-writing, and the techniques for adult and youth groups described in Kelly (1948) can readily be adapted for use in school. What is essential is that the starting-point should be not an attempt at a written script, but a group discussion of plot and characterisation followed by an un-scripted 'trying-out' of the various possibilities. Only thus can the average class achieve dialogue which is natural and unstilted, and a shape for their play which is genuinely dramatic and not merely narrative or 'literary'. This work is probably best done in fairly small groups (not too large at any rate to provide a part for each member of the group); and at an appropriate stage in the play's growth, one member of the group will be deputed to write down and polish a script which can then be 'fixed' and learned. Since it is at this point in their school career that children begin to feel the need for an audience as an incentive to bring forth their best effort, it is a good plan to arrange for them to present their final version not merely to the rest of the form, but if possible to their parallel form (or forms) as well. But whether or not this kind of follow-up proves successful we can be certain that earlier experience of dramatic improvisation will be of inestimable value when our classes move on to the acting of 'real plays'.

(iii) DRAMA FROM A TEXT

The reading of Shakespeare forms a part of the ordinary curriculum of English-speaking school children. Read in the ordinary way by a class of children sitting at desks, out of a horrid little school edition provided with the sort of notes that one can be examined on, a play by Shakespeare seems meaningless and dull. Naturally; Shakespeare did not write his plays to be read, with notes, by children sitting at desks; he wrote them to be acted. Children who have read the plays dramatically, who have lived through them with their whole imaginative being, acquire an understanding of Shakespeare, a feeling for the poetry, denied to those who have ploughed through them in class and passed, even with honours, an examination in the notes.

ALDOUS HUXLEY, *Proper Studies* (1927)

So far our discussion has emphasised mainly the satisfactions available to the individual child in the acting of his own allotted role; in drama lessons 'from a text' these satisfactions persist, but increas-ingly they are merged into something deeper and more far-reaching, which we can only term the active experience of drama as an artistic medium. Our overriding concern now is the satisfaction the children can gain through 'taking in' the play as a unified imaginative experience—an experience (originally that of the dramatist himself) which has been given permanent significance and value by its organisation into dramatic form. Henceforth our activity is inter- pretative rather than purely creative, and the words of the dramatist's script become the arbiter in all that we do. They are the authority to which we must keep referring back, since they embody and control the kind of realisation which is possible and permissible in the acting. The key question which continually proposes itself is no longer 'How would this character feel?' but instead 'How *does* he feel?'—'How does he feel, that is, in the scene as it is defined for us by the text of the play?' I suppose one can assume fairly general agreement that in English lessons a play is to be treated as a play— and that this means it must be acted. Among English teachers of today there cannot be left many of the old school who used obligingly to read all the parts themselves, one after another; and even those who have never got further than allowing the children to read the parts seated in their desks must surely be a dwindling minority. The accepted practice is, thank goodness, to 'have them out in front to act it'; and it is increasingly realised that drama, far from being merely another branch of literature, is, rather, a combined art-form in which the words themselves are only one among a number of components, so that a play, like a score in music, comes fully to life only when it is performed.

Of course the class-room sets its own limits to how far we can get in the direction of 'performance'. We cannot supply any scenery (though this shouldn't be missed if the play is Shakespeare), we have to make do with fairly rudimentary substitutes for properties and costume (certainly the more of these the better), and the actors will be hampered by having to read their parts, book in hand. But in practice these limitations prove far less of a hindrance than might be feared. What we want is that our lessons should resemble more than anything else an early rehearsal for a co-operative form of dramatic production—a production which would be, in the result, not the interpretation of a single mind (the teacher-producer) but the collec- tive interpretation of the group. It is a cardinal principle that the children start acting the play straight away, wasting the barest minimum of time upon casting or other preliminaries. We do not require them first to read through the scene seated in their desks in order to get an idea of what it is about, nor does the teacher take up time explaining what is going to happen, what the characters are like, or even how the stage should be set — for these are the very things the children are to find out for themselves in the course of their acting. The value of the lesson for them is to lie precisely in this process of interpretation, of bringing the text to life; and this work must not therefore be done for them. If it is a new play we are starting we may look briefly at the list of dramatis personae to discover from it all that we can about the characters and the relationships between them (if the play is Sheridan or Goldsmith the names alone will tell us a good deal); or we may glance at the author's initial stage directions (not necessarily, after all, as exiguous as those in the Shakespearean canon) to glean what we can about the best way to lay out our acting area. But apart from this the sooner we are launched upon the acting the better.

Once the first run-through has started, the teacher's conduct of the lesson has to be guided by two conflicting considerations. On the one hand he will want to give the actors a chance to build up a sense of the flow and rhythm of the scene, and to develop the impetus which will carry them over many difficulties (of language, for instance) which would otherwise cause them to stumble. With this in mind he will feel inclined to interrupt them only if they are going wildly astray — if, for instance, an actor is on the stage when he shouldn't be, or is reading the wrong part, or is addressing his remarks to the wrong character. But on the other hand the teacher will be acutely aware that improvement will not come of its own accord. If the actors are failing hopelessly to bring the scene to life, little is gained by letting them plod on wearily to the end of it. All that results from this is that the rest of the class grow bored, and the actors themselves become dispirited. For this reason the teacher will often feel the need to intervene in the same way that a producer would at an early rehearsal.

What kind of intervention, though? It is certainly true that in the class-room, as in rehearsals for an actual production, the road to improvement lies through careful attention to significant detail; but we cannot be satisfied (as some producers might) merely to tell them, or even to show them, what gestures to use, what expression or intonation to adopt. It is not the end-result (the acting proficiency) but the process of getting there that is educationally valuable. On the other hand, generalised exhortation or instruction is fruitless, and tends to remove the problem on to the merely verbal plane. Habit-hardened to the question 'What was wrong with that scene?' the children remain content to parrot, with weary confidence, 'Not enough life in it', or 'Please, sir, they should have put more expression in it' – clichés which the teacher learns, in time, to recognise as a damaging (if unintended) criticism of his previous procedures. In the earlier stages, at any rate, what we have to do, as we work over, discuss, and act again selected bits of the text, is to find ways of helping the actors to break down their task into manageable units, which they can then master one at a time with the understanding which comes from getting increasingly inside the dramatic situation.

In general terms the questions we need are those which will focus the children's attention on the dramatic qualities implicit in the dramatist's unique arrangement of words on the printed page. This means that the questions asked should not be concerned with the meaning of a word, or a phrase, or even with the meaning of a whole speech, *unless* the speech is one which has vital *dramatic* significance for the action of the play. Nor should they deal with character, or events, or plot, *except in so far as these emerge in dramatic terms in the actual scene in hand.* More positively, we can say that the questions which will be found effective are likely to tend towards the pattern suggested in the following:

Who is this character A is talking to now? How do we know? What is he doing while he says this? (Or what has he done just before saying it?) How do we know? What is this other character B doing while A talks? How do we know? What is A feeling when he says this? How do we know? How could he have shown this so that we in the audience would have realised it? By his posture? By his facial expression? In his movements? In the pitch of his voice? By speaking fast? Or slowly? By pausing? If so, where?

Similarly, what is this other character B thinking or feeling while A says this? How do we know? How could *he* have shown it?

And so on. Clearly the teacher has to decide beforehand where and in what way these questions are relevant to the particular material in hand, and also to settle in his own mind their relative order of importance. For equally clearly, he won't decide to ask all the questions which occur to him while preparing the scene. If an actor has grasped a point on his own there will be no need to mention it, except perhaps in a brief word of commendation ('Did you notice how Malvolio showed us so-and-so?'); while at other times it will be necessary to let slip many of the finer shades of interpretation and be content to establish merely the most obvious and centrally important aspects. Again it will be seen that the recurrent question 'How do we know?' implies a continual reference-back to the text itself; an insistence on this should eventually exclude the merely fanciful or eccentric embellishment so much in favour with modern Shakespearean producers. And finally it should be emphasised that this discussion needs to be kept in close contact with the attempt to act. Any piece of insight or enlightenment gained verbally must be immediately transferred to the plane of practice, by asking the actor to attempt the relevant fragment again; if he fails badly, another child can be asked to try it (there will usually be no lack of volunteers). Sometimes the miming of an action can be helpful as a step towards the achievement required; and once the more limited goal has been reached the mimed action can be fitted again into the total dramatic context. In ways such as this the dramatic life of the scene can be built up and enriched gradually, piece by piece.

The teacher who remains uncertain as to precisely what is meant by the term *dramatic qualities* in the above argument may care to study the following brief and self-contained extract from Ben Jonson's brilliant comedy *The Silent Woman*. The Parson here makes his only appearance in the play; he has been called in to officiate at Morose's 'marriage' to Epicene. By this point in the dramatic action Morose's character has been firmly established, and we know that his 'humour' is to be completely unable to endure any noise except the sound of his own voice.

Scene: *A Room in* MOROSE'S *House*

[Enter MOROSE, EPICOENE, PARSON and CUTBEARD]

MOROSE. Sir, there's an angel for yourself, and a brace of angels for your cold. Muse not at this manage of my bounty. It is fit we should thank fortune for any benefit she confers upon us; besides, it is your imperfection, but my solace.

PARSON (*speaks as having a cold*). I thank your worship; so it is mine, now.

MOROSE. What says he, Cutbeard?

CUTBEARD. He says, proesto, sir, whensoever your worship needs him, he can be ready with the like. He got this cold with sitting up late, and singing catches with cloth-workers.

MOROSE. No more. I thank him.

PARSON. God keep your worship, and give you much joy with your fair spouse!—uh! uh! uh!

MOROSE. O, O! stay, Cutbeard! let him give me five shillings of my money

back. As it is bounty to reward benefits, so it is equity to mulct injuries.
I will have it. What says he?
CUTBEARD. He cannot change it, sir.
MOROSE. It must be changed.
CUTBEARD. Cough again. [*Aside to* PARSON]
MOROSE. What says he?
CUTBEARD. He will cough out the rest, sir.
PARSON. Uh, uh, uh!
MOROSE. Away, away with him! stop his mouth! away! I forgive it.

[*Exit* CUTBEARD, *thrusting out the* PARSON]

If we read this over two or three times with the kind of attention
we would have to give it in preparing to produce the play, we shall be
astonished by the extraordinarily full and specific instructions (for
producer and actors alike) which the skilled hand of a master-
dramatist has managed to incorporate in the dialogue — instructions
as to the actions, gestures and reactions of the characters, their
movements and positioning on the stage relative to one another, the
way they are to deliver their lines, the facial expressions which are to
accompany them. Whereas a modern playwright (J. B. Priestley, for
example) will liberally besprinkle his pages with helpfully explana-
tory stage directions (as though he had started out to write a novel
and changed his mind half-way through), it is clear that for Jonson —
as indeed for Shakespeare — every scene has been conceived from
the beginning as something to be represented by actors on a stage.
The 'qualities' inherent in dramatic writing such as this can be
examined, in the extract quoted, virtually in isolation; in *Volpone* (or
in *Hamlet*) they might be cloaked from us, at first, by the magnifi-
cence of the poetry, but practice will enable us to uncover them and
to realise how firmly the permissible range of interpretation has been
structured and defined by the texture of the writing itself.

Of course, in the class-room itself we have to concentrate on those
'dramatic qualities' which are well within the scope of the children's
realisation. Commonly enough those which fulfil this condition are
intermingled, in the plays we use in school, with others which don't;
and one must be careful to adapt one's treatment, by selection and
weight of emphasis, to suit the capabilities of the class and the degree
of maturity they have attained. There is no point in trying to move
forward through the play always at the same even undiscriminating
pace. There will be some scenes, or parts of scenes, which can be

dealt with cursorily, or even cut completely, thus leaving more time for other sections which will repay more expansive treatment. In a first approach to Shakespeare it is more profitable to concentrate on the parts which are potentially well within the children's reach (with a first or second form the mechanicals' scenes in *A Midsummer Night's Dream*, or with a third or fourth form the scenes in *Twelfth Night* involving Sir Toby, Sir Andrew and Malvolio); while in *The Rivals* we shall do well to play down the dullish and somewhat undramatic scenes between Julia and Faulkland. If the section in hand offers rich dramatic possibilities which are within the children's range (in *Twelfth Night* the duel scene, for instance, or even, with a good form, the more difficult letter scene), it is often sound procedure to act it through three times within the same lesson. On the first occasion the children will run through it without help or interruption; next will come the detailed working-over with interrupting questions and repetition of acting practice; and finally the children will act straight through again to incorporate the detailed improvements into the dramatic flow and life of the scene. At other times the nature of the dramatic material may well suggest a different form of compromise between continuity of acting and detailed improvement.

Let us take, as a further illustration of how our principles might work out in practice, the scene in *The Merchant of Venice* in which Shylock makes his first appearance (Act I, Scene iii). This is central to the action of the play, since in it Antonio agrees to the 'merry bond' proposed by Shylock, and it also exemplifies the way in which even the less spectacularly dramatic scenes in Shakespeare may offer distinct possibilities for class-room acting, if one takes the trouble to look for them. If we are taking this with a second or third form, I shall be inclined to cut out the thirty-odd lines (lines 72–103)[1] (difficult to follow, and not really essential at this level) in which Shylock and Antonio debate the scriptural precedent for usury. All the teacher needs to do is to tell the class, before starting the scene, that they are to leave out these lines because they are not very important at present. What is now left of the scene falls quite naturally into two distinct sub-units, separated by the entry of Antonio (line 40). If we are so lucky as to have two exceptionally good actors for Bassanio and Shylock we may find that they do well enough with the opening section to be allowed to go on to the end of it uninterrupted.

[1] The line-numbering used here relates to W. J. Craig's edition of the complete works of Shakespeare, published by the Oxford University Press.

It is more likely, however, that the first few speeches will be read uncomprehendingly and without any grasp of what is implied dramatically by Shylock's repeated interjection 'Well?'. If so, we had better stop and try to build up piecemeal a sense of the dramatic context which will help the actors to enter more fully into the situation as they proceed.

What (we may ask) is Bassanio asking Shylock to do for him? What is Shylock's attitude to the request? (On the surface he seems at this point to be hesitating, and debating with himself whether his money would be safe; it is not until his soliloquy later in the scene that we get an indication that his hesitation may be only a pretence, designed to lead Bassanio on, and make Antonio more ready to accept his terms.) How might Shylock show his hesitation? By what gesture or facial expression? (Demonstrations, please.) How would he make the repeated word 'Well' sound hesitating? How does Bassanio react to Shylock's 'stalling'? Which speech first shows that he is becoming impatient? At what point can we see that he is not merely impatient but actually angry? (And why?)

We shall not want to spend too long over this questioning, otherwise the class themselves will grow impatient to get on with the action. When once the actors have begun to grasp what is going on, they should be better able to interpret for themselves the subsequent developments – including perhaps (though this introduces a fresh element) the outburst of resentment which escapes from Shylock when he is invited to dine. A sense of continuity can be restored if we now ask the actors to go back to the beginning of the scene and act straight through past Antonio's entry.

[Enter ANTONIO]
BASSANIO. This is Signor Antonio.
SHYLOCK. How like a fawning publican he looks!
(aside)   I hate him for he is a Christian;
    But more for that in low simplicity
    He lends out money gratis, and brings down
    The rate of usance here with us in Venice.
    If I can catch him once upon the hip,
    I will feed fat the ancient grudge I bear him.
    He hates our sacred nation, and he rails,
    Even there where merchants most do congregate,

On me, my bargains, and my well-won thrift,
Which he calls interest. Cursed be my tribe,
If I forgive him!
BASSANIO. Shylock, do you hear?
SHYLOCK. I am debating of my present store,
And by the near guess of my memory,
I cannot instantly raise up the gross
Of full three thousand ducats. What of that?
Tubal, a wealthy Hebrew of my tribe,
Will furnish me. But soft! how many months
Do you desire? (*To* ANTONIO) Rest you fair, good signior,
Your worship was the last man in our mouths.

Here we may need to give some attention to the management of
Shylock's prolonged aside. On the simplest level there is the positioning of the actors to be sorted out. 'What are Bassanio and
Antonio doing while Shylock says all this?' Evidently they must be
absorbed in their own conversation, while standing far enough away
from Shylock to make it plausible that they do not hear what he is
saying. From the actor's point of view we shall need, too, to bring
out the contrast between the venom which Shylock gives vent to in
his aside and the mask which he has worn earlier and which he
resumes (his pretence of deliberation and hesitation) when Bassanio
walks over to him again.

A little later in the scene we come on one of the long speeches
which often prove a stumbling-block in a form's early approaches to
Shakespeare.

ANTONIO. Well, Shylock, shall we be beholding to you?
SHYLOCK. Signior Antonio, many a time and oft
In the Rialto you have rated me
About my moneys and my usances:
Still have I borne it with a patient shrug,
For sufferance is the badge of all our tribe.
You call me misbeliever, cut-throat dog,
And spet upon my Jewish gaberdine,
And all for use of that which is mine own.
Well then, it now appears you need my help:
Go to then; you come to me, and you say,
'Shylock, we would have moneys': you say so;
You, that did void your rheum upon my beard,
And foot me as you spurn a stranger cur
Over your threshold: moneys is your suit.

What should I say to you? Should I not say,
'Hath a dog money? Is it possible
A cur can lend three thousand ducats?' or
Shall I bend low, and in a bondman's key,
With bated breath, and whispering humbleness,
Say this:—
'Fair sir, you spet on me on Wednesday last;
You spurn'd me such a day; another time
You call'd me dog; and for these courtesies
I'll lend you thus much moneys?'

This is certainly difficult, and it is primarily to the dramatic context that we must turn for help. It does not seem to be in keeping with Shylock's intentions as revealed elsewhere in the scene that he should deliberately set out to display his bitterness against the Christians at this point; in fact, the immediate effect of his tirade is an outburst of temper from Antonio whom Shylock then has to placate. The most plausible (though not necessarily the only) interpretation is that in thinking about his grievances Shylock allows his indignation to express itself against his original conscious intention. It may be better therefore to go on a little further, at least as far as the explicit mention of the bond, and then return to this speech to explore its significance more fully in the light of what follows it. ('What is Shylock trying to do in this scene? Do you think he would want, at this point, to show Bassanio and Antonio just how much he hates them? How does Antonio react to the speech, and what does Shylock find he has to do about it. If Shylock doesn't mean to show his true feelings, why do you think he nevertheless does so? Would he, then, say the whole speech in the same tone? Would he be equally vehement all the way through it? If he starts calmly and quietly and then gradually works himself up over his wrongs, at what point does his anger first come out into the open? At the words "misbeliever, cut-throat dog", perhaps? At what point is he most vehement in expressing his resentment?') What I want to stress is that the dramatic approach—the question 'How ought we to act it?' —is the most powerful lever we can find to open up all the difficulties (even of language) which really matter. It is often helpful to break down a long speech into the segments which mark its dramatic progression. 'Is he talking about the same thing all the time in this speech? Is he talking to the same person all the time? Are his feelings the same all the way through? Where do you think his feelings change? How might you show his different feelings?' In this particular speech of Shylock's there is a clear separation and contrast between the two possible answers which Shylock rehearses at the end, and each of these calls for its own characteristic expression and gesture. The rest of the speech seems to be more a matter of a single steady crescendo of feeling; though it could be argued (the point is no doubt too subtle for any but an exceptional form) that at the line, 'Well then, it now appears you need my help', he makes an effort to rein in his feelings, in spite of which they only break out again more vehemently a line or two later.

As far as the rest of the scene is concerned we need only refer here to the contrast at its close between Antonio's credulous acceptance of the Jew's goodwill, and Bassanio's continuing suspicion—a point that can be effectively brought out in terms of the acting. The scene as a whole has enough good dramatic 'meat' in it to make it well worth while to act it straight through again if lesson time allows.

(iv) SOME PROBLEMS AND OBJECTIONS

One objection to all this is certain to make itself heard. 'Surely if the children don't *read* the play first, they won't understand it enough to be able to act it?' This reveals a failure of understanding so fundamental that it must be dealt with at some length. In the first place it assumes that the class can already do the very thing we are trying to train them to do; and it overlooks the fact that the adult ability to form a mental conception of a play's dramatic life while reading it recumbent in an armchair depends upon an experience of theatre-going (and school dramatics!) which the child simply does not possess. Let us suppose that, yielding to this ill-founded suggestion, we do spend the first half of the lesson with the children reading their parts seated in their desks. Whether or not this is accompanied by comments on the meaning of words, on the poetry, or the characterisation, or the events, we shall normally find that when they 'come out in front' afterwards they are no further forward in their acting than if they were starting from scratch. Usually, indeed, the only effect of the preliminary read-through is to take the edge off their enthusiasm a little. The fact is that a non-dramatic reading which distorts the play into a substitute for continuous narrative (like a novel with everything but the conversation suppressed) is bound to neglect essential dramatic qualities which only the attempt at acting can bring out. This failure to grasp the all-important distinction between the dramatic and the narrative mode vitiates a good deal of drama teaching, even of the kind which starts out with the best of intentions. Here is a small example, by way of illustration. When Malvolio, in the letter scene, says, 'By your leave, wax. Soft! and the impressure her Lucrece, with which she uses to seal: 'tis my lady,' the dramatic meaning of these lines – the one which counts – is that in opening the letter Malvolio has noticed on the wax securing it the imprint of Olivia's seal. (Won't he have pointed to it with his forefinger as·well?). On the other hand the footnote describing the particular kind of seal called a Lucrece represents the kind of explanation of meaning we shall be led into by a non-dramatic reading of the scene, and it is surely singularly little to the purpose.

In general it can be asserted that to plunge straightaway into an attempt at acting (however fumbling the attempt may be at first) is the only way to come to grips with the problems of meaning which belong properly to the medium of drama. The sound general principle should not, of course, be turned into a fetish. If the actors, knowing the parts allocated them for the next lesson, choose to read the scene on their own beforehand, I shall applaud their initiative; what I deprecate is the use of valuable lesson-time for a reading which at best is fruitless and at worst is liable to distort the direction of the class's approach to understanding.

Even so, I am aware that some reader may quote against me instances where the dramatic approach has been tried and has failed dismally. To diagnose confidently one would need to observe the symptoms at first hand, but I would say that in ninety-nine cases out of a hundred this is the result of choosing a play whose language is too far in advance of the class's reading capacity. It is my own experience that a thoroughgoing dramatic handling will often enable weak readers to get further with difficult material than they could by any other method. Just as a developing sense of the narrative context makes it easier to read a story, so the sense of dramatic context gradually built up through the acting makes the dramatic language easier to interpret. There are limits to this, however. If the purely linguistic difficulties are too overwhelming (too many words the children don't know, too many syntactical constructions that are unfamiliar), the actors will have no attention free for anything else. In the first year (and with many secondary modern classes in the second year as well) it is best to concentrate almost entirely upon unscripted drama; when the class are ready for it, a start can be made with suitable one-act plays (what a pity that so many school collections of these are padded out with dreary and incompetent rubbish!), and then, for a grammar-school stream, a ruthlessly cut version of *A Midsummer Night's Dream*. Further material for a second-year class can be found in modernised adaptations of medieval mystery plays, in Maeterlinck's *The Bluebird*, Galsworthy's *The Little Man* and (for an able group) *The Merchant of Venice*. For a third year one might try Sean O'Casey's *A Pound on Demand*, Obey's *Noah*, Gogol's *The Government Inspector*, *She Stoops to Conquer*, and *Julius Caesar*. In the fourth year the choice is naturally much wider; among the possibilities which are readily available in cheap editions I will mention only *Strife*, *The Rivals*, *Androcles and the Lion*, *Pygmalion*, *You Never Can Tell*, *Twelfth Night*, *Macbeth*, *The School for Scandal*, and *The Importance of Being Earnest*.

It is implied in this list of titles that Shakespeare should be the culmination of the school drama syllabus rather than its staple ingredient. The tradition which says, in effect, 'Shakespeare or nothing' is understandable enough in a way. Because Shakespeare is not only our supreme poet but also our supreme dramatist, English teachers are naturally preoccupied with the ambition to make their children acquainted with some at least of the plays before they leave school. Yet how many of his plays are there which really come within the linguistic and emotional range of the young adolescent? To those mentioned already one could perhaps add for grammar school forms *King Henry IV*, *Part I* (with boys) and *As You Like It* (with girls); but even these, along with *Macbeth* and *Twelfth Night*, would often be enjoyed more fully if they could be reserved for the fifth year. (Of course it is characteristic of Shakespeare's genius that he can be appreciated on many different levels, and even the relatively crude response of the groundlings is not to be sneered at; consequently if examination requirements mean that the fifth year has to be devoted entirely to a single play, there is much to be said for giving the class a chance to take what they can from other plays during the preceding terms.) In the secondary modern school the difficulties inevitably loom much larger, though for a determined teacher they need not prove insuperable. The cutting will need to be still more radical; and it may help with the intricacies and unfamiliarity of the Shakespearean idiom if the teacher takes a turn at reading some of the more difficult parts, giving thus a 'lift' to the life of the particular scene in hand, and also providing through the example of his reading a sense

F

of how Shakespearean verse should be spoken. (The Marlowe Society's recorded versions of the plays can also be extremely useful in this respect.) One further device is worth trying. Before tackling a given scene the teacher gives an outline of the characters and events in it, and the class try to construct and act their own version in their own language. To the extent that the situation has come alive for them as drama in the course of this, the class will then be better placed for their attempt to bring to life the drama of the Shakespearean version. I believe there are few secondary forms which couldn't gain something from work on these lines with *The Merchant of Venice* and *Julius Caesar*, at least; but if they obviously don't, we had better cut our losses and abandon Shakespeare in favour of simpler dramatic material. An introduction which doesn't lead to a desire for further acquaintance does no service either to Shakespeare or to the children.

One or two practical problems have still to be mentioned. First, on what basis should we allot parts? We need to maintain a standard of acting which does not impair the interest and enjoyment of the class as a whole; on the other hand, to rely always on a few good readers is unfair to the others and does not give them a chance to develop. Not that justice is to be equated with a blind egalitarianism. The fair procedure is to give the more difficult roles to children who can do them justice, and to find for the weaker readers parts in which they can at least acquit themselves honourably; at the same time we need to be on the look-out for opportunities to bring forward the less talented, so that when they have gained confidence in the discharge of limited tasks they may graduate to more exacting ones. We shall also want to meet the children's own wishes whenever we can, bearing in mind that the fulfilment of emotional needs through acting is part of the value not only of free drama but also of scripted drama as well. It is therefore a good idea to consult the class at times ('Who would like to be Jessica? Who do you think we should have for Shylock?'), though it is a mistake to be drawn into a full-dress debate about casting when we ought to be pressing on with the acting.

In the early stages it will usually be found that the children are all desperately keen to act, showing disappointment and restlessness when no part is found for them. In these circumstances it is advisable to change the cast frequently within the same lesson, since at this age children's horizons do not readily extend beyond the immediate present. In time they will grow more able to contain their impatience, having learnt that their turn will come round next week even if it does not do so this. However, the audience itself (i.e. the rest of the class) should have a function that is active and not merely passive. We have to make them aware that they share responsibility for the common task of dramatic realisation, and we must train them to divide their attention (just as a producer would have to) between the text open in front of them and the actor's attempts to breathe life into it.[1] In the first place we make it clear that we expect spectators as well as actors to be ready with answers to the detailed type of questioning illustrated in the previous section. Secondly we make a point of asking the audience at the end of each scene to give their opinion of the acting and to make suggestions for its improvement. 'Did you enjoy the way they acted that? What was good about it?' If they are slow to respond, the teacher himself can refer to some part of the scene that deserved praise. 'Let's have that bit done over again, so that this time you can notice the good points in it.' Later, when the positive aspect of the critical function has been sufficiently stressed, we may ask, 'Did you notice any points that the actors missed? Were there any bits that they might have done better? You come out and show us how *you* would have done it.' In this way we can gradually devolve responsibility from the teacher's shoulders on to those of the children. The first step is to induce them to ask for themselves the questions which in the beginning had to be formulated by the teacher. Later we delegate to certain carefully chosen pupils some of the functions of producer, stage-manager and property-man, following this up by dividing the form into groups, each under its own producer. As a final stage we can establish within the form two (or more) semi-permanent 'acting-companies' which then take responsibility for casting, preparing and performing either different scenes or rival versions of the same scene.

One danger that must be avoided is an over-emphasis upon what we may call 'stage-technique'. With some classes it is noticeable that discussion regularly resolves itself into such comments as 'Please, sir, they weren't spread out enough' or 'Jones had his back to the audience', and one can't help feeling that this must reflect a misconceived pseudo-professionalism on the part of their teacher at

[1] There will, however, be times, usually during the final uninterrupted run-through at the end of a lesson, when we vary this by telling them to close their books and concentrate on the actors alone.

some period. It can be pointed out that these particular shibboleths have no universal validity anyway, and that such prescriptive force as they have is confined to productions on a modern proscenium stage; if we use an arena stage for our school productions, or if we arrange our class-room audience around three sides of the acting-space (as in an Elizabethan playhouse) we shall be forced to think these issues out afresh. It is the place of technique in general that needs clarifying, however. Certainly class-room drama must aim to improve the children's command of acting technique; but it is, of course, the ability to *use* technical accomplishments (not to talk—about them) that is required. I believe that this is best secured by working towards the accomplishment covertly, from within the situation of the play, rather than by expecting the child actor both to be 'inside' his part and at the same time to visualise himself from the outside as seen from an auditorium. The combination of self-consciousness and self-forgetfulness, detachment and involvement, which this would call for is a more sophisticated requirement than we may realise. Thus failures of grouping (a tendency to bunch together, or to stand strung out in a line like boy scouts on parade) can be tackled by questions concerned with the dramatic relation-ships existing between the characters at this point in the scene. 'Would they all be standing close together? Which would stand close together? Which would keep apart from one another? Which characters are talking, and which are merely looking on?' And the actor who ought not (at this point) to be standing with his back to the audience can be asked, tactfully: 'What is this character feeling? How could he show it? Can he show it if we can't see his face?' A similar approach will apply to other skills that we need to develop: natural stage movement, variations of pace, the ability to build up to a climax.

There has been heated controversy at times over the place to be occupied, in school drama, by the public or semi-public perfor-mance. It has been said, quite truthfully, that the annual 'school play' is often put on for irrelevant reasons of prestige (to impress the parents or the Governors); that, in order to make the evening's entertainment tolerable to an audience seated on hard chairs in a draughty hall, too much emphasis has to be given to the purely technical level of achievement which can be imposed by an ex-perienced producer, at the expense of the first-hand exploration of dramatic roles which is educationally valuable; and that the educational benefit is in any case confined to the comparatively small number who actually take part in the production, and sometimes only to a few star performers. These strictures apply with most force when the school production is an isolated event which does not arise naturally out of a varied and vigorous dramatic life in the school as a whole; and when it is undertaken with pupils who are too young to gain much from it. Certainly there can be no place for the public performance in the junior school, nor yet with junior forms in the secondary school. At this stage of development dramatic play is still an absorbing and satisfying activity in itself, and the children feel of their own accord no need for an audience beyond that of their own immediate circle. Around the age of thirteen or fourteen, however, many children grow dissatisfied with dramatic activity which does not at times take to itself a more serious and adult justification. At this point the occasional performance for another form or for a school Drama Festival can supply the incentive for more determined and disciplined effort, and at the same time add a related sense of purposefulness to the normal run of dramatic activity in the class-room. And if the more ambitious school play develops out of this kind of experience, and is produced with a due sense of what the actors ought to gain from it as well as the audience, it can have great value both as an ultimate goal for the dramatically-inclined and as an indication of attainable standards of achievement.

The end-result of class-room drama is not to be looked for only in the sphere of production and performance, however. A vital dramatic tradition will show itself above all as an enrichment and deepening of the study of drama which takes place in upper forms. I suspect that there are still many teachers who regard the approach to a play via acting as primarily a concession to immaturity, something to be jettisoned as soon as the class are old enough to get down to serious study. Nothing could be more mistaken. It is not merely Shakespeare's comic interludes which call for class-room acting (we have stressed these earlier because they typify the kind of Shakespeare material which children usually find it easier to start with). In the fifth and even the sixth form the first experience of a play should always come through acting it, and much of the subsequent de-tailed study — examination of the poetry, the characterisation, the dramatic structure, the thematic development — is best carried out within the context of continued attempts at dramatic realisation. The extent to which Shakespeare's central meanings are conveyed in essentially dramatic terms has perhaps been obscured for many of us by the distressing aberrations currently characteristic of Shakespearean productions on the professional stage. We have too often seen irrelevant stage-business thrust into the limelight, the drama inherent in the poet's words ignored, the poetry itself mangled, or drowned by off-stage music and intrusive sound-effects, and the dramatist's unifying intention butchered to make a producer's field-day; so that our most rewarding experience of Shakespeare has usually had to come through solitary effort. Occasionally we may be fortunate enough to see a production which has been dedicated not to spurious 'originality' but to faithful interpretation, and then the difference comes as a revelation. So it is that I remember from a decade ago a performance of *Macbeth* by the Mermaid Theatre in which the words took their full weight, the action moved forward uninterruptedly on a bare platform stage, and there was an attempt, scholarly but not pedantic, to recreate an acting style similar to that used in the Elizabethan playhouse. Such experiences ought not to be as exceptional as they are; for the fact is that Shakespeare's poetry is essentially dramatic poetry, needing to be approached first and foremost by way of the dramatic qualities implicit within it. Take Macbeth's 'dagger' soliloquy as an obvious case in point—a speech which fairly demands that we come to it through a consideration of how the actor is to speak the lines, and how (by phrasing and gesture) he is to show Macbeth's shifts in mood. Or look at the following excerpt (it comes just after Duncan's murder):

LADY MACBETH. Who was it that thus cried? Why, worthy thane,
You do unbend your noble strength to think
So brainsickly of things. Go get some water,
And wash this filthy witness from your hand.
Why did you bring these daggers from the place?
They must lie there: go carry them, and smear
The sleepy grooms with blood.

MACBETH. I'll go no more:
I am afraid to think what I have done;
Look on't again I dare not.

LADY MACBETH. Infirm of purpose!
Give me the daggers. The sleeping and the dead
Are but as pictures; 'tis the eye of childhood
That fears a painted devil. If he do bleed
I'll gild the faces of the grooms withal,
For it must seem their guilt.

Here, even with a fifth form, it is the endeavour to improve the acting that will provide the incentive for examining the poet's language, and in particular the metaphors ('brainsickly', 'infirm of purpose', 'the eye of childhood') which help to define Lady Macbeth's attitude to her husband. From the same starting-point we can go on to follow up the implications of 'unbend your noble strength' (with its possible reminiscence of Lady Macbeth's earlier image 'But screw your courage to the sticking-place') for our understanding of Macbeth's condition, and explore some of the further light thrown on Lady Macbeth's frame of mind by her word-play on 'gild' and 'guilt'. A further advantage is that we shall not easily make the Bradleyan mistake of seeing the characters as flesh-and-blood human beings whose history and psychology can be pursued in abstraction from the words of the play, for we shall be aware all the time that they move and have their being only as personae within the nexus of an acted drama. And when in the sixth form we advance to a study of that organisation of poetic texture which justifies us in thinking of each play as (in part at least) 'an expanded metaphor', this further level of understanding will fall naturally into place as part of an awareness of the drama as an organic whole.

Chapter 5

TALKING AND WRITING

(i)

'The way the world is now,' Levin said, 'I sometimes feel I'm engaged in a great irrelevancy, teaching people how to write who don't know what to write. I can give them subjects but not subject matter. I worry I'm not teaching how to keep civilisation from destroying itself. . . . I have the strongest compulsion to be involved with such thoughts in the classroom, if you know what I mean.'

'I do,' said Bucket, 'but if we all did that who'd be teaching composition?'

BERNARD MALAMUD, *A New Life*

'ENGLISH composition' is one of those fragments of educational jargon which hang round our neck like the albatross. We can't get away from it, and can't, apparently, manage without it; yet it has associations and implications which are gravely misleading. The associations are a matter of educational history, for the word 'composition' itself is part of what we inherit from the nineteenth-century teaching of classics. The implication, hard to escape, is that writing (to be equated with 'composition') is a matter of *putting together* words and phrases in accordance with certain clearly defined rules or clearly definable principles. With Latin the rules were those derived from study of the golden age of Ciceronian prose; in our case they are thought of, less explicitly, as the rules of grammar and of correct English usage. Thus it is that so many 'composition' courses assume that what the pupil has to acquire is a conscious mechanical skill essentially synthetic in nature, a progressive sequence of techniques for combining words into sentences, sentences into paragraphs, paragraphs into an essay. The teacher's role is that of *preceptor*, dispensing the general rules and principles which the pupil must first master and then learn to apply by incessant practice or 'drill'.

Does this sound reasonable? Do we ourselves, when we speak or write our native language, spend our time thinking about either grammatical rules or stylistic principles? Do we, for that matter, give any of our conscious attention to the words and constructions we are using *as such*? Don't we rather have to focus our mind on the content of our communication – on just what it is that we have to say? 'Write a description of the sea on a stormy day,' says the course-book, 'and remember to use plenty of vivid interesting adjectives.' 'Rubbish!' any practising author would retort. 'What you must do is go and look at the sea on a stormy day and really observe it – notice exactly what it looks like, what colours and shapes it assumes, what sounds it makes, what feelings it induces in you. Then you must concentrate on conveying your experience in words so that the reader will share it just as if he had been there with you. If you try hard enough to visualise the scene you will find afterwards that you have indeed used many vivid and appropriate words, adjectives included. But if you clutter up your mind with ideas about the *kind* of word you ought to use, then you will be lost, for this kind of consciousness is sure to come between you and your real task.'

The fact is that language is so intimately bound up with the human capacity for thought and feeling that we cannot profitably isolate the one from the other. In composition lessons the focus of attention must always be on the thoughts, the feelings, the experience that have to be communicated; the basic requirement is that the writer should be able to hold these in his mind, clearly grasped, sharply realised, vividly imagined. 'If a man's thoughts are clear,' observed Swift, 'the properest words will generally present themselves first.' And it is evident that Coleridge in his rather different idiom was saying something very similar when he remarked that before he could write he had to have 'a body of thought'. Compare, too, Charles Darwin: 'I never study style; all that I do is try to get the subject as clear as I can in my head, and express it in the commonest language which occurs to me. But I generally have to think a good deal before the simplest arrangement occurs to me.'

Admittedly we must beware of overstressing (as these quotations might seem to do) the purely intellectual aspect of the process: it is not merely 'thought', in the narrower sense, for which words have to be found. Nevertheless, the central truth remains – that it is first and foremost the *content* of his children's speech and writing with which the teacher has to concern himself. It is to this area that the pupils' powers of concentration must be directed; it is within this area that they need, and benefit from, stimulation and guidance — help in gathering together their ideas and feelings and impressions, in refining and making more precise their perceptions, in organising and giving shape to their inward store of experience.

Of course it would be wrong to suggest that teacher and pupil should *never* give deliberate attention to forms of expression on the verbal level. (For the adult writer, does not this kind of attention come in at the stage when he revises his first draft, sets out to produce a fair copy?) The point to stress for the moment, however, is that the ability to communicate experience to others in one's native language develops not through conscious awareness of precepts, but primarily through practice in so communicating. 'Children learn to write by writing.' The first task is to ensure that all our pupils have plentiful experience of using the medium of writing for purposes with which they fully identify themselves; and the teacher's main role is to establish the conditions under which this regular practice will be most fully conducive to improvement.

In considering how to do this, the fruitful parallel to examine is not the learning of a second language (let alone a dead one) but rather the first stages by which a child gains a command of his native tongue. There are important differences, of course, and the analogy must not be pressed too far; nevertheless I believe that the secondary teacher can learn a good deal from studying the manner in which the small child's first acquisition of speech takes place. A. N. Whitehead once described this as the most difficult intellectual task which any human being undertakes in the course of his whole lifetime; yet, in all save a minute percentage of exceptional cases, the task is accomplished with amazing efficiency in the first five years of a child's life. By the age of five or six the normal child has learnt to manipulate almost all the structures of his native language, and, at a very conservative estimate, is able to use in conversation something between 2,000 and 3,000 words. This generalisation applies to all known languages and cultures, whether 'primitive' or civilised.

From many points of view, the learning of the complex systems through which human communications goes on — language, kinesics (or gestures and motions), and vocalisations (the phenomena generally referred to as 'tone of voice') — is the greatest intellectual achievement any of us ever makes. And yet these systems are thoroughly learned and internalised by all physiologically normal human beings in all cultures at about five and a half years of age! Individuals learn the systems at different rates and in different orders, but from the point of view of the culturologist, the important fact is that about 98 per cent of all our species are in full control of the *structure* of their group's communication systems at about the same age. (Smith, 1956).

In the case of children in the United States (and it seems likely that the figures for children in Great Britain would be closely similar) we can also state, with rather more precision, that the average child of six knows some meanings for about 15,000 words. (Smith, 1941; Templin, 1957.) This remarkable achievement is, of course, only 'natural' in the sense that it is not the result of any deliberately planned course of learning; we must clearly regard it as the end-product of many thousands of years of social evolution.

How is it done? We can note here only a few points which seem particularly relevant to our own concerns. In the first place the child's early speech does not appear suddenly out of the blue; his first words and sentences represent rather a drawing-together of a diverse complex of activities which have been going on almost since the very first weeks of life. Thus, the extraordinarily wide range of articulations which the baby produces during his first year – all the cooings and grunts and babblings – are the necessary precursors of speech; they include all the different consonant and vowel-sounds which are used in any of the known languages of the world. From these the child has to learn eventually to select the particular sounds which are used to convey meaning in his mother-tongue (the *phonemes* of the language); and in this learning the central role is played by the activity of listening. We know this because babies who have been institutionalised in the early months and thus deprived of normal opportunities of listening to the talk of the family circle become severely retarded in their vocalisations; similarly, backwardness in listening to and understanding the talk of those around him is one of the first and surest indications that a child will later prove to be backward in talking.

In this gathering together of different and apparently separate activities into the unique achievement of speech, we can see clearly at work the process we have already referred to as maturation. In a normal family environment all children follow, at their own differing rates, the same inevitable sequence. Certain levels of muscular control and auditory discrimination are necessary before the child can launch his first meaningful utterances. When he does, his first utterances are invariably single words; and he is likely to have a couple of dozen or more of these at his command by his second birthday, the majority of them almost certainly either proper names or nouns. (Perhaps, however, it would be more correct to regard these first words as compressed equivalents for sentences, 'Milk' thus representing the command 'Give me some milk', and 'Doggy' the statement 'There is a dog' or 'That is a dog'.) A few months later he will have moved on to the stage of simple sentences, advancing later to a grasp of verb forms indicating tense and person, later still to a mastery of the personal pronouns, and so on. And it seems to be generally accepted that there would be no point in trying to hurry the child through the necessary sequence of stages; in the normal home the child is allowed to develop his powers of speech at his own rate.

In this development, conscious deliberate effort (the kind of effort generally held to be an indispensable accompaniment of 'learning' in any school situation) plays virtually no part. The process is not so much one of learning as of *acquiring*: listening, followed by imitation, unconscious assimilation, and intuitive adaptation. The small child is not, for instance, called upon to master intellectually any rules for combining sounds (phonemes) together to make up words. The first 'pieces' of language which the infant gets a real grasp of are not isolated vowel or consonant sounds, but complete units of a larger kind; and in the earlier stages these words or small phrases seem to be quite indissoluble. The baby draws upon his repertoire of sounds to produce the word, but the individual sound (the 'd' in 'dadda' or the 'm' in 'mama') has no separate existence for him as such. We can see some evidence of this in the confusing-together of pairs of words which is quite common in children around the ages of two and three. Obviously enough, whereas there are some words which are quite easily distinguishable in sound, there are other pairs of words which may sound quite different to the adult ear but much less so to the infant's. For one of the writer's children one pair of this kind was 'doggy' and 'Daddy'; during his second year he used a sort of intermediate form of 'Doddy' for some time before he finally separated the two words out. Another confusion belonging to around the same period was between 'mummy' and 'bunny'; but in this case the word he already knew did duty for the new word which resembled it, so that for some weeks he went around referring to his new stuffed toy as a 'mummy-rabbit'. Only a good deal later does there come any consciousness of the individual elements of which words are compounded. In the case of this particular child we saw the first clear sign of this awareness about a year later when he started to play around with consonants and transpose them experimentally in nursery rhymes that he already knew well, so that we would hear from time to time versions of 'Little Bo-Peep' such as 'Dittle Do-Peep has dost her deep', and so on. In a similar way the patterns and structure of sentences are in the first place picked up as wholes, and are not built up by deliberate synthesis. Certainly the regularities which are inherent in syntactical structuring must become embedded in the patterning of the child's own mental processes; but only occasionally can we trace any explicit consciousness of the nature of these regularities. Thus it is that intelligent children around the age of four or so can sometimes be observed formulating to themselves their own home-made generalisations about the past tense of English verbs. The trend of their thinking only comes to light because they try to apply its results to the irregular forms of the so-called 'strong' verbs. A child who has for some time used *knew* and *saw*, in their rightful contexts, will suddenly start saying *knowed* and *seed* (and perhaps *hitted*!) instead; he may even say *knew* automatically and then stop and 'correct' himself. The main point here is that such mental systematisation as is needed shapes itself during the process of using the language; mastery of the complex and varying patterns of the language does not require prior knowledge of the principles which underlie the patterns, and the whole process of mastery seems to take place at an intuitive rather than at a conscious level.

The child's first command of speech, then, is acquired rather than deliberately learnt; it is picked up gradually, unconsciously, and effortlessly as the child tries to use language in order to communicate with the other human beings around him. What should also be stressed is the extreme urgency of the small child's desire to achieve such communication through language. All parents will have witnessed at one time or another the extraordinarily acute frustration of the infant whose mother or father has failed to understand what he is trying to say. The motives and purposes which impel a small child towards speech are exceptionally intense, because they arise in relation to vital needs and interests that really matter to him, and because they are directed towards the members of the family circle on whom all his emotional life is centred. Some writers have stressed in particular the practical or pragmatic purposes which motivate the infant's use of language, believing this to provide the main (if not indeed the sole) incentive to linguistic growth. [See especially Lewis (1957, 1963).] Certainly the most obvious benefit a child gains from articulate speech is the power to secure for himself specific kinds of attention—to compel the adult to produce for him the particular food, drink, or toy that he wants. I have formed the impression, however, that this operational use of language comes comparatively late in the development of many children; and that most of the earlier manifestations of speech have a less utilitarian function. Anthropologists have shown us that in any community, whether primitive or civilised, an astonishingly large proportion of the total linguistic activity is devoted primarily to establishing, preserving and strengthening the bonds of relationship between people—to acting, in fact, as a kind of 'social cement'. Malinowski (1923) even invented a special term for this type of linguistic functioning— 'phatic communion'. Time and again, one can see a small child's first attempts at speech doing precisely this. Pointing to the cat on the hearth or the felt toy or the picture in his book, the child says 'Pussy', the mother repeats the word after him, and a smile lights up both faces. The utterance has linked the two human beings in a shared relationship towards the named object, and this is its true function and, indeed, its 'meaning'. As with so much that forms part of our everyday adult converse ('Good morning', 'How do you do?', 'Nice to see you') no practical consequence follows; the motive for speech is essentially the urge to create this delighted mutuality of experience. Again, much of the child's early speech is governed not so much by the pragmatic purposes of actual living, as by the imagined ones of play. We have seen already how these activities we call play (spontaneously undertaken for their own sake, and with no ostensible justification other than the immediate pleasure they bring) prove in the long run to have a vital significance for children's development towards maturity; and it is not therefore surprising that they should play an equally important role in the development of language. The greater part of the infant's babbling is indeed imitative play—it goes on regardless of whether other people are present or not, and is really a kind of 'playing at talking'. Nevertheless in the course of it one can hear the child gradually mastering the basic 'tunes' or intonation-patterns of the language, so that an English child's babbling will come in the end to sound distinctively English, even though it contains as yet no specifically English words or syllables. And for most children an immense amount of their early speech is bound up with their play-world of nursery rhymes, games with dolls and toys, picture-books, stories and so on.

In any case whether the small child's purposes in using language are practical, emotional or imaginative, we shall all agree that he cares intensely about them. To achieve rapport with his mother by producing the right sounds; to communicate his requirements or wishes; to talk to his teddy-bear exactly as his father talks to him—these are all things that he really *wants* to do. This strong motivation, and the persistence it gives rise to, are reinforced by the atmosphere of encouragement which surrounds his efforts. In the normal home there is no question of commenting on or correcting faults and imperfections. As a rule parents cheerfully go more than halfway to meet the child in his first attempts at communication; indeed one often finds that a fond mother will proudly claim to understand 'words' of which an outsider could make nothing.

This is a convenient point at which to return to the problems of the secondary school. Do we pay enough attention in our composition lessons to the child's need for encouragement? Do we realise, I wonder, how profoundly *dis*couraging he must often find our transparent lack of interest in what he has to tell us, and our consistent over-anxiety about errors, mistakes and imperfections in the way that he tells it? We cannot imagine a mother saying to her infant: 'You mustn't say "baba"; you must say "baby". Now say it correctly—*ten times!*'; nor is it any more conceivable that a parent would warn a toddler: 'If you try to talk a lot, you'll only make a lot of mistakes; you must just say one sentence, but *mind you say it correctly*.' Yet similar adjurations in regard to writing are by no means uncommon in the secondary school class-room. The contrast between the two milieux is certainly striking. It may have some bearing on the fact that so many children fail in learning to write whereas so few fail in learning to talk.

There are other ways in which our observation of children's early speech seems to me to have relevance for the later stage of learning to write. In the first place, writing (like speech) is not an isolable or suddenly-acquired 'new' ability; it represents rather the culmination of a number of other skills and experiences. Sometimes, even in the secondary school, we need to spend far more time than we do in developing such essential prior accomplishments as flexible and expressive speech, or wide experience of reading; only if there is a sure foundation here, in these aspects of linguistic growth, can we expect a boy or girl to make satisfactory progress in the more complex and exacting task of writing. Secondly, we ought to recognise that maturation plays a part in learning to write just as it does in learning to talk, and that here too we reap no benefit by trying to 'jump' necessary stages in natural development. There is one very broad application of this truth which is often ignored. Children need at first (in the junior school and in junior forms of the secondary school) to have plenty of experience of writing copiously, no matter how inaccurately. This is the right stage for extensive practice at 'babbling' and 'chattering' in ink. Only later (at thirteen or fourteen, say) can they profit from sustained conscious attention to the forms of written expression; and the reshaping, rewriting and refining which properly belongs to this later stage needs as its raw material a readiness of expression which is too often lacking in classes which have been restricted earlier on to writing 'only one paragraph' or 'not more than a page'. More specifically, the principle of readiness applies in a very obvious way over the whole field of 'correctness' or 'technical accuracy' in writing; and here too it is all too often signally neglected. At what stage does it begin to be useful to discuss with children the principles of paragraph construction? (Most series of course-books get in their little homily good and early and go on repeating it each year a little more impatiently, in the hope that at some point or other in the child's school career it may perhaps sink in.) Is there much point in teaching children of eleven or twelve to combine simple sentences together into more complex constructions, when a year or two later they will, in the majority of cases, start to use complex sentences in their writing anyway, whether they have been 'taught' them or not? Do we expect our pupils to master the intricacies of punctuation at one fell swoop, or as a progressive sequence? These instances could be multiplied almost indefinitely. It is my own belief that many of the common errors which persist so ineradicably in children's writing have become entrenched there because the rule or usage in question was introduced too early. When a pupil is not yet old enough to understand the principle involved or to see the point of it, instruction on such points leaves behind only a sense of failure and inadequacy. A mental or emotional blockage then arises which even the most skilled and sympathetic teaching will find very difficult to break down. A few years ago the examiners' report on the G.C.E. Ordinary Level English Language paper of one examining board referred to one candidate who was so paralysed by the fear of omitting some of the requisite punctuation marks that he played safe and inserted a full stop after every single word! I find it hard not to link this in my mind with another engaging anecdote, this time about a junior school. A teacher had been busy in previous weeks implanting in her class certain taboos (discredited by now, one would have hoped) about the use of 'And' and 'But'. 'What is it,' she asked, 'that we must not start a sentence with?' One small girl's hand shot up promptly. 'Please, miss,' she cried confidently, 'a full stop!'

There is still one final lesson to be learnt from our parallel with small children: the overwhelming importance of strong motivation. In writing as in speaking, what matters more than anything else is that one should have something to say that one really cares about saying. It is this powerful impetus from within that is essential in order to carry the prentice writer past the obstacles and difficulties of his task; yet all too often this is entirely missing from the attitude with which the secondary school child approaches his weekly composition homework. The first aim of the teacher must be to manœuvre the child into a position where he feels this impetus within himself; somehow he has to engender in his pupils an urgently felt impulse towards communication—towards that particular type of communication, moreover, which demands for its fulfilment the permanence of the written form of language. It is easy to say this. How is it to be done?

(ii)

Henry Sweet, the greatest of English linguists, once defined language as 'the expression of thought by means of speech sounds'. In its intellectual emphasis, as well as in its dualistic philosophical implications, this phrase shows that he was still, to some extent, the prisoner of those nineteenth-century habits of thought about language which he did so much to revolutionise. 'Expression of thought', or (Jespersen's way of putting it) 'the effort of one human being to make himself understood and of the other to understand'—this does certainly fit a good deal (though not all) of what is going on when we use the written form of our language. But only intermittently can it be applied to the living speech from which writing derives, in the last analysis, all its meaning. Consider the following examples:

'How do you do?'

'It's an ill wind that blows nobody any good.'

'Love, forty.'

'I do solemnly swear to tell the truth, the whole truth, and nothing but the truth, so help me God.'

'Sudso washes whiter than white.'

'God Save Our Gracious Queen.'

'Our Father which art in Heaven, Hallowed be Thy Name.'

For each of these utterances the reader will find it easy to think up a plausible context of human use — a situation in which someone speaks or hears them every day. They are not, however, used to express thought.

We can see today that the outlook of nineteenth-century linguistics was distorted by its historical preoccupations; the language of written documents is the only form in which the language of past ages can be studied, but it is also something of a special case. In the present century our perspectives have become wider, largely as a result of the work of cultural anthropologists who have felt the need to record and analyse the language of pre-literate communities in remote parts of the world. In these circumstances the basic, indeed the sole, raw material for linguistic study consists of 'people talking'. In observing and classifying such data one is forced to realise that language is a form of social activity which is very intimately bound up with social behaviour. People talk always in specific social situations, and their speech may serve a variety of functions, of which the communication of thought is only one. (To attain some practical operational objective; to communicate feelings; to establish social contact; to score while playing a game; to give solemn legal force to a statement or contract; to persuade; to unite in a ritual community of allegiance; to worship or to pray — this list offers no more than a sample.)

Moreover, once we have left behind the familiar *mores* of our own culture, it is brought home to us that more often than not people's 'talk' can only be understood *within the context of the situation in which it occurs*. Malinowski found this to be so true of the speech of Trobriand Islanders on their fishing expeditions that he was led to conclude that: 'Utterance and situation are bound up inextricably with one another, and the context of situation is indispensable for the understanding of the words.'[1] This generalisation seems to be true also of a surprising amount of the speech that goes on in more

---

[1] Malinowski (1923). See also Malinowski (1934).

complex and literate civilisations such as our own. To 'understand the words' we need to know who is present, who is speaking and who is spoken to, what actions accompany the words and what effect follows them. We can see this even at the most routine or formulaic level of language. When an Englishman, for instance, says 'Black or white?' the meaning of the question is clearly inseparable from the situation, a situation so typical that in this case we can infer from the words alone all its essential features—the conclusion of a meal, the minimum socio-economic status of the eaters, the presence of cups and saucers, the consequential pouring-out of a cup of coffee.[1]

The example may seem trivial; but the principle it illustrates is a fundamental one. The experience of language which children have stored within themselves is less abstract than we sometimes realise. Because it is predominantly spoken in form, it has its roots in social action and social relationships, and represents the accumulated residue from a kaleidoscopic sequence of concrete situations in each of which there was an impelling purpose to affect a known audience in some highly specific way. The notion of writing for an anonymous undefined public is still alien to the mind of the young secondary school pupil; for him the image of the 'common reader' needs to have a face painted on before he can visualise it. The concept of 'situation' (a concept which implies a known audience and a recognised purpose in relation to that audience) is, in fact, an indispensable aid when we are teaching children of this age. Rightly understood, it can do much to supply the compelling motive for writing which we know to be essential but which is often missing.

Of course it may be said that in the class-room situation the 'audience' is always and inescapably the teacher, and that this is just as should be. Certainly in the primary school the common and sufficient motive for the children's writing is their desire to share experience with a trusted parent-figure, and to earn sanction and approval from the quasi-omnipotent adult whose judgment is,

[1] Cf. Firth (1957): 'A context of situation for linguistic work brings into relation the following categories:
  A. The relevant features of participants: persons, personalities.
      (i) The verbal action of the participants.
      (ii) The non-verbal action of the participants.
  B. The relevant objects.
  C. The effect of the verbal action.'
In illustration Professor Firth offers one brief sentence representing 'a typical Cockney event', namely: 'Ahng gunna gi' wun fer Ber' (I'm going to get one for Bert). The reader may like to test for himself whether he can 'provide a typical context of situation in which it would be the verbal action of one of the participants'.

within the four walls of the class-room, the only one which really counts. In any case the intense rivalry for affection and recognition which seems to be invariable among young children prevents them from taking at this age a sustained interest in anyone's writing but their own, and only very slowly do they learn to tolerate realistic comparison between their own achievement in any field and that of other children. In the secondary school the same need for a 'teacher-centred' approach to the composition lesson may persist among slow-developing pupils, or in relation to the more personal kind of writing which involves intimate self-revelation. But in general the greater objectivity which the twelve-year-old class begins to be capable of indicates a readiness to develop a greater degree of self-reliance in the standards they apply to their own writing. In addition their growing sense of realism about their own childish limitations makes it increasingly difficult for the teacher to provide, in his own person, a wholly satisfactory audience. Are not his standards of judgment (they feel) somehow bafflingly different from their own? Can he be sincere when his kindly commendation is so widely distributed? Isn't his experience of life so much wider than theirs that anything they write can only be a matter of telling him the road he knows already? (Of course, the artificiality of the class-room 'situation' *can* be sensed by younger children as well. I cannot resist repeating Dr. P. B. Ballard's anecdote of an old-style 'conversation lesson' with an infant class. The subject was cats. 'How many feet has a cat?' asked the teacher, 'Where are his whiskers?', and so on. In the end the new little girl, unable to contain her surprise any longer, burst out with the question, 'Ain't you ever seen a cat, miss?'.)

For these reasons it is often preferable at this stage to make the other members of the class the 'audience' aimed at. Certainly when the children are writing 'stories' it is their own estimate of what is exciting or entertaining that we should appeal to. Narrative makes up much the greater part of their reading (it is also what they most often choose to write if given the chance), and they have begun to form intuitively their own criteria for such writing, cruder, maybe, than those of the teacher, certainly different. Similarly if we offer on occasion the incentive of writing for a class magazine or wall-display, we shall find that the target of publication before an actual and known audience lends so much zest to the task that much of it will cheerfully be done outside lesson-time.

At other times we may construct in the class-room a fictitious situation with an imagined audience, relying upon the traces of the play-instinct which persist in twelve- or thirteen-year-old children to invest this situation with imaginative validity; if it is presented in the right way, 'make-believe' can still at this age seem real enough to spur them on to animated speech or vital writing. This expedient works best if the situation is one which has a recognisable prototype in the world outside the school. 'Here,' we may say, placing a bottle of coloured pills on the teacher's desk, 'is some highly dangerous poison which has been missed from a doctor's car while it was parked in the High Street; describe what you see in front of you as accurately as you can, in the form of a police warning to be read out over the wireless.' Over and above the fact that children can mobilise greater energy and assurance when they see the point of what they are trying to do, an approach of this kind has a further important advantage. It delimits and defines the nature of the task to be accomplished, reducing the bewildering multiplicity of possibilities which otherwise confront the unpractised writer.

As an illustration of this, we might consider the complex choices we find ourselves obliged to make whenever we have to write about other people. 'Describe someone you know', or 'Write a character-sketch of one of your neighbours', says the course-book airily—but nine times out of ten the young writer doesn't know where to begin. Caldwell Cook used to persuade his third forms at the Perse School to write character-sketches (of a policeman, an auctioneer, a good salesman, a politician) after the manner of the seventeenth-century character-writers; and admittedly there are occasions when a model taken not too directly from literature may help to mark out possible paths—though there is always the danger that any but the exceptionally able pupil will be enslaved rather than liberated by good example. Suppose we try instead to think of some circumstances in the world of today when 'describing someone' might be called for. A friend or acquaintance has disappeared, and the police enlist your help in framing a 'Missing from her home' appeal; you have chanced to witness a bank raid, and are asked to help compose a 'Wanted for Murder' notice; you are travelling to London or Paris for the first time and have to write a letter which makes it certain that you will be recognised at a crowded railway station by a relative who has never seen you before. In each of these cases what is required is an exact record of physical appearances—height, build, colouring, facial characteristics, clothes. Quite different is the situation which arises when a headmaster has to write a letter of reference to a prospective employer; he will exclude outward appearance, and confine himself to the applicant's abilities and qualities of character. Slightly different again is the case of the school-girl writing to ask a pen-friend organisation to match her with a correspondent in another country; in this self-description it is tastes, interests, outlook on life that will be in question. At other times, a combination of physical traits with other characteristics may be relevant. A school-girl writes to a friend in hospital telling her what the new form-teacher is like; a casting agency files information about a young actor or actress; a marriage bureau compiles a dossier on a would-be husband. It is clear that in each instance which has been mentioned the writer must select and arrange his material differently; the specific situation imposes its own requirements and its own inherent discipline.

In the class-room, then, the virtue of the 'imagined situation' is that it can provide a strong incentive to many different purposes in writing, each of which holds within itself the criterion by which the pupil can estimate his own success. At the simplest level we can observe this effect when we reconstruct with a first-year class a 'Lost Property Office'. (In the interest of verisimilitude the exercise this time had better be spoken rather than written, since we do not write letters to a Lost Property Office except as a last resort.) The teacher gathers together a number of small possessions from different members of the form — pocket-knives, pens and pencils, watches, spectacles in their cases. Children take it in turn to impersonate the railway official to whom the owner of each article has to describe what he has lost with such precision that it can be identified at the first attempt. The task here is a straightforward one, and the yard-stick for achievement unmistakable. But the same principle can be set to work more subtly at other levels whenever a felt sense of 'purpose' prompts the young writer to ask himself, 'How far would this succeed in affecting my audience in the way I intended?' And the objectives he sets before himself at different times must, of course, be varied and wide-ranging — not only to describe accurately or evocatively, but also (for instance) to give instructions unambiguously, to evoke or communicate a feeling, to explain clearly the working of a process or of a machine, to persuade to a course of action, or to present a reasoned argument.

I have argued that we need to give thought to the young writer's relationship to his audience—to be clear in our own mind what the audience is to be for any given piece of writing, and to arrange, as unostentatiously as possible, that the nature of this audience shall be present in the pupil's consciousness as well, where it can work, unseen yet cogent, to shape and direct the movement of his thought and therefore of his pen. It is not less important, however, to think about the young writer's relationship to his subject-matter. What kind of topic may we expect to stimulate good writing at different ages and stages? Unfortunately this perennial question, 'What shall I set?' is less susceptible to generalisation than any other major issue which arises in English teaching. The teacher is obliged to grapple with it afresh for every single class he takes, aware that the subject which worked well with 2A may well fail to strike a spark in 2B and will very likely prove a complete flop with another 2A in twelve months' time. Consequently the discussion of principles which follows can be tentative only, and is to be taken as a provocation to thought rather than as an attempt to do any teacher's thinking for him.

In the first place we cannot expect anyone to write well unless he is keenly interested in what he is writing about. Platitudinous enough, this, in all conscience (did not Aristotle say, many centuries ago, that 'intellect works not alone but incited by the emotions and directed by the will'?); yet surely more difficult to apply in practice than we usually admit. For one thing, if we study our children's interests with patience and insight we shall find that where they penetrate deepest they are highly individual. How often can we hope to find a single subject which will strike oil with all the thirty-odd members of our class simultaneously? Of course there are occasions and events which bring the whole form together in a buzz of fascinated alertness (Guy Fawkes' night; the visiting circus; the opening of a new swimming-pool; local blizzards or floods or conflagrations; the latest exploit in space-travel) and we should not hesitate to exploit such topicalities when they offer themselves. More generally, perhaps, the most we can do in mitigation is to offer the class a choice of two or three subjects, or of two or three approaches to the same subject, and add the rider that anyone who wants to write about something different may do so.

A related difficulty is that the enthusiasm which is held in common often shrinks, on closer inspection, to a rootless triviality. It is worn in unthinking conformity as a badge of childish or teen-age gregariousness, and since it has called for no special skill, knowledge or involvement, the young enthusiast has nothing to say about it that is worth saying. Thus boys are often excited at the prospect of writing about football, yet prove, when it comes to the point, disconcertingly inarticulate about it. Similarly unrewarding are the ephemeral 'cults' which commercial interests sedulously foster in fifteen- or sixteen-year-olds. The fourth form may sit up with alacrity at mention of the current pop-singer or of the newest vogue in clothing and hair-style; but since the *raison d'être* of these phenomena is to band together teen-agers everywhere in a comforting uniformity, their contribution to discussion of them will seldom rise above cliché. No doubt the shoddiness or vacuity of our mass-culture's artefacts is, in such cases, a further reason for tongue-tiedness; anyone who has watched 'Juke-Box Jury' will have noticed how frequently the 'experts' themselves can find no more to say about the new hit record than: 'I like it—yes, I like it.' For all that, such enthusiasms loom large, at times, in the consciousness of our pupils, and the wise teacher will not avoid them entirely, but will see them rather as a challenge to his own ingenuity and resourcefulness. Thus we might try to catch in words what it feels like to play football on a wet, muddy day—or on a frost-bound pitch with a wintry sun setting behind one of the goal-posts. (How would tactics and techniques be adapted to the differing conditions?) Or we might imagine ourselves caught up in a football game somewhere near the Equator —played *without boots*. Again, the record from the 'Top Ten' could be played over in the class-room with the determination to get beyond the stock reactions of 'I couldn't hear the words' or 'I like the backing'. (What instruments can you hear as part of the backing? Which are playing or elaborating the tune and which are providing the beat? How important are the words in making a tune a hit, and what feelings must they appeal to in order to do so?) Or the class might pool their knowledge of the publicity techniques which launch a new pop-singer (one of Stan Freberg's satirical records could be a provocative starting-point here), and then go away to do further research before writing the success-story of a teen-age idol of their own creation. Whatever the device employed, the teacher's role is to lead his pupils beyond unthinking enthusiasm to a point where they are prepared to exercise observation and reasoning, and to question conventionally accepted attitudes.

For here is the second essential. The writer must not only be interested in his subject; he must also know, *really* know, something about it. Clearly, direct first-hand experience is the most valuable kind for our purpose; and there is fortunately a class of topic which offers children the opportunity to draw upon this to the full. I mean those which have been described by J. H. Walsh as 'topics which relate to the experiences of the children's own lives, and especially to those experiences which, because they are accompanied by emotion or strong feeling, are lived with an intensity which makes easier their subsequent recapture in words'. The teacher who is worth his salt will have no difficulty in identifying an almost endless variety of topics which fall (for his own class) into this category.[1] Often his point of departure will be the highly-charged relationships within the family group which loom so large in children's lives; and the feelings which give a clear edge to memory will be those of delight (family festivals, family outings) or relief (mother home from hospital) or resentment (restrictions, quarrels, injustices) or jealousy (a sibling's envied successes or coveted birthday presents). At other times the feelings tapped will be those of alarm or discomfort (visits to dentist or hospital, days spent in bed with measles or influenza) or of absorbing interest and enthusiasm (holiday pursuits, hobbies, camping, cycling, mountaineering, sailing). At other times again he will find his pupils re-creating an experience vividly because of its novelty (first day in a new house, new school or new foreign country, first sea voyage or aeroplane journey) or its unexpectedness (a road accident, the day our house was burgled). Subjects of this kind are particularly fruitful during the first two or three years of the secondary course. Naturally they demand for success a relationship of trust between pupil and teacher — a confidence that whatever is revealed about the writer or his family will be treated with respect and sympathy.

By comparison with the sincere and vivid writing which these 'real-life' experiences often elicit, the 'stories' which children of this age delight in turning out may well seem a regrettable second-best. Thrown back upon a second-hand vision of life filtered through the medium of film, television or children's book, they draw heavily upon stock conventions for character, incident and setting, and resort unwittingly to turns of phrase borrowed all too repetitively from third-rate models. Nevertheless the desire to write narrative of the kind they themselves enjoy reading is too intense to be repressed or

[1] Walsh (1965), pp. 31-32, gives a long list of examples.

ignored. At the very least we can use it to develop fluency and confidence; and if we are prepared to be patient with writing which has more appeal for the writer's classmates than for his teacher, there is much we can do to foster progress away from stereotypes towards individuality. Certainly we should not make the mistake of issuing prohibitive fiats ('No murders this week, no secret passages, no dormitory feasts, no buried treasure'). The aim should rather be to extend the areas which show genuine imaginative grasp, by indicating ways in which the story can become more exciting, believable, clearly visualised. If pirates are the craze of the moment, we may ask for more detail in the setting of the scene. ('What kind of ship? What rig, how navigated, how provisioned, what weapons, what quarters for captain and crew? What latitude and longitude, flora and fauna, for the inevitable desert island? What can we learn from the library about the careers of Morgan, Kydd and other historical pirates?') Or in the school or 'holiday adventure' story we may suggest the desirability of aiming at more lifelike dialogue or credible characterisation. Indeed, one of the great advantages of the narrative framework (particularly if we extend its length to stretch over several homeworks) is the varied opportunity it offers for introducing different kinds of writing – description of setting and of characters, conversation, climactic incident, messages, letters, explanations of how things are done, creation of atmosphere, and so on.

The same power to enforce a need for varied types of writing is what some teachers value particularly in the form magazine. Here responsibility for different features (news, book reviews, letters, stories, women's page, etc.) can be delegated gradually to individual pupils, each section perhaps being allotted to a group of four or five children who select and 'vet' for final publication the best among their own contributions. No less diverse are the opportunities thrown up by the composition project which extends over several weeks a topic such as 'Our Desert Island', 'Our Village' or 'Our Railway Station'. For the village project the children invent the village; draw a map of it; write the penny-plain account of it which appears in the country guide-book (and also perhaps the more coloured description which would be offered in a tourist agency's publicity, in a travel-book by a foreign author, or in a letter from a newly-arrived visitor); they write letters from one villager to another; act out conversations in the village shop or bus queue; tape-record telephone interchanges;

draw up notices for village events (the jumble sale, the annual fête, the elections to the parish council) and write reports of them for the local newspaper; they write letters of complaint about bus services or refuse collection; make up stories; and so on. For the written work each child may keep and illustrate his own folder; or alternatively a form compilation may be the repository which preserves the best efforts. The topic for such a project needs to be chosen with care to suit the abilities and background of a given class; city children confronted with the village assignment might rely too heavily at first upon cosy stereotypes from Ambridge—though they can often be weaned away from this by tactful discussion, and there is usually some first-hand experience within the class to be drawn upon. With an able class a more recondite and exotic theme can sometimes be attempted (an African, Eskimo or Red Indian village, for instance), provided some research is done beforehand in the school library.

It will be noticed that in such projects the work moves easily back and forth between writing and speech, and this is perhaps the point at which to emphasise that throughout the secondary school course oral and written composition should go on side by side, mutually complementing and supporting each other. As Dr. P. B. Ballard put it, 'oral' must not be seen as merely the handmaiden to 'written'. In the modern world young people need more than ever before a ready and flexible command of their spoken language; yet the conditions of urban life (the crowded tube-train, the noisy street, the living-room with the television set as its focus) have become increasingly inimical to the development of modes of speech which are subtly modulated or finely expressive. Even less do they favour the growth of that delight in the spoken word as an instrument of civilisation which (as we can sense from reading such a book as George Sturt's *A Farmer's Life*) must have been widely diffused in the more leisurely and stable rural community of the recent past. Secondary school pupils need continued practice in talking as well as in writing, and the occasions which we can provide, in English lessons, for such practice fall into three main categories.

In the first place, there will be much that is incidental and wholly informal. I am thinking here of the discussion which takes place in small groups in the course of preparing an improvised play, working together on a composition project, or pooling ideas about a poem or a 'home reader'. The talk here will be impromptu, and the role of the teacher inconspicuous, confined largely to helping the children to listen to each other, to speak quietly, one at a time, and to keep to the point.

Secondly, there is the slightly more extended and semi-formal class-room activity which corresponds roughly to those occasions in adult life when a consecutive ordered statement is called for (relating one's symptoms to the doctor, undergoing interview for a job, making a complaint to a store manager, giving evidence in the witness-box). Here we must give opportunity for preparation and preliminary thought, perhaps even for note-making. At times this work may take the form of the brief three-minute talk or lecturette (on 'My Hobby' or 'How to do it' or 'How it Works'); but less articulate children need the support of a make-believe situation which permits the interplay of dialogue or the prompting of the interviewer's questions. Models come to hand readily enough, either from adult life (the demonstrator explaining to the housewife how to use the new washing-machine or vacuum-cleaner or automatic cooker, the policeman telling a pedestrian the way to the railway station) or from television and radio programmes (the interviewing of a celebrity in 'In Town Today' or of the man-in-the-street in 'Tonight', the panel technique for the expression of opinion as in 'Any Questions'). For such lessons a tape-recorder is invaluable, and helpful suggestions for its use can be found in Methold (1959).

Finally there is the more formal type of oral composition which has the function of preparing the future citizen of a democracy to take part in the affairs of his trade union branch, political or religious organisation, or community centre. Apart from the occasional mock trial or mock election it is customary to rely here upon the importation into the class-room of the framework and ritual trappings of the debating society. It should be recognised, however, that debating is a difficult art (some might object that it is also a slightly crooked one); it calls for an ability to sustain a reasoned argument and to distinguish the logical relevance of objections which is seldom much in evidence before the age of fifteen or sixteen. With third or fourth forms it is preferable to start less ambitiously with say a 'For and Against' session in which a number of controversial issues are dealt with briefly by one speaker on each side. We do best to begin with relatively simple topics which bear closely on our pupils' lives. ('Should dogs be kept in large towns?' 'Is it better to spend one's money on several E.P. records or on one L.P.?' 'Are transistor wireless sets anti-social?' 'Should there be restrictions on part-time jobs for schoolboys?' 'Should bicycles be taxed?' 'Should the keeping of a cat require a licence?' 'Is it better to spend one's holiday in a holiday-camp or in youth hostels?') moving only gradually to more abstract but more important issues ('Should stag-hunting be prohibited?' 'Are there too many flag-days?' 'Should Britain give up the H-bomb?'). Written preparation is essential here, but speeches must never, of course, be *read*; and we shall have to show our pupils how to draw up the concise 'brief' in note-form which most speakers need as an aide-memoire.

Generally speaking, the progression to be aimed at in all our pupils' speaking and writing is one that leads gradually through the concrete topic, the narrative framework, the speech or writing that is closely bound up with a specific situation, towards discourse which is more generalised and more abstract in its terms of reference.

But the capacity to handle thought on an abstract level is one that develops more slowly than we sometimes realise; many secondary modern children have acquired it hardly at all by the age at which they are about to leave school. We must do for such young people as much as we can; and it may be worth concluding this section by describing a variant of the dramatic method which I have seen used to strikingly good effect with less able pupils during their final year in school. Suitable situations are acted out by different groups in the class-room: a teen-ager is involved in a family dispute about clothes, or choice of job, or staying out late at night; a girl is left at home to look after her small brother while the parents go out to the pictures; a housewife is over-persuaded by a hire-purchase salesman. In each case the dramatic realisation of the episode is taken seriously for its own sake; but it is followed also by a discussion of the issue which it has raised. ('On what grounds should one choose one's clothes or one's job?' 'What are the most sensible ways of looking after or disciplining young children?' 'How much of the weekly wage is it reasonable to commit to hire-purchase payments?'). With the immediacy of the personalised dramatic presentation still present to the inward eye, the class become able to formulate the problem more impersonally and to talk about their reactions to it more objectively. And if we find it hard to say whether lessons of this kind are 'teaching English' or 'educating for living', that surely is just as it should be.

(iii)

Self-expression has become one of the icons of our time, almost as revered by the Republic as the Community Chest, but it is ignored too easily that self-expression usually ends as therapy. What is detestable about a bad style is that the author is cleaning his own nervous system at the expense of mucking our own in the psychic sediments of his taste.

NORMAN MAILER, *Advertisements for Myself*

We have seen that the human need for language cannot be narrowed down to mere communication; and that even communication of an intellectual or utilitarian kind must draw its energy from deeper levels of personality—in Lawrence's words, from that 'intuitional consciousness . . . which alone relates us in direct awareness to physical things and substantial presences'. As this insight has become more widely diffused, teachers have increasingly broadened the scope of the writing they demand or expect from children. The stress now falls (very rightly) on 'spontaneity' and on a 'personal and involved handling of private material' in which children write out of themselves about things that really matter to them. In the course of such writing most children can show a creative potential which would surprise the English teacher of a former generation, and many of them also fall quite naturally into a poetic mode of expression when their mood and subject-matter calls for this. This unforced approach to the writing of poems is undoubtedly the right one. Children should always feel free to choose the form of expression which suits what they have to say, though the teacher may also on occasion devise ways of encouraging them to experiment with the heightened cadences and bolder imagery which belong more specifically to poetry.[1] It should be realised, too, that the less able children sometimes find free verse a medium which they can handle more easily than prose, since its short lines and relatively loose syntax liberate them from the sense that an extended and rationally coherent verbal structure is necessarily required of them.

Clearly then the spread of creative writing in schools is something to be welcomed wholeheartedly—the more so in that there are still far too many schools where it has penetrated hardly at all. At the

[1] At the earlier ages the choice of an emotionally-charged topic will sometimes be stimulus enough in itself; another fruitful jumping-off point can be the reading of short *vers-libre* poems (Arthur Waley's translations from the Chinese are particularly useful here). Explicit instruction in the techniques of verse-composition should be avoided as far as possible, since preoccupation with the difficulties of rhyme and metre can so easily become a distraction and a discouragement. There may be a place occasionally, however, for the very simple kind of exercise which consists of adding fresh couplets or verses to a ballad-type sequence (see Reeves, 1958, pp. 55–58, for examples), since this can embolden some children to try out possibilities which would not otherwise occur to them. For further suggestions and helpful discussion of a practical kind, see Druce (1965).

same time honesty compels me to record that 'creativity' has now developed something of a cult around it (psychologists are even busy constructing tests to measure it), and that some of the implications of this cult are a little disturbing. We can perhaps pass over briefly the more extreme manifestations of gush, of the kind that introduced the publication in the United States a few years ago of a new magazine of writings by children ('Here in this unique magazine the editors of *Swing* will bring you every season another green fresh draught from that mystic fount of excitement, that depthless well of longing.') Less easily shrugged off is the annual publication of prize-winning entries from the *Daily Mirror* Children's Literary Competition, with an introduction by Sir Herbert Read claiming that 'the successful entries show that in rare cases the child is capable of a quality of expression that is to be judged and accepted by the highest standards of literature'; or the readiness of publishers to offer to the public collections in which children's poems are presented, *tout court*, as 'poems in their own right'. The most extensive of these (*Poems by Children, 1950–1961*) has an introduction in which the editor Michael Baldwin actually writes of its contents: 'None of them may be a great poem – the word is irrelevant – but they are all of them good poems, and they have been a part of my growth these last months no less than the works of the mature poets I have been able to come to freshly during the same period . . .' The tone of this should perhaps prepare us for the shock when a few pages later we find Mr. Baldwin disparaging a great poet ('the adolescent flavour of Eliot's *Marina*') by exalting at his expense an accomplished piece of adolescent versifying which seems to have no point of comparison with *Marina* apart from the inclusion of a few boat-builder's terms.

A rather similar falsification of values can be detected at times in the more recent writings of David Holbrook. (In *English from Maturity* the chapter on 'Making Things Up' seems, fortunately, to have been free from this defect.) Thus in a broadcast talk reprinted in *The Listener* (October 25, 1962) he quotes the following poem by a girl who came to the secondary school 'with the remark on her Primary School Record Card, "Has no originality or imagination" – I.Q. 76.'

A poem

A little yellow bird sat on my window sill
He hop and poped about

He wisheld he cherped.
I trid to chach my little yellow brid
but he flew in to the golden yellow sun,
O how I wish that was my yellow brid.

Yes, we shall agree, an admirable achievement for this child, and one that should warn us never to write off any pupil's potential merely because of his measured intelligence. But does it quite justify Mr. Holbrook's accompanying claim that: 'Those we call "low-stream" pupils are often capable of fluency and creative phantasy of a fine quality – sincere, moving, beautiful'? (One wonders, indeed, how far the exaggerated valuation may have been influenced by the mis-spelling of 'bird' and an unconscious association of 'brid' with the atmosphere of medieval folksong and carol.) Again, in an article in *The Guardian* (September 16, 1963) Mr. Holbrook relates how 'a withdrawn, difficult, unco-operative child suddenly produces some-thing terrifyingly penetratingly Blakean about human nature' when asked by a student teacher to 'free associate' about Fire. This 'terrifyingly penetratingly Blakean' piece of writing is the following:

Fire is not understanding; he is reckless and ruthless. He bites when you touch him, he is angry. Why? Why does he roar when devouring one thing and purr when devouring another? He is a giver of heat but he doesn't want you to take it. The naked tongues of flame reach high into the sky as if searching for food.

He hates the wind and the rain, the wind makes him curl up and hide and the rain makes him spit in a fury of rain and smoke.

What makes him so reckless? Why does he find pleasure in destroying things? Why does he gnash his teeth in anger at metallic objects? He is so powerful, he stops at nothing.

(A boy aged thirteen)

In this case, too, the educative activity is certainly commendable; does this excuse the rhetorical exaggeration which mars Mr. Hol-brook's description of the educational product?

As it happens, Mr. Holbrook's comments on this piece of prose are worth quoting at some length, because they reveal the nature of the muddle we seem to be getting ourselves into. He continues:

The piece is remarkable enough for a previously unco-operative pupil. It is also very beautiful as a piece of prose. Its fluency will change his whole literacy for the better, and now makes it possible for him to begin to draw on literature if it is presented to him in a relevant way. But some-thing deeper is here, too. The boy was unco-operative because he was afraid of his own inward aggressiveness, the inward destructiveness in his psyche. To write about these, as aspects of human nature, as Blake does in his 'Tyger', will help the child to come to terms with them, to include his assertiveness in his personality, and thus become more efficient in his living, and, possibly, happier.

Surely it is clear that this confuses two distinct (though possibly related) issues. On the one hand, there is the quality of the child's writing as such ('very beautiful as a piece of prose'); on the other, its presumed effect on the development of the writer's personality. Why do we (apparently) find it so difficult to believe in the importance of the latter without losing our sense of proportion over the former?

Flora J. Arnstein was, I believe, the first writer to document at all fully the creative powers which children can develop in their writing, and also one of the earliest to elaborate the ways in which children, through gaining access to their own creativity, may be helped to grow as people. In *Adventure into Poetry* (1946) she summed up the benefits of her poetry classes as follows: 'the release that comes through writing, through sharing ideas and feelings; the integration that accompanies the deliberating upon, and evaluating of our experience in the world around us; the building up of self-confidence by acceptance; and, finally, the social good that comes of feeling ourselves one with others and of the recognition that other people's ideas as well as our own are worthy of thoughtful consideration.' Earlier in the same chapter she drew attention to the fact that for children it is 'the doing, the creating' that is important rather than 'the actual product, the poem'; and she had some wise things to say about the unfavourable effects which may follow if we shift the emphasis from creation to product. It is precisely this shift in emphasis that gives ground for anxiety at the present time. It is leading to a blurring of necessary distinctions—an unnoticed assumption that if the act of writing has brought the child 'release' and 'integration', then what he has written is, by virtue of that very fact, endued with literary merit.[1] The mischief is that this exaltation of writing which is 'therapeutic' for its author can be accomplished only by 'playing down' in importance those qualities which distinguish the permanent from the ephemeral in literature.

Obviously a critical heresy of this kind could take root and flourish

[1] Cf. James Britton in *Young Writers, Young Readers*, p. 75: 'When language assists in such exploration (i.e. exploration of "dark and difficult corners of experience"), what the children write will often be poetry. It will be poetry by virtue of its power to alter, in a certain way, the children's "accumulated feelings about themselves" . . .'

G

only within a specifically favourable 'climate of opinion'; and it may be worth while to stand back for a moment from the teaching situation in order to place this malaise within a broader historical perspective. We may take as our point of reference the observation by M. H. Abrams in *The Mirror and the Lamp* that the distinctive feature of Romantic and early nineteenth-century critical theories is that they all explain the nature and criteria of poetry in terms of the writer himself. Professor Abrams argues convincingly that there are four elements in the total situation which a critical theory must necessarily take account of: the work of art, the universe from which it draws its subject-matter, the artist, and the audience. Any critical theory tends to emphasise *one* of these four. Rarest (at any rate in the field of literary criticism) are the 'objective' or 'aesthetic' theories which see the work of art as 'a self-sufficient entity constituted by its parts in their internal relations', and therefore to be judged 'by criteria intrinsic to its own mode of being'. More central in critical history from Plato onwards are the various forms of mimetic theory which see the work of art as primarily an imitation of aspects of the universe (in eighteenth-century terminology, 'Nature'). For such theories the characteristic metaphor (the one which came naturally to Dr. Johnson) is that of 'the mirror'. Of this Professor Abrams observes that:

> For better or worse, the analogy helped focus interest on the subject matter of a work and its models in nature, to the comparative neglect of the shaping influence of artistic conventions, the inherent requirements of the single work of art, and the individuality of the author . . . and it fostered a preoccupation with the 'truth' of art, or its correspondence, in some fashion, to the matters it is held to reflect.

Most typically, however, the English critical tradition has combined the mimetic with the pragmatic, so that the doctrine of imitation has gone hand in hand with an emphasis upon the effect of the work of art upon its audience. This (sometimes rather arbitrary) conjunction can be illustrated on the one hand by Sidney's 'poesy is an arte of imitation . . . with this end, to teach and delight', on the other by Dr. Johnson's 'Nothing can please many or please long but just representations of general nature'. Much eighteenth-century critical theorising, in fact, consisted of attempts to redefine 'nature' in such a way that its 'representation' could be justified in terms of the didactic work-audience relationship which had now become (whether overtly or not) the main focus of critical attention; Dr. Johnson, for instance, held it necessary 'to distinguish those parts of nature which are most proper for imitation'.

By contrast, the revolutionary feature of Romantic critical theory was the overwhelming stress it laid on the writer's own experience. No longer did critics ask about a work of art: 'Is it true to nature?' Instead they demanded: 'Is it sincere? Is it genuine? Does it match the intention, the feeling, and the actual state of mind of the poet when writing?' Wordsworth, we recall, asserted with confidence that 'Poetry is the spontaneous overflow of powerful feelings'. It is true that, having his roots firmly in the eighteenth century,

> Wordsworth himself anchored his theory to the external world by maintaining that 'I have at all times endeavoured to look steadily at my subject', and declared that the emotion was recollected in tranquillity and that the spontaneity of its overflow was merely the reward of a prior process of deliberate thought. He reasoned also that since this thought has found and rendered instinctive the connection of the poet's feelings to matters really important to men, the final overflow cannot but accomplish a 'worthy purpose' with respect to the poet's audience [Abrams (1953), pp. 47–48].

But as the Romantic movement gained impetus, such checks and balances were rapidly discarded; within a few decades such critics as Keble, Carlyle, and John Stuart Mill had eliminated 'for all practical purposes . . . the conditions of the given world, the requirements of the audience, and the control by conscious purpose and art as important determinants of a poem' (op. cit., p. 48).

It seems to me that the distortions I have noted in current evaluations of children's writing belong with the tag-end of this same critical tradition; they are unwitting offshoots of those expressive theories which take as the exclusive criterion of a poem its 'sincerity',[1] its faithfulness to the poet's 'inner vision', or its relationship to the writer's personality. Thus it is that an anthology of children's writing can proclaim an ambition to 'have chosen writings which were in some way satisfying not to parents or examiners or even, in the first place, teachers, but to the writers themselves.' (*And When You Are Young*, 1960, collected by the London Association for the Teaching of English, and published by the Joint Council for Education through Art.) Thus it is that teachers are led to seek out, as trophies signalling

---

[1] According to Robert Graves the 'touchstone' for true poetry.

a very special pedagogic achievement, those pieces which have been for the child-writer therapeutic or have served for him, in Marjorie Hourd's words, as 'a way towards unconscious integration'. (Would not a teacher, by the way, need to have a remarkably intimate knowledge of the pupil before he could feel at all confident that such was in fact the case?)

A further, and even more extreme, example of this disabling onesidedness is the now fashionable movement known as 'Free Writing'. Under this régime the children are presented with some specific and immediate stimulus—a suggestive verbal fragment, either of prose or of poetry; a picture; a snatch of music; an object of some kind which has been taken into the class-room (a fossil, a vase, a potato). They are then asked to set down on paper for a quarter of an hour or so whatever comes into their minds. Although some of the results may later be read aloud, it is made clear that what they write does not need to be in any sense a communication; it will not be 'marked' or 'corrected', and logical sequence can be abandoned entirely if the writer feels so impelled.

Now experience shows that this procedure can, in the short run, have an unmistakable therapeutic effect upon some classes. It seems that it frees the child from the oppressive sense that resented adult expectations circumscribe and diminish his power to write. After a series of such lessons from one of my own students, a class of thirteen-year-old girls were unanimous that they enjoyed 'free writing' (previously all composition lessons had been anathema to them); and one of their number advanced as her reason: 'You can write whatever you think and what you write is all your own.' This is surely the 'mental set' we want our pupils to have towards writing; and a teacher need feel no scruples about using 'free writing' as a short-term expedient if he finds himself confronted by a class who groan in deep-felt despair the moment writing is suggested. But once this 'loosening-up' has been accomplished, what then? To be satisfied with private and uncontrolled 'free association' is to exclude all too resolutely the depersonalising and socialising function which is inherent in the very nature of language itself. As well as being 'all our own', our writing has to serve as a bridge, linking us with other people: to unburden ourselves of unwanted images or to discharge unwanted tensions is not enough. As teachers we shall have to broaden our criteria to include the other three elements which belong to the total critical situation. If they are to develop in and through their writing, our children will need to meet the challenge of an audience; they must be led to feel the urge to match their descriptions, and narratives, and expositions, with that objective reality which the eighteenth century called 'Nature'; they should even experience at times the exacting discipline of the medium in which they are working—that 'intolerable wrestle/With words and meanings' through which alone we can achieve phrases and sentences which are right, 'where every word is at home/Taking its place to support the others'. It is right that we should be aware of the extent to which children's writing may be fertilised, nourished and shaped by impulses arising from the deeper levels of the mind;[1] but we cannot afford to indulge in the now-fashionable narrowing of vision which would convert us from teachers into amateur psycho-therapists. Only if our standards of evaluation are broadly based and firmly held, can we give our child-writers the guidance they will need in their growth towards genuine maturity.

(iv)

It is common practice to give some lesson-time to 'oral preparation' before the class start the actual writing of their compositions; indeed many teachers think such a warming-up period indispensable. The great virtue of this informal preliminary discussion is that it can help each child to the conviction that he has within himself an ample stock of ideas and experiences bearing upon the topic in hand. It may also enable him to adumbrate, somewhere in the background of his consciousness, the sequence of development which will emerge from his material when he begins to write; but we should not make the mistake of setting up as our objective an agreed 'scheme' for the composition, with paragraph-headings neatly numbered and docketed. The writer's grasp of the shape a subject can have for him is very much a personal matter, and children (like adults) usually arrive at it intuitively rather than cerebrally. To record the insight when it arrives may be found helpful by some, but this formal plan-of-campaign should never be demanded as a compulsory

---

[1] Cf. one contemporary novelist's way of putting it: 'Thought begins somewhere deep in the unconscious. . . . Out of each human being's vast and mighty unconscious, perhaps from the depths of our life itself, up over all the forbidding powerful and subterranean mental mountain ranges which forbid expression, rises from the mysterious source of our knowledge, the small self-fertilisation of thought, conscious thought. But for a thought to live (and so give us dignity) before it disappears, unexpressed and perhaps never to be thought again, it must be told to someone else—to one's mate, to a good friend, or occasionally to a stranger.' Norman Mailer, *Advertisements for Myself*, p. 216.

requirement since there are many whom it will only hamper and constrain. A further benefit which may result from oral preparation is that as the class talk around the subject, the words, phrases, and technical terms appropriate to it are brought forward into consciousness, and made ready, as it were, for subsequent use. Sometimes words known only to a few are contributed to the common pool and thereby made available to others who did not previously know them; more frequently, what happens is that the to-and-fro of discussion enables children to bring forward items from their passive 'recognition' vocabulary and place them in a context of mental associations which fits them for active use. In general it is better to allow this enrichment of verbal resource to develop of its own accord, as a by-product of the main aim of the discussion; the teacher may at times choose to write some of the more unusual words on the blackboard (correctly spelt), but if he does this there is a danger that the same words will shine forth, like newly acquired gems, from composition after composition.

The advantages to be derived from oral preparation are, then, real enough; at the same time, I would hesitate to recommend it as an invariable prerequisite. Much depends on the topic, the ability and temperament of the class, and the stage of development they have reached. Most teachers will have had the experience at some time or other of guiltily tossing a subject to their class in the last few minutes of a lesson, only to find later that the resulting batch of compositions turns out, through some fortunate combination of circumstances, to be way above their usual standard. And in any event we should always be on our guard against prolonging the preliminary discussion beyond the stage at which it has served its real purpose. Once the majority of the class feel ready to write, we should stand out of their way and let them get on with it. We need to be able to recognise the point at which the ferment of ideas in the class-room has come to the boil, and stop then; if we keep on with the discussion after this, the ideas will only boil away.

Let us move now to the stage when the preliminaries are over, and the compositions have been written and collected in. Whatever the term may mean in relation to other subjects, the 'marking' which now waits to be done is no simple matter. Any English teacher worth his salt knows how fallible and inconsistent his judgment will often be, and how biased and subjective it can easily become. Yet he will know also that, if he is to give his children the help they need, he cannot confine himself to assigning a numerical mark to each composition nor yet be satisfied with scoring through in red pencil all the mistakes in spelling and syntax. Despite the difficulty of the task, he must attempt first of all to evaluate each child's effort sympathetically, sensitively and objectively, identifying the qualities (good and bad) which are actually there, and keeping his eye firmly upon the important issues rather than upon the trivia. Any such act of 'practical criticism' is onerous enough in itself, as was demonstrated independently a good many years ago by I. A. Richards in England and E. G. Biaggini in Australia.[1] For the English teacher it is complicated still further by the need to bring his findings into relationship with all that he knows about the writer's past and present development. What matters ultimately is not the worth of a child's composition *per se* but its value as achievement — its import, that is, for the writer himself at his own particular stage of growth.

This reference to development implies certain expectations of progress in children's writing that deserve further analysis. We do certainly expect our pupils to improve, throughout their years in the secondary school, in their command over the ancillary skills of written expression; we shall be right to feel dissatisfied if spelling, punctuation and syntax are no more accurate at the age of fifteen than at the age of eleven. But surely we look also for more than this — for an advance in the quality of experience communicated and in the writer's ability to grasp and order his thoughts and feelings, for progress, in fact, in writing *as* writing? From this wider point of view the benefits conferred by our lessons in composition may well appear somewhat tenuous. Certainly there is often a marked contrast between the freshness and spontaneity which characterise the writing of the ten- or eleven-year-old and the constricted sentiments or conventional narrative which are so typical of the thirteen-year-old. The progress we can regularly observe in our children's writing is clearly not a straightforward movement from simple to more complex, crude to more refined.

Our perspectives may become clearer if we face the fact that the writing of junior school children is peculiarly attractive to most adults for two reasons. First there is the newness, to children of this age, of their own perceptions. They are still seeing many aspects of the world around them for the first time, undulled by habit. Being unconstrained by any compulsion to fit their observations into the

<hr />

[1] Richards (1929) and Biaggini (1933).

framework of larger generalised categories they look at the phenomenon as a thing-in-itself, with a curiosity and delight which forges
its own engaging vivacity of linguistic form. We can often note
similar verbal felicities in the speech of the under-fives, particularly
in their novel coinage of metaphor. Who could fail to be touched and
heartened, for instance, by the three-year-old who looks out of the
window one misty summer morning, the first he has ever really
noticed, and cries: 'Why, it's all fizzy'? Secondly the adult may, for
his own reasons, find an especial charm in the artless and unself-
conscious quality which attaches to the young child's expression of
his own feelings. Enmeshed as we are in our own social obligations,
it is hardly surprising if we take a keen delight in the naivety of those
who feel as yet no need to worry about what other people are going
to think.

It is obvious that these qualities are bound to fade away with the
approach towards maturity, though they may still occur sporadically
in the writing of early adolescence. In my own experience the really
good writing which we may get from the age of twelve or thirteen
onwards (writing, that is, to which the teacher can respond with
genuine and unforced enthusiasm) tends to fall into three categories.
In the first place there is the work of the small minority of exceptionally gifted pupils. Since these children's innate endowments may
well be equal or superior to those of the teacher, he needs to recognise the stringent demand which their presence in his class-room will
make upon his mental flexibility; he can perhaps console himself
with the thought that they will probably find their own way forward
whatever he does or does not do for them. Secondly there is the
piece of writing which has been, for the child himself, therapeutic.
An opportunity has been provided for the writer to work over, in
words, some acutely felt experience from his own past life, usually
one which was so disturbing at the time that it was hard to assimilate.
Early hospitalisation provides a theme which recurs frequently in
compositions of this type; but we may also encounter a variety of
other family crises, or childish catastrophes. (One unforgettable
instance from some years ago was an account of a fly-bomb raid on
London in which the writer was having tea at a neighbour's house
a few doors down the street and so escaped the direct hit which
killed her mother and sister.) As we can often sense in the texture of
the writing, the child finds unmistakable cathartic value in going
back over the emotions which once agitated him, and in bringing

order into them through the controlling medium of the written word; the benefit is analogous, in its own lesser degree, to that which comes from 'working through' past experience in the course of psycho-analytic treatment.[1] For the most part, of course, such writing is far too personal and intimate for public display; and the role of the teacher is simply to provide the support of his own acceptance and commendation. The example which follows (from a girl in a Secondary Modern School, Fourth Year) falls, I think, just within the fringe of this category, dealing as it does with an episode which, at the time when it was experienced, was moderately rather than acutely disturbing:

A.

Fainting

That cut on my hand. How did it get there? It's very deep and there's sand in it. They say I must wash it but not with sea water. It makes me feel sick. They're deciding what to do.

'Is there a doctor near?'

'No! But there is a first-aid hut farther along the beach.'

Oh why can't they decide quickly. I want to sit down. My legs are weak and I can't stand up much longer. My arms are heavy and my head is spinning. That's funny. The sand is going round and round and up and down. It doesn't usually do that. At least I don't think so. What does it matter? I can't hear what they are saying. Everything seems so distant. Where has everyone gone? It's all so peaceful. It's a lovely feeling; as though I am on a switch back at the fairground. Round and round and up and down. I think I've got a pair of shoes in my hand. Heavens! They do feel heavy. I'd better put them down on the sand. Why should I bother? I'll drop them!

Everything is black but I can hear voices.

'She fainted'

'What's happened?'

'Quick! Some water'

'It's her hand!'

---

[1] 'Freud has postulated the process of *working through* as an essential part of psycho-analytic procedure. To put it in a nutshell, this means enabling the patient to experience his emotions, anxieties, and past situations over and over again both in relation to the analyst and to different people and situations in the patient's present and past life. There is, however, a working through occurring to some extent in normal individual development. Adaptation to external reality increases and with it the infant achieves a less phantastic picture of the world around him. . . . In this way he gradually works through his early fears and comes to terms with his conflicting impulses and emotions.' [Klein (1960), pp. 9–10].

My eyes are opening. I feel very refreshed. As though after a long
  sleep.
It's all so bright.
It's all so peaceful.

This has a good deal of the vividness and clarity of focus which we
find when children are 'writing out of themselves' a traumatic
experience; although in this case the experience as presented has no
raw edges to it, but is controlled and distanced in a way which
suggests that by now the writer has succeeded in coming to terms
with it.

In the third of my categories come those compositions in which
the writer's intense absorption in his subject-matter has lifted him
far above his customary level. The first example is one quoted by
James Britton in *Young Writers, Young Readers* (p. 54):

B.

There is something in woodwork that just enlightens me, it is nothing
very special, it just is something . . .
In woodwork there are many things that I delight in, but seeing an
article slowly take shape from a plank or pieces of wood is, I think, a most
joy giving experience. Another thing which always is most important in
preparing wood for use is planing, to me it is a lovely sight to see, possibly
a dirty piece of wood going under the plane, engaging the sharp cutting
blade from which curls up a thin sheet of wood so neatly rolled up, then
from underneath the back of the plane coming a smooth flat river of clean
wood. Here I have described it slowly but in reality the whole movement
is fast and the noise it makes is not a note it is a beautiful clean cutting
sound peculiar only to that one tool.

(Sixteen-year-old boy)

I have encountered writing with this intentness of involvement on
a wide variety of active hobbies or pursuits, such as fishing, bird-
watching or sailing; and I have noticed that the writer's feeling for
his chosen interest often shows itself not only in an unwonted
perspicuity and vitality of expression, but also in an unaccustomedly
sure handling of the mechanics of writing. On the other hand it must
be admitted that in my second example (by a thirteen-year-old boy
in a low stream in a secondary modern school) any improvement in
techniques is not very conspicuous, though the writer's absorption
in his subject is conveyed unmistakably:

186

TALKING AND WRITING

C.

Going Fishing

In Summer I usualy go fishing with my friend Melvyn. I get out of bed at $\frac{1}{2}$ past 5 and have my breackfast then I get all my cit ready. I have got three fishing rods one 13' another 11' and the other 7' I have a new fishing basket which I got for christmas it was a tray in it to seperate the food from my tatle. About 7 month ago my grandad bought me a landing net and keep net.

I put on a pair of old jeans and my leather jaket and set off to the station. Me and my friend get a 3/– ticket to Crowl or Kidby we usualy play cards on the train or chess when the train stops at Doncaster we get off and have a cup of coffee and some chocolate out of the machine. and get back on the train. When we are in Kidby we make for the drains their is a lot of other people fishing so I find a spot away from everyone else and tattle up I don't like tattling up when every one else is fishing because if I make a nois it will disturbe the fish and spoil it for other people I cast out until I have got my float in the right place and then put my rod on the idal-back I have to wait a long time before I get a bite at last I get a fish It is not a very big one but it puts up a fight I get my landing net out and when the fish is close enough to the bank I get it in my net and land it. If the fish is seven inch or over I take it home and eat it but if it is smaller than seven inch I throw it back into the water.

It is, I believe, from writing of these three types that the teacher will derive most of his own personal satisfaction and encouragement; and within certain limits he may hope to extend the provenance of such writing by wise choice and introduction of topics, by careful observation of his children's deeper interests, and by creating in his class-room an atmosphere of the kind known as 'permissive'. But it must be admitted that much of the writing turned in by most secondary school children will come nowhere near to this level; relatively speaking, it is bound to be undistinguished and unmemorable. Here the teacher will have to discipline himself to search patiently for the qualities which deserve commendation, either because they are good in their own way, or because they represent a step forward in achievement, or because they indicate a potentiality for future development. In the examples that follow I have tried to represent adequately these typical run-of-the-mill compositions (the kind which are never likely to figure in any anthology of children's writing) since it is in this area that the teacher's most intractable problems are usually to be found.

187

Here then are two contrasting examples, from a first-year class in a grammar school, of what our starting-point may be:

D.

A Windy Day

A watery, pale sun, looked down coldly on a late Autumn Morning. The North wind was having a fine game with our hair; as we swept up the brilliant carpet of leaves away from the door. Now and again, the sun would dissapear, behind a playful cloud, and the wind would blow more harshly than before. As the sun dissapeared once more, the leaves danced and whirled about our feet, the grey clouds formed overhead, and the wind tore even more leaves off the nearly bare trees. We fastened our coat collars around our necks, and tied our scarves more tightly. Our leaf pile was scattered far and wide. We gave up all hope of making the windswept garden look tidy, and went blue with cold inside to get ourselves warm. The large willow tree looked as though it was going to snap, it was so low. The crysanthemums were blown this way and that, their petals ripped ruthlessly off the tattered stalks. We watched, silently, despaired to see the remains of our leaf pile. We recieved thankfully cups of steaming cocoa, feeling glad we were not at sea!

This is for the most part 'correct' and 'acceptable' insofar as techniques are concerned; but it lacks individuality, and the writer's involvement in her subject-matter is surely no more than perfunctory. We cannot doubt that this girl has ability and even perhaps a certain verbal flair (witness such a sentence as 'The crysanthemums were blown this way and that, their petals ripped ruthlessly off the tattered stalks.'); but she has been led to believe, presumably in her primary school, that a certain kind of writing is 'officially' expected, and so she dutifully shuffles her cards around to produce a winning hand. We feel that such phrases as 'having a fine game with our hair', 'brilliant carpet of leaves' or 'playful cloud' reflect this conventional conception of 'good writing' rather than any direct apprehension of experience.

The next piece, from another member of the same first-year class, is far less accomplished:

E.

A Windy Day

I clipped the dogs lead to his collar, ready for his walk. Then stepped out, what a wind! Clash! went the dustbin lid, bang! went the door behind me.

In spite of the weather I decieded to carry on with my intentions, of taking the dog for a walk. My berry slipped off of my head, and was blown a hundred yards ahead, and finally landed in a hedge, I ran after it letting the dogs led slip out of my hands, A disastrous movment, for as soon as I let go he saw a cat, and being a dog, chased it.

I ran down to the hedge, recovered my hat, and with my hair about my face, and my skirt flying in the wind, I went to get the dog. I finally found him barking by a tree, in which sat a ginger cat. I tugged at his lead, and pulled him away.

The wind howled in the trees blowing them this way and that, leaves of golden, brown and red, danced pilouettes along the road, twisting and turning in the wind. Then came bits of newspaper, sweet rappers and bags dancing hand in hand to the whistling music.

The dog gave a tug at the lead and turned towards home. Soon the dustbin lid welcomed us at the door, by landing at our feet with a clatter.

Despite the obvious defects, we can recognise, in the penultimate paragraph particularly, a genuine attempt to render the writer's own observations—an attempt which is apparent not only in the ambition of 'pilouettes' but also in the apt yet unself-conscious 'twisting and turning' or 'bits of newspaper, sweet rappers and bags'. Writing of this kind can be the starting-point for immediate development, whereas the writer of D will need loosening up and redirecting before a fruitful advance can be made.

Next come two examples of the way in which first-hand observation can act as a leaven in the writing of children of no more than average ability. F is from a second year pupil in a secondary modern school, while G comes from the third year of the same school:

F.

The Snake

I was standing in the 'Reptile House' in London Zoo watching a snake as he coiled round a branch in his glass cage.

The light from the back of the cage was shining on the snake's skin making it glisten; instead of the browny grey and dirty white of his skin, he became suddenly alight. He slithered slowly off the branch with a graceful movement and came to the window of his cage with his forked tongue projecting from his mouth. His head began to sway gently as he stared at me with his evil eyes, yet he looked sorrowful somehow, as if he longed for the blazing sun and the dark jungles of Africa.

While I watched him in the lonelinness of his cage, someone hit my hand

and as it hit the glass of the cage, the snake suddenly came to life and darted as quick as lightning behind a stone in his cage.

G.

Dawn Light

I have walked down this street every day this summer and for many others as well; but to-day as I turn into the street everything looks different. It is still quite early in the morning but there is a greyish light slipping between the houses and creeping over the gardens. Usually the downward sloping gardens make the houses look light and airy but now they are all dark and quiet with curtains tightly closed to shut out the days first beautiful light. The street lamps on; and with a lamp behind it and dawn light swimming round it, the plain tree looks quite lovely as if there is the finest layer of frost on its boughs.

I walked into my house and upstairs to my room to take one more look at the beautiful scene but in the short time I had been indoors, the street light had been put out and the sun was rising up; it is going to be another lovely day, The street looks normal, the houses solid and the plants and trees, brightly colored, waving in the breeze, a perfect bright summery day, lovely, but nothing like that beautiful pale light of an hour ago.

In both these cases, we may note, it is the feeling sensibility which guides the perceptions of the writer: in G the feelings being those awoken by seeing a familiar scene in an unaccustomed light, while in F they may well draw some of their energy from unconscious associations with the snake as a sexual symbol.

By contrast the next piece reveals its second-hand origins unmistakably. It is an extract from a long story *Journey to the Moon* written at the end of the writer's second year in a grammar school:

H.

Chapter 7. *They go exploring*

. . . In the morning they awoke and had their breakfast. When they had had it. They prepared for going outside. 'Get your space suits on men, have you got your camera, Jack?' 'Yes, Prof.' said Harry. 'Right open the airlock Jack.' There was a hum and the airlock door opened. 'Do you mind if you stay behind Harry?' asked Prof. 'All right I will stay but you'd better hurry up because I want to go outside too.' So he shut the airlock door when they had gone through. Then he opened the main door. 'Now Peter. You will be the first man to step on to the moon.' Peter hesitated and then he stepped down from the ship and gazed around. He saw a grey world of craters. By this time the others had joined him. 'Gosh,' he said 'To think we are really on the moon.' 'Yes! Good heavens! What's that?' Prof. gazed into space. 'Its another spaceship and its only a thousand miles away.' They all gazed at it. 'Well what shall we do?' said Tom. 'Go back to our ship.' said Prof. 'It may be someone connected with Scarface.' They all ran back to the ship and got inside. They told Harry what they had seen. 'I'll have a look through the telescope,' said Harry. 'What can you see?' said Jack. 'Nothing at all, I don't believe you saw anything,' 'But I tell you I did,' said Peter. 'Well if there's nothing out there now you could not have seen anything,' said Harry. 'But I tell you I saw it. We all saw it except you,' said Peter 'All right, all right you two, break it up,' shouted Jack. 'We don't want to talk about it now.' 'Let's turn in,' said Prof. They went to their bunks and climed in and they all fell asleep.

Chapter 8. *An Exciting Find*

In the morning they woke up and they decided to leave Tom behind. The put their space suits and went out. Then they walked over to a large crater, then Harry said, 'Shall we go exploring in the crater,' he made for the crater, 'I'm going way,' and he started running towards the crater. 'Come back' shouted Prof. But Harry went on running, and Prof saw that it was no use calling him back so he shouted 'Don't run,' Harry heard him and slowed down. He reached the crater, and went inside and the others followed him. The crater was large inside and made of the same grey rock as the other craters. 'Look,' said Prof. 'What's that stuff there, it looks like gold dust.' 'Yes, it does. We'd better take a sample. Have you got a test tube Prof?' said Jac. 'Yes,' said Prof. 'here you are,' and he gave him the test tube. Jack got a sample and they went back to the ship.

This was written at the height of a space-travel vogue, and the writer has clearly enjoyed himself. All the same the teacher will be hard put to it to find anything more than unthinking reproduction of stereotypes from the cheapest of juvenile fiction, tumbled out in haste with scant regard for narrative coherence, time-values, paragraphing or punctuation. The shoddiness of the model shows forth in the downgrading of the moon to a mere setting for gangster-type conflicts with 'Scarface', in which the reward of lunar exploration is to be neither more nor less than a haul of gold-dust.

The next venture in the same genre might seem, at a hasty glance, to be indistinguishable from the first. A more careful reading, however, will show that it does offer some foothold to the teacher:

J.

From (another) *Journey to the Moon*

Chapter 3. *Landing on the Moon*

The clock on the wall showed 1 p m and the space-ship had passed through the gravity of the moon without coming to any harm or damage. In a few minutes time they would make an attempt to land on the moon. Every minute the ground seemed to come nearer, till they were 100 yds above it, then 50 yds until, with a grating crack they came to a sudden standstill and they were literally thrown on the floor. They had landed on the moon! It was hard to believe that it was only 24 hours since they had first taken off.

Neil Merritt volanteered to venture outside the space-ship, fitted on his special oxygen mask, slipped into a rain proof space-suit and carried a compass, a gun and knife with him. They all wished him 'good luck' as he stepped through the door and disappeared into the rather thick mist, which now became noticeable. During the time Neil was gone, Graham inspected the ship for any damage caused by the landing, when reaching the lower floor, he discovered to his horror a huge hole in the excact spot where the meteorite had scraped it, only it was much larger, and naturally more serious. He called to the remaining three men who hurried down, wondering what was wrong. When they saw the accident they gasped, for it would take at least 12 hours to repair it, as they were only at the moment four men.

Then the Doctor realised that their food would not last all that time, as the time scheduled for them to stay on the moon was only, at the maximum, 4 hours. After about 2 hours hard work the men suddenly realised that Neil has not returned. What a mess they were in! Not enough food, Neil disappeared and still a lot of repair work to do!

Chapter 4. *Neil Returns*

Eventually, after about 4 hours, Neil arrived looking very exhausted. When he had been revived with a strong cup of tea, he had a very strange story to relate. After walking arround for about a quarter of an hour he remembered to collect specimens of the material on the moon. Most of the stone, made up into deep crevaces, steep, unclimable mountains, potholes and caves, was a dull grey, but suddenly he spied a peculair green-colourd rock which he began to climb up to. He reached it without any mishap, cut away a small chunk, and decided to come down a different route. He slipped a little and he sat down heavily. After a brief rest he decided to explore further, but when he moved, in the attempt to get up, he realised to his horror that a giant clam-like structure had a firm grip of his foot! After getting over this shock he examined it carefully, and was glad to find that, where his foot was held, it was a little worn so he set to work to try and cut it away with his knife. After an hour of very hard work, he at last managed to make a large enough hole for his foot to slip through, which was very bruised and scratched. He carried on, down this steep-sided hill for little while, very slowly as his foot and leg were very painful, until, of all the bad luck, he slipped on a loose stone and felt himself falling, then everything turned black, as he lost consciencness. When he regained consciecness he was puzzled as to where he was lying, then it all flooded back into his memory, journeying in the space-ship, landing on the moon and then him exploring it and finally slipping. As he was making an effort to stand up, he found he couldn't. His foot and leg were covered in blood, a result from the fall and the giant clam, his face and hands were all scratched although they were protected, and his back started to ache. As he couldn't walk he was forced to crawl, and did this for about a mile till finally he came to the welcome sight of the space-ship where he was brought in by the other men. When his adventure was finished, Doctor Cook immediately cleansed Neil's wounds and he was ordered to rest, if not sleep in his bunk.

The writer here has made some attempt to grapple with the problems which a story of this kind must raise for the inventive imagination; he has tried to think out and record a number of details about the atmosphere, the equipment and provisioning of the expedition, the landscape on the moon, the time-scale of events. Where implausibilities result, they are an outcome of the writer's willingness to show his hand, instead of relying upon mere bluff. Discussion of probabilities will have, in this case, something to bite upon; and can thus avoid the appearance of carping fault-finding. The 'giant clam-like structure' is evidently a half-remembered residue from the writer's past reading; and it fails to carry any conviction largely because the model from which it derives must clearly have been such a shabby one—a representative example of the threadbare hackwork which (*pace* Mr. Kingsley Amis) exposes the term 'science-fiction' as an egregious misnomer.

The next two pieces similarly remind us of the close link that may exist at this age between writing and reading:

K.

Report on Mars (Future)

We were on a Rocket ship heading for Mars. there were small stars around us everywhere. Suddenly the pilot yelled 'put your space helmets on everybody we are going to land.' 'Crash' we were nearly jolted out of our skins. Slowly I sat up feeling carefully to see if any bones were broken. We tumbled to the door. Everyone got down the steps safely exept me. I tripped over the first step and fell. But to my great surprise I floated softly to the ground. Our leader laughed. I found out later that there was not nearly as much gravity on Mars as there was on the earth. 'Right now, scatter men' yelled the pilot. 'If you find something, whistle three times.' I made my way to a forest. Which looked from here about half a mile away. I found it difficult to walk, because I felt that any minute I would float on air. Otherwise everything was much the same as on earth. But when I arrived at the forest things were as different as they possibly could be. The atmosphere was hot and damp, almost as though I was in the coal forests of long ago. At first I could hardly see, the tall trees kept away the sun so. But as my eyes got used to the dark, I could see huge fern-like structures almost as tall as the trees. Suddenly something flitted past my ear. I whipped round, and gasped in astonishment. I began to wonder whether I really was on the earth in the coal forests of long ago. For there right in fron of my eyes was a 'thing' something like the very first bird on earth, for instead of wings there were huge claws with pieces of skin stretched between them. In Its sharp beak, I could see rows and rows of huge teeth. This creature, which altogether was big as an average man, stood on a rotting tree stump and stared at me unwinkingly. I shivered, It seemed so uncanny. Then, suddenly, the creature gave a squawk, and flew off. I sighed with relief. Then suddenly I heard a plop just ahead of me. Cautiously I parted the thick undergrowth and peered through there, just beside me was a great swamp, with oozy black mud in it. I put a foot gingerly down upon it, there was a squelching noise and I felt my foot being sucked down. I pulled it out quickly. Then suddenly there was a squelching noise and a very small head with a great long neck popped out of the mud. I was to terrified to move as the 'thing' slowly and ponderously stepped out of the swamp. Altogether it was about 88 feet in length. Suddenly I collected my senses, and ran for my life, tripping over the dense undergrowth. At last panting for breath I arrived in the open. I gave three short sharp whistles . . .

I am glad to say that I am now safe on earth again.

(Grammar School, Second Year)

The teacher's attitude to this will be influenced by the fact that this time the literary prototype (presumably Conan Doyle's *The Lost World*) is one towards which he can feel rather more goodwill. Even allowing for this, however, it seems a fair comment that the writer has ingested her source material more fully and worked over it more strenuously. The principal episode is certainly constructed out of elements drawn from reading, but these constituents have been reassembled into an individual pattern by the writer's own mental activity, so that the total effect is that of a genuine imaginative entry into the situation presented. (In a similar way, the incident contrived to illustrate weightlessness, though far from novel in its main outline, strikes us as having been thought out afresh here, rather than merely remembered.) This piece as a whole seems to me convincing evidence for the view that second-hand experience derived from reading can at times help forward the young writer's development in ways which the teacher cannot afford to despise. If further demonstration of this is needed, here is another composition written by the same child a couple of terms later:

L.

Catastrophe!

In the year 1974, a certain event took place which could not be called anything else but one of the worst catastrophies that the world had ever known. It started in 1964 simply with a certain disease . . .

Everyone knew that in some parts of the world the rabbit population did great damage to the crops. So some years ago Britain imported a deadly disease namely myxamatosis to kill all rabbits. Most of the farmers were delighted. No longer would their crops be ruined by the rabbits. The main body of people regarded with indifference the paragraphs written of the terrible lingering deaths among the rabbit population. Nobody had any really strong feelings against it except maybe the occasional child mourning over it's dead pet.

Then other countries started asking for the disease to be exported to them and within ten years, the rabbit population had become extinct. A few weeks later, the newspaper headlines provided the answer as to what the weasels and stoats were now feeding on. The chicken population was decreasing rapidly.

The minister of Food Supply expressed great concern at the alarming situation.

The weasels and stoats continued their raids on domestic fowls and with the change of diet grew bigger and more fearless. A week later it was stated that a pack of weasels had killed three dogs and already the stoats had attacked the cat population. Then a few weeks later the horror-stricken public read that a man had been attacked by weasels in the new forest and had been killed! This had been witnessed by a terrified child who had been feeding the wild ponies and had stayed out of sight behind some bushes. He had then stumbled home, petrified with fear, and told the story to the newspapers. 'Who knows,' concluded the Editor of a great national newspaper, 'Some day weasels and stoats may rule the world, and man himself may be extinct.'

(Grammar School, Third Year, by the same writer as K.)

This surely raises in acute form the question of what we mean, as teachers, by the term 'originality'. *Catastrophe* clearly takes off from H. G. Wells (we may suspect that *The Food of the Gods* lies somewhere in the background), but the writer is using her stimuli, drawn in part from current happenings and in part from fictional reading, for her own purposes, to dramatise a sense of moral outrage. Strong feelings are evidently involved, but they have here been given outlet in a form which is commendably mature and 'depersonalised' for a thirteen-year-old.

Finally, here are two pieces of writing by slightly older pupils which fill out in more detail the observation made earlier that children's progress in writing can never be in an uninterrupted straight line. Both M and N were written by girls in their fourth year in a secondary modern school:

M.

The Enjoyment of Man

The lighting is very dim, soft music is playing, and mingled with the sweat of perspiring bodies comes the smell of cigars, liquers, and from somewhere an exotic perfume.

Couples are linked together shuffling along a crowded floor; as if they were afraid at any minute they might be torn apart from each other.

The band is seated on a low platform in blue silk suits and black bowties; a dusky singer is crooning into the microphone. The time could be anything from ten p.m. to four a.m.; the day any night of the week.

Later on there will be a cabaret; the girls have already been on, but were sent off as a drunkard didn't know how to behave himself. More and more drinks will be ordered until the proprietor will call through the microphone, 'Time please, see you again tomorrow night,' then crack some corny joke.

Outside cars will be waiting; big cars, little busses, anything from a chauffeur driven Rolls to a mini-car. Minks will quiver in the cool of the morning as their owners hurry home to sleep off the effects of the night in the few sleeping hours left.

The next night the same thing will occur; the same doorman will shuffle to open the car door; the same cloakroom attendant will sniffle and sneeze as she hands us the cloakroom tickets; the crooner will once again croone into her beloved mike, and the smell will remain. How long will this continue you may ask; for as long as women and men have the same attraction to one-another; and there is wine in which to down ones cares and worries.

N.

A Crowded Place

The room was noisey and crowded, girls and boys in trousers and large jumpers sat in the half lit and extremely smokey atmosphere listening to an excentric jazz band.

As the music started everyone got up to dance, even though half the time they could not see who their partner was through this artificial smog.

In amongst them was like being in the middle of a herd of sheep, everyone pushed for space, either to dance in, stand in or mierly get some air. But all the same everyone was happy, you could talk to anyone—and have never seen them before and they will be friendly. I felt as though I belonged here in the mass of moving heat and smoke. I found that, here amongst all these people, what they felt, I felt; as their excitment grew for the music I felt mine growing—as if our minds and hearts were joined by the closeness of our bodies.

As the strong beat of the drums hit against us in the last tune we all clapped a couple who danced in amongst us and a large circular space was automatically cleared for them; here again no order was given the feeling was automatic to everyone.

Then suddenly it was all over the crowd had gone the atmosphere had gone, it was almost as if I had left something behind as I walked away, but there was always next week and maybe the week after . . .

M is fluent and will certainly have to be given a fairly high mark for its technical competence. Yet what claim can its content make upon our esteem when the values, vision and vocabulary are drawn so predominantly from the glossy advertisement and the mass circulation woman's magazine? N besides being technically faulty is both fumbling and incoherent; the writer seldom seems able to find the word or phrase she really wants. Nevertheless one can feel within it an attempt to seize and render a real experience which has meant something to the writer. Are we not justified in thinking that this attempt to take hold of experience (an attempt which seems to have been made with some earnestness and effort) will have been valuable to the writer's own development towards self-knowledge, even though its result is not, as writing, successful?

On the other hand, as compared with the writer of N who has kept close to the teen-age world she herself knows, the writer of M can be seen to have handicapped herself by the attempt to deal with aspects of adult living about which she can as yet know little. We have to keep in mind that the adolescent must at some stage make this attempt to move forward and outward from the enclosed world of childish experience within which an accumulated weight of past living can make perceptions acute and valuations sure; the movement is in a real sense a step forward, even though it has to be made at a price which entails, for the time being, a coarsening of sensitivity and an increased reliance on mass-produced observations and attitudes. This stage of development presents the teacher with delicate and perplexing problems of assessment and guidance. We can evade them if we like (many do) by running for cover under the umbrella of external examinations, with their seemingly inevitable stress upon correctness and propriety as the all-important goals; but if we do so we are guilty of a betrayal. The teaching of English is concerned with more than words, and in helping our pupils to write we have also to help them in their groping towards the values and standards by which they can live, in this disrupted and irresponsible society of ours, the life of mature, responsible and truly civilised human beings.

So far all I have done is to exemplify the evaluative process which must be at the centre of the teacher's response as he reads his pupils' compositions. Over and above this the teacher's approach must at the same time be diagnostic; besides looking for qualities which deserve praise and commendation, he must also seek out and decide upon the qualities which are capable of development or improvement, and which call therefore either for immediate discussion or for planned attention in subsequent composition lessons. I can best illustrate the kind of thinking I have in mind by quoting another piece of writing by a child in her first year at a grammar school:

O.

A Visit to the Circus

There was a loud aplaud as the band struck up a merry tune and the hall was plunged into darkness, save for the lights of the circus ring. There was even more cheers and claps as Mr. Tom Arnold appeared and addressed the audiance and then the animals trooped in one by one.

The first performance was by the horses. They jumped and galloped and pranced in the most facinating way. When the were clapped etc. they all bowed there heads very politely.

The elephants were very good also and the lions were rather terrifying. One lion would not do as it was supposed to do and the ring master had to pick up a chair and face the legs at the lion.

The monkeys were very funny in there little frocks and suits. They would not perform until they were clapped twice over. They played a minature piano and pretended to fight. There was a mother monkey who fed the children and put the babies to bed.

When the trapeze artists and tight-rope walkers came on every-body held his or her breath. The trapeze artists swung from ropes when they were upside down and jumped from bar to bar.

Last of all came the clowns. They spilt buckets of water over themselves and fell off of ladders. They really were funny. When everything was over the National Anthem was sung and everybody departed from a a fine performance.

Adequate but unexciting, one may say. There are signs that (as one might expect) the topic has aroused the writer's interest, but this interest can be felt in the writing only intermittently. Certain of the verbs used, for instance, communicate some liveliness of apprehension — 'plunged into darkness', 'trooped in', 'jumped and galloped and pranced'. (In the hands of a more mature writer these might incur the stigma of cliché, but not surely when used by an eleven-year-old.) Again the writer has produced an ordered account which moves forward smoothly in time-sequence — an achievement which, unambitious though it may seem, is not always at the command of the eleven-year-old. Perhaps the title has cast its net rather too wide, in this instance; a less scrappy, more fully realised piece of work might have resulted if the subject had been angled or limited slightly more ('The turn I enjoyed most at the circus'; 'Before the lights go down'). In any event we can see that the writer's grip upon some of the incidents is too uncertain, her mental picture of them too imprecise. It is this which accounts for the lameness of 'The elephants were very good also', and the confused failure of communication in the description of the lions. What is needed is that the child should visualise the events in fuller detail, call to mind more exactly what it was that happened, and how she felt about it. ('Can you tell me in what way the elephants were "good"?' 'I don't quite understand what it was the lions were supposed to do; could you tell me more about their act, so that I shall be able to imagine it clearly?') As so often at this age, in fact, the essential for progress is that the writer should be given the opportunity and the stimulus to clarify and bring to focus in her own mind the content of what she has to communicate.

Ideally one would like to be able to talk over each composition with its author personally and privately, if only for a few minutes; and even under present-day class-room conditions we can usually arrange that each week some half-dozen children shall have the benefit of this kind of individual discussion at the teacher's desk, while the remainder of the class are either reading silently or getting on with further written work. But with classes of between thirty and forty, and an allowance of no more than five or six English lessons a week, we are compelled as a rule to devise some compromise procedure that will make class-teaching possible. (This can also have the advantage of making it easier for the teacher to move away gradually from the situation in which he is the sole recipient of the child's communication, and its unquestioned arbiter.) The first step is to select, after reading each set of compositions, one or at most two issues discussion of which will be helpful at this stage to a number of pupils. In the case of narrative, the qualities to be considered may be at various times such matters as the selection of events, their order and arrangement, the choice of expressive words to convey actions, the writing of natural dialogue, the revelation of people's feelings, the portrayal of character, the setting of the scene for a new episode, or the way to build up towards a climax in the story. Or for descriptive writing we may concern ourselves with vividness of detail, with choosing and maintaining a single standpoint from which the room or the street or the landscape is to be described, or, more subtly, with the 'slanting' of a description to evoke a particular feeling or atmosphere. (I would exclude for the moment purely technical problems of punctuation, syntax or spelling, since I believe that these are better dealt with separately in ways to be outlined in the final section of this chapter.) Having made our choice, we must next find two or three relevant compositions, or extracts from compositions, to read out to the class. Much will depend on the judicious selection of these extracts, since in the discussion that follows the aim is to develop the children's ability to notice and analyse differences and to formulate their own independent critical opinion and judgment. The teacher's guidance therefore has to be exercised not via his own comment but through his skill in bringing together and placing before the class passages whose contrasting qualities will force attention into the desired direction. As a rule, it is best to use 'good' and 'less good' attempts to achieve a similar or comparable effect; it is a mistake to pillory the really inferior production, even *pour encourager les autres*. Desirable though it might be (ideally) to duplicate copies of these extracts for the class to have in front of them, it is seldom practicable. If we have to rely upon reading them aloud, one practical point is worth remembering. Through the ear alone it is more difficult than is sometimes realised to take in a passage fully and keep it in mind as a whole. Extracts should therefore be as short as possible, and may need to be read over two or three times before discussion can get going on a secure foundation.

Here are two extracts which might be chosen to initiate a discussion of 'tone' – the way in which a writer's relationship to his audience may shape the texture of his writing, including his choice of words and the rhythm of his sentences. Both are taken from 'letters' written by girls in their third year in a grammar school:

P.

. . . Soon we reached the farm which was Monica's home. As we walked up the path leading to the front door I noticed that the whole garden was a mass of beautiful flowers. We soon reached the front door which had been left hospitably open, and I was taken into a warm, bearlike embrace, by a plump motherly sort of woman, who Monica told me was her mother. The inside of the farmhouse was really charming and Olde Worlde. The rooms were gabled, and the windows were latticed. In the centre of the kitchen was a large table covered with a snow-white cloth and upon which was spread one of the most magnificent feasts I have ever seen.

There was two jugs of pure cream, a batch of hot loaves, which her mother informed me had just come out of the oven. Then we had trout which had been caught in the stream which runs at the back of the garden, there were many other delicious dishes, which I can't begin to describe, we finished our meal with an enormous dish of fruit, covered with pure, thick, white cream. After I had finished I could hardly move, but Monica insisted, and we spent a happy afternoon on the shore, peering into the many small pools, and searching for gull's nests.

Q.

. . . As you know we are staying with Gillian's aunt on her farm which is just outside St. Ives. It took ages to get here and we were both beginning to think we never would. When we got off the train we just missed a bus and we had to wait half an hour before another came. We arrived just after seven and there was a lovely dinner waiting for us. Mrs. Brown certainly knows how to feed hungry people. I should think Mrs. Brown knows everyone for miles around, because the first evening she told us about all of them, and there were well over twenty.

The farm is a big rambling place and it is supposed to be haunted. Gill and I havn't heard any ghosts yet any way. Last night we sat up in the hope of hearing or seeing one but we had no luck. The farm stands on about twelve acres of land. The chickens are allowed to run all over the house and no one seems to mind, not even the cats and dogs.

P contains a good deal of well-realised detail, even though rather too much of it comes over in the vocabulary of the popular woman's magazine ('charming and Olde Worlde'; 'snow-white cloth'; 'warm bear-like embrace'; 'plump motherly sort of woman'). But unquestionably the tone is too stiff and meticulous for a letter to a friend, and one has the impression that the writer has never escaped from her awareness of the teacher hovering in the background with his red pencil poised. In Q, on the other hand, the tone is casual, conversational, almost racy—and this is surely right for a letter of this kind. But the informality has lapsed here into a too-easy tolerance of the inexpressive reach-me-down phrase ('it took ages'; 'a lovely dinner'), together with an absence of ordered sequence. Starting from a comparison of these two attempts, a third-year form should be able to formulate for themselves the problem of how to achieve the appropriate tone for an informal letter without sacrificing precision and vitality of expression.

Frequently in these discussions the teacher's endeavour will be to induce the class to apprehend more clearly the *purpose* of the particular piece of writing which has been attempted—to visualise its audience, and to become more sharply aware, for instance, of how much this audience knows already, what it needs to know, how it is to be led to feel, and so on. At other times (and more especially perhaps with younger classes) the objective may be to persuade the children to think more fully and accurately about the *content* of their writing. 'Does it really look, feel, smell, taste, like that? Is that really the way it works? Is that really what he would do?' Or, to take a more specific instance, if the topic, for a first form, has been 'A Snowball Fight' we may ask: 'What movements do you make with your hands when you're about to make and throw a snowball?' (A case even for mime here, if the verbal answers lack precision.) 'How far can you throw a snowball?' 'What exactly do you feel when a snowball hits your shoulder, cheek, hair?' On such occasions the teacher need have no qualms about deviating into what looks for the time being more like a lesson in geography, history, biology, physics or chemistry than one in English; nor should he feel any guilt at concentrating attention for the time being on things rather than words. He must have confidence in the old maxim of Quintilian: 'Seize firmly the matter, words will follow.'[1]

The insights gained in the course of such discussion will be fixed in the consciousness of those who need them most only if they have opportunity immediately to put them into practice. This means that we must induce them, in the same lesson, to write one brief section (no more than a paragraph, perhaps) in which they tackle a problem closely similar to that which has been discussed. Thus to pursue the examples we have just used, the first form might follow up their discussions of snowball-fighting by writing a short account of making a snowman; or the third form, with their ideas about 'tone' fresh in mind, might write an extract from a letter to the same friend describing the journey home after their holiday. These practice-compositions will not normally be collected in, but the teacher will move around the class-room to look at what is being achieved, and a few of the better attempts should be read aloud to the class before the lesson ends. To cram all this into a single 'giving-back lesson' of only forty minutes will need careful (and indeed ruthless) organisation. Nevertheless by concentrating on a single problem, it can be done; this focusing of energies is, I am convinced, far more profitable than dissipating the same amount of time in fleeting glances at a number of different and unrelated issues.

(v)

Shortly after the Second World War Sir Winston Churchill, while on a visit to the United States, made a special recording of his voice in which he addressed the workers of the Soundscriber Corporation factory as follows: 'This is me, Winston Churchill, speaking himself to you . . .' To quote from the account of the episode given in *The Development of Modern English*:[2]

This seemingly innocent remark created a considerable flutter for some weeks. An editor of the *New York Times* commented with obvious dis-

[1] Quoted in Gurrey (1954).
[2] Robertson and Cassidy (1954).

approval that this was a 'remarkable sentence', and when *Time* reported the incident, letters from readers berated the Prime Minister for his 'bad grammar', the most extreme of all seeing in such language a general reflection of the decay of the British Empire . . .

Clearly 'correctness' in language is an explosive issue. Many people (in Great Britain as well as in the U.S.) are ready to express strong views about it, and the emotional vehemence with which they utter them is usually in inverse proportion to their understanding of what is involved. One common cause of confusion is the fact that the language spoken by any community has an innate tendency to change, whereas the ordinary person has been led to believe (often, alas, by school-teachers!) that it ought not to. Thus ever since the beginning of the nineteenth century, successive generations of school-masters have tried earnestly to check the spread of the locution, 'This is me', together with that of the more frequently occurring form, 'It's me'. Fortunately, perhaps, they have had little success; indeed it has been said that their only achievement has been to lead some anxious speakers to over-insure against error by saying 'Between you and I . . .'[1]

This Canute-like resistance to linguistic change is not, of course, limited to idiom or syntactic constructions. It extends to pronunciation as well. We have all met the teacher who takes it upon himself to tell his class that 'interesting' ought to have four syllables, 'extra-ordinary' six, and that it is a solecism to pronounce 'waistcoat' as though it contained only one 't', or 'often' as if it contained none. Still more benighted is the widespread pedagogic superstition that the original meaning of a word is fixed for all time as its 'true', or even its only permissible, meaning. In my own childhood I was made to feel indiscriminately guilty about the word 'nice'; no nice person, I was led to understand, would ever dream of using it, unless perhaps in the cliché 'That's a nice distinction'. Even today there are teachers with a self-appointed mission to protect the word 'aggravate' from misuse; if anyone dares to point out that over a century ago Dickens was already using it as a near-synonym for 'annoy' — well, that only goes to show that Dickens was a vulgarian anyway.

It is noticeable that those who would like to command the tide of linguistic change to turn round and flow backwards are modest

[1] Perhaps they should be credited also with the following conversation reported a few years ago by Professor Randolph Quirk: 'And Janet is going too,' said one well-dressed young woman. 'Oh,' said the other, with a nervously perfect drawl, 'Janet whom?'

enough to want it to flow back only so far. No one seems to have thought of demanding that the words 'candour' and 'candid' should revert to their eighteenth-century signification, which was almost directly opposite to the one which is invariable today; nor is it counted as one of Jane Austen's virtues that she was a linguistic conservative who found it natural to represent Elizabeth Bennet as saying to her elder sister: 'Affectation of candour is common enough; one meets it everywhere. But to be candid without ostentation or design—to take the good of everybody's character and make it still better, and say nothing of the bad—belongs to you alone.' (Jane Austen's lifetime spanned almost exactly the decisive period in the history of these two words. The change seems to have stemmed initially from Mrs. Candour's example in *The School for Scandal*, first performed in 1777; in her novels written between 1800 and 1817 Maria Edgworth veers from one usage to the other, with no detectable concern for consistency.) Again, the locution 'It's me' has itself a longer history than the pedants seem to realise. In Old English the corresponding idiom was *Ic hit eom*. In Middle English this became *Hit am I*; but eventually, as word-order came to be an increasingly important element in syntax, it began to seem unnatural for the subject to follow its verb in this way. The verb was therefore altered to *is*; and the phrase became *It is I*. As early as the sixteenth century, however, *me* occurs as an alternative to *I* in this new phrase; and it was not until the late eighteenth century that authoritarian-minded grammarians invented the idea that one of the two variant forms in this divided usage was to be condemned as 'incorrect'.

This example is a reminder that many of our most persistent superstitions about 'correct English' are, in fact, a legacy from eighteenth-century ways of thinking about language—the tabu on the so-called 'split infinitive', for instance, or the fanciful set of rules about *shall* and *will* which are almost universally disregarded in actual speech. The Augustan determination (typified in *The Spectator*) to reform manners went hand in hand with an ambition to 'improve' and 'refine' the native tongue. The aim was to establish, for English, a single and universally-held standard of propriety; ideally this would be as authoritative and unchanging as that of the Latin which had co-existed as a learned language alongside the vernacular for so many centuries and with such high prestige. Thus Dr. Johnson, while recognising that 'language is only the instrument of science, and words are but the signs of ideas', nevertheless wished 'that the instrument might be less apt to decay, and that signs might be permanent'; and he continued to believe that his design to 'fix' the language was a worthy one even after his work on his Dictionary had led him to doubt whether it was possible of attainment.

Because of the prestige accorded to learned Latin, much of this effort at standardisation took the form of an attempt to force English into an alien classical mould. Revealing, in this respect, is the story of how Dryden saddled us for more than two centuries with the shibboleth that a sentence must not end with a preposition. Realising suddenly that in Latin the preposition never comes last in the sentence, he was moved 'to recast the English sentences of his prefaces in order to eliminate what he had come to feel as barbarous' [Robertson & Cassidy (1954), p. 319]. A further and related influence was the belief that language ought to be logical; holding that there are universal and immutable laws of thought (grounded in 'nature') which ought to be reflected in a 'universal grammar', eighteenth-century grammarians and lexicographers claimed explicitly that their corrections and improvements followed the 'principles of reason'. For all that, it is evident to us today that these reforming efforts were in essence an attempt to give universal sanction and authority to the linguistic standards of a small social group. In preserving (as Dr. Johnson put it) 'the purity of the English idiom' the criterion appealed to was that of the 'polite' — the usage of the educated eighteenth-century gentleman, reinforced, where convenient, by the practice of such earlier authors as the eighteenth-century gentleman judged by his own standards to be 'polite writers'.

Here, of course, we come near to the crux of the whole matter. It is not 'divided usage' as such which incites indignant letters to the daily or Sunday papers. What rouses strong passions (now as in the eighteenth century) is the fact that one or other of the two variants is felt to carry with it a low social assessment, and to mark off its user as belonging to a despised or feared social stratum. Concern for 'good speech' or 'correct writing' is, alas, almost invariably an expression of concealed social prejudice.

Yet the notion of an absolute standard of correctness which once gave sanction to such attitudes is now utterly exploded. Modern linguistic science is unanimous in holding that grammar-books and dictionaries can never properly be thought of as normative or prescriptive, and that there is no possible source of authority in language other than the usage of those who actually speak it and write it. In

the words of Henry Sweet himself (writing in 1891, be it noted!):
'The rules of grammar have no value except as statements of facts:
whatever is in general use in a language is for that very reason
grammatically correct. A vulgarism and the corresponding standard
or polite expression are equally grammatical – each in its own sphere
– if only they are in general use.' Most linguistic scholars today
would prefer either to leave out the word *standard* in this quotation,
or put it inside inverted commas, since it has increasingly come to be
accepted that 'All languages and dialects are of equal merit, each in
its own way' (Hall, 1950). With this in mind we can perhaps savour
the full force of another American professor's racy comment that 'when
English teachers condemn *ain't* they are promoting a class dialect'.

Linguistic relativity of this kind is to many people intensely disturbing, so that it may be as well to insist that its adoption by the
experts is not an academic whim, but a necessity enforced by the
results of many decades of factual descriptive and comparative study
of many hundreds of languages. Any language (the facts compel us to
recognise) is an arbitrary set of conventions in which the items have
the value and meaning they do have solely because the speakers in
question use them in that way. There cannot in the nature of things
be any intrinsically *linguistic* stigma inherent in such forms as *ain't*
or *you was*; after all, such expressions are perfectly well understood
even by those who condemn them. They are objected to, quite
simply, because in Great Britain today they occur solely in the speech
of groups of people whose social prestige stands low in the eyes of the
community in general. Moreover such social evaluations are highly
ephemeral. At the beginning of the nineteenth century Jane Austen
regularly used in her letters, and presumably in her speech as well,
the form *ain't*; while a few decades earlier the form *you was* occurs
repeatedly in the letters of Sir Charles Grandison, a character
depicted by Richardson as the very model of aristocratic propriety,
and universally accepted as such. The function of dictionaries and
grammar-books is to record the ways in which people actually speak
and write; whenever a community changes its language-habits, it is
incumbent on them to follow and record the changed practice. Their
limitation as a source of authority is that they can never do complete
justice to the variety and complexity of the phenomena they describe,
and that they are always bound to be a little out of date.[1]

---

[1] Cf. Hall (1950), p. 6: 'A dictionary or grammar is not as good an authority for your
own speech as the way you speak yourself.'

There follow from this brief discussion of 'correctness' a few very important principles for our practice as teachers. In the first place, our language-habits are always changing, and it is no part of the English teacher's job to try to stop them from doing so. It is current English that we want our pupils to speak and write, not that of some earlier generation. Secondly, we need to lower the emotional temperature in our class-room discussion of variant linguistic forms. At present far too many children are made to feel inferior, ashamed, or even sinful, because they find it natural to speak the same group-language as their parents. Pronunciation, dialect, local idiom, colloquialisms and slang should be considered dispassionately, with the tone that belongs to a sociological inquiry and not to a linguistic witch-hunt. Thirdly, we must abandon the mythical unitary ideal of 'correctness' and try instead for the almost infinitely variable one of *appropriateness*. Good English is the possession of those who are able to adapt their speech or writing to the needs of the particular situation – to be at the very least acceptable to their audience; at best, pleasing, forceful, effective.

In the light of these principles let us consider for a moment the now widely accepted view that, as far as speech is concerned, we must expect many children to be bilingual, using one set of language-forms in the home, playground and street, and a different one in the more formal atmosphere of the class-room. While this degree of liberal-mindedness is welcome as far as it goes, its limitations should be recognised. It narrows down the concept of linguistic flexibility to a single dimension – the dimension of what one can only call the class-aspect of language. What is meant is that we ought to be tolerant of local working-class lingo so long as the speaker is also able on occasion to adopt forms of utterance which are in some degree recognisably akin to those of a B.B.C. announcer. Let me repeat that the judgments implied in this attitude are social, not linguistic, ones. To be 'well-spoken' in common parlance means to be a middle-class speaker. The pressure for schools to inculcate 'good speech' in this sense (it comes from employers and parents as well as from teachers) is associated with the long tradition in English education which has established the secondary school as an agent for what the sociologists call 'upward social mobility'. If, in the present era of free secondary education for all, we are ever to disentangle the muddle which this tradition has left us in, we shall have to face the fact that the language of Bermondsey, Birmingham or Bristol is just as good, *qua* language, as that of Broadcasting House. (We must not try to evade the issue either by making a false distinction between rural dialects which have a long history and the more recently established idiom of the large cities; antiquity confers no special merit on a language, and there is no justification linguistically for rating the speech of the South Yorkshire coalfield – 'uncouth, slovenly, not a true dialect' – below that of the remote North Yorkshire dale – 'picturesque and therefore respectable'.) There may be cogent social reasons (English society being what it is) for taking pains in school to enable some children to speak a different group-language from that of their home-circle; we ought to be quite clear what these reasons are, and why they deserve to be found compelling.

Unfortunately many teachers (head-teachers especially) are obsessed by the class-aspect of speech differences, to the virtual neglect of those other qualities in children's speech (freshness, fittingness, vigour) which in reality matter so much more than conformity to middle-class *mores*. In their obsession they surely underestimate the tolerance nowadays shown, in practice, in the world outside the school. Do employers really prefer the nicely-spoken dunderhead to the lad who is aitchless but capable? Moreover it seems unlikely that the school by itself, however hard it tries, can alter pupils' vowel and consonant sounds as much as the fanatics seem to expect. Not long ago a sixteen-year-old girl paid a return visit to the high school which she had left six months earlier to take up a job in a hairdressing parlour. One of her former teachers remarked afterwards: 'There now, did you notice how her speech has altered? You wouldn't think it could be the same person. I was always on at her about her accent while she was with us, but of course she wouldn't take any notice. I knew she could speak properly if she tried.' The moral drawn from the incident by this teacher should have been rather different. The fact is that the way we speak is inevitably a product of the way we live; the decisive influence is that of the group (or groups) of people we mix with and work with and identify ourselves with. Mutually incomprehensible dialects or accents are the outcome of social distance. If we *want* to acquire the speech of a group other than our own the surest way is to spend as much time as possible in their company. And conversely if we are thrown together constantly with an unfamiliar speech-group, we soon find ourselves wanting to assimilate ourselves to those around us – to tone down obtrusive differences and to acquire as

H

much as possible of the 'group-smell'. Many middle-class speakers who served in the ranks during the last war will testify that a few months spent in a barrack-room produced quite remarkable (though impermanent) changes in both their vocabulary and their pronunciation; the motive force towards conformity in this case was partly a matter of good manners, partly of nervous self-defence. In general, formal educational institutions[1] have had, and can be expected to have, only a minor influence upon the speech-habits of our society as a whole. Certainly there is an observable trend today towards greater uniformity .in speech-patterns throughout Great Britain. Dialectal and class variations are increasingly becoming less marked and less extreme; and regional speech is everywhere being modified by more youthful speakers in the direction of Received Pronunciation, at the same time as R.P. itself loses a good deal of its former status-value. But these changes must be attributed almost wholly to corresponding changes in our way of life: the more democratic mingling of different social classes on more or less equal terms, easier communications and means of travel, the great geographical mobility of many types of worker, the increase in holidays taken away from home, the spread of the telephone, the pace-setting by radio and television. Generally speaking, the minority of pupils who *need* to adopt a new group-language after leaving school (in order to fit in with either the new job or the new locality) will find in their changed environment all the opportunity and incentive they need. What the school can do to help is to develop an over-all flexibility in their children's speech, by cultivating a good ear and encouraging a relaxed attitude which is based upon informed understanding of the nature of linguistic variation. (Class-room drama is, of course, invaluable here; the appropriate role enables the working-class child to 'talk posh' without self-consciousness, since he is doing so under cover of a *persona* other than his own.) 'Going on at' children about their accent, on the other hand, usually does more harm than good. We all feel that our own speech is intensely and intimately identified with our own personality, and under criticism we tend to dig our heels in resentfully. As so often happens in education, the teacher who

---

[1] The exception to this is the residential university or the boarding-school where enforced seclusion in a small enclosed community can give rise to a way of speech which is highly distinctive, not to say idiosyncratic, and which its possessors cling to tenaciously throughout life as a marker of social prestige. The late Professor J. R. Firth claimed to have an unerring flair for identifying the speech of what he called a 'double Wykehamist'—a man for whom Winchester had been the scene of both his own and his father's schooling.

gets his values inverted is in danger of making the worst of both worlds.

* * *

When we turn to the written form of our language, the problem of 'correctness' raises slightly different issues. Written English has its own conventions, different from those of speech, and on the whole much more uniform and inflexible. English spelling was fixed in its present monolithic mould by the eighteenth-century dictionary makers; since the mid-nineteenth century a rigid code of rules for punctuation has been imposed upon us by the printing trade. In these respects we have no option but to conform, even in our private correspondence; we know that if we deviate markedly from the customary norms we shall be judged either eccentric or uneducated. It is true that in choice of words and in certain aspects of syntax and sentence structure a wider lattitude is left to the individual writer, who remains free to adopt a more or less unbuttoned tone to suit his particular purpose and audience. We do not apply the same standards of expectation to a headline as to a leading article, and a friendly letter would seem oddly stilted if it stood on as much ceremony as an official testimonial. Even here, nevertheless, the range of permissible variation in the written language is a relatively narrow one, and a feeling for the boundaries which delimit acceptability is something which all children need to acquire, albeit gradually. For the young child writing tends to be a matter of putting down on paper the words he would say; the school-leaver, by contrast, should be aware that many idioms and constructions can appear in print only if they are between inverted commas.[1]

In the written language, then, certain aspects of correctness need

[1] This does not, of course, give anyone the warrant to apply standards which are unrealistic and archaic; as has been said already, it is *current* usage which determines *current* acceptability. Unfortunately the fuddy-duddy attitude towards language dies hard. Not many years ago I was present at a G.C.E. examiners' meeting where the chief examiner proclaimed himself a liberal in linguistic matters, prepared therefore to tolerate a certain measure of colloquialism in the candidates' writing. 'Does that mean,' asked one teacher innocently, 'that you wouldn't object to the sentence in one of my scripts where the girl writes in a letter to her friend that she was "told off" by her teacher?' To my amazement the chief examiner back-pedalled hastily, justifying himself by the extraordinary statement that 'told off' was not colloquial but slang! Soon afterwards I observed Lord Attlee writing as follows in a respectable Sunday newspaper: 'As Prime Minister, I myself had to give him [Lord Montgomery] more than one tick-off, and once I had to give him a really good raspberry.' If 'tick-off' is acceptable usage in this context, why on earth should we expect a schoolgirl to write 'I was reprimanded' in an informal letter? Surely we ought to avoid at all costs the pedantry of inventing errors with which to find fault.

to be mastered by all children because they are indispensable ancillaries to ease of communication in the modern world. But how can we, in fact, help our pupils to achieve this kind of competence? By giving the class every day a list of ten words whose spelling must be committed to memory? By constant practice in punctuation exercises? By incessant drill in the correcting of common errors? At present a vast amount of time is devoted in English lessons to precisely this kind of direct attack upon the mechanics of written English; and for the most part it is time utterly wasted. For the direct attack which involves conscious effort and deliberate learning is not in reality the *main* way in which we acquire competence in these aspects of English; we acquire it, on the contrary, as the end result of a long process of unconscious accumulation of experience – in the young child the experience of listening to and absorbing the patterns of speech, in the older child the experience of wide reading which builds up gradually an intuitive sense of the patterns and structure of the written language. In the secondary school no amount of direct teaching of the mechanics will get anywhere unless it draws support from this background experience of wide reading. Head teachers who find that they are continually complaining about their pupils' spelling and punctuation should ask themselves whether they are really doing all they might to promote the reading-habit within their school. Even from the most narrowly utilitarian point of view most of the time and money now spent on exercises, drills, tests and textbooks would be much better diverted to the reading of real books.

Incidental learning as a by-product of reading is the all-important factor; and we need to have more confidence in what it can do for our pupils. This is not to deny, however, that most of them need in addition a certain amount of deliberately planned attention to their weaknesses in spelling, punctuation, syntax and usage. The point is that direct teaching on such matters has to be seen as a means of dealing with instances where, for one reason or another, the normal processes of learning are not taking place. All too often at present we give the child a spelling or a rule to learn at a time predetermined by the textbook, not at the time when he is in need of it, can see the benefit of it, and will therefore make it his own possession. We ignore, in fact, the natural sequence of unconscious learning which we can observe in any child who has formed the reading-habit, and as a result our class-room instruction often does more harm than good. Direct teaching should be concerned with mistakes which the children are making in their current writing and composition work; even more important, it should not try to deal with *all* the mistakes at once, but only with those which, at any given point in time, the children can readily learn to avoid.

Clearly the right kind of selectivity calls for careful and sensitive observation of the developmental sequence of particular children; and I can do no more here than illustrate some of the considerations which the good teacher will have in mind when deciding which mistakes to concentrate on and which to ignore. If we look back at 'A Visit to the Circus' (pp. 198–9) by an eleven-year-old grammar school child we shall see that the dozen or so errors in this piece of writing are not all of a piece. There is at least one mistake (*the* for *they*) of the kind we usually call careless; though actually we are all liable to make slips of this kind occasionally, especially if we are writing hurriedly or if our thoughts have run ahead of our manipulative skill with pen or typewriter. The writer knows that a mistake has been made as soon as he can succeed in focusing his eyes to take in what he actually wrote as opposed to what he intended to write. All that is called for here is greater care in 'proof-reading', and to foster this we shall do well always to provide time for reading through and self-correction before any piece of writing is handed in. At the opposite extreme there are some spelling mistakes (*minature* and *facinating*, possibly also *aplaud* and *audiance*) which seem to have resulted from a reaching-out towards a more ambitious level of expression than that which the writer has full command over. This calls for positive commendation, not discouragement; and it would be utterly wrong to penalise verbal initiative by demanding that such mis-spellings be written out correctly five times. Would it even be psychologically sound for the teacher to write in the correct spelling himself in red ink? The answer to this would depend, no doubt, on one's knowledge of the particular child's temperament, and the extent of his need for encouragement; there seems to be no good reason, however, for expecting a child always to spell a word correctly the first time he uses it, and little ground for fearing that unless a mis-spelling is pointed out at once, it is bound to persist indefinitely.

Somewhere between these two extremes there are those defects which fall short, in varying degree, of the level of competence that could reasonably be expected in a grammar school pupil of this age. Some of these (the hyphen in *every-body*, the clumsiness of *etc.* and *his or her*) probably reflect inexperience of the conventions of the printed medium, and could perhaps be expected to disappear within a few terms even without overt teaching. One (*off of*) typifies the socially sub-standard colloquialism which can prove singularly difficult to dislodge from a child's speech if it is deeply rooted in the language of the home circle; nevertheless its unacceptibility in the written form of the language is something which can and should be explained to the pupil at this stage. There remains the use of *there was* instead of *there were* in the second sentence (is this another carry-over from 'sub-standard colloquial', or is it a slip which the child would quickly recognise if asked to read the sentence over again aloud?); and the mis-spelling (twice) of *their*—a confusion which certainly needs to be cleared up without delay for a grammar school pupil of this age.

I have been suggesting that different types of error need different treatment; and this piece of writing, in which the mistakes are fairly thin on the ground, has the advantage of enabling us to distinguish clearly the main categories into which they fall. In fact I suppose that in this case a teacher might 'correct' all the dozen errors quite indiscriminately without running much danger of drowning the pupil's self-confidence under the flow of red ink. On the other hand one obviously could not say the same about 'Going Fishing', the composition on p. 187 by a thirteen-year-old low-stream secondary modern schoolboy; to score through all the forty-odd errors in these two paragraphs would be a ritual which might relieve the teacher's feelings but could do absolutely no service to the writer. To consider these errors more closely is to realise how complex a task of diagnosis the conscientious English teacher may often have to face. First it may be worth making the point that, outlandish though this piece of writing may appear, it contains nothing that is either un-English or non-English; the idioms, structures and vocabulary are those in current use in working-class speech in a South Yorkshire industrial town. For this reason, despite the boy's persistent mishandling of the conventions by which it is customary to represent such speech in writing, the defects do not in fact act as a barrier to communication; we may feel prejudiced against making the effort to understand what he is saying, but we find it perfectly possible to do so. Looking next at the mis-spellings we can say with certainty that to ask a pupil of this ability-level to relearn all thirteen of them at one fell swoop will only flummox him. We must select a few of the most important ones, and ignore the others for the time being. I would be inclined to pick out in the first instance *cit* (for *kit*) and *tatle* (for *tackle*), since these indicate a failure to grasp fundamental sound-letter relationships and also differ from all the other mis-spellings in that they offer a genuine obstacle to the reader's comprehension. Next in priority might come *usualy* since the spelling-pattern in question here (doubling the final *l* in an adjective to form an adverb) is one with a wide applicability. Among the other miscellaneous defects I suggest we ought to concentrate solely on the writer's failure to separate sentences by the use of full stop and capital letter. This failure is repeated a dozen times, and it is an important one; experience shows, moreover, that the principle involved is one which a boy of this age should be able to master successfully, given careful explanation and enough practice in reading aloud what he has written. And this surely would be enough. With a pupil such as this it is a mistake to comment on or even to underline more errors than this at any one time. Better that he should really learn a few points thoroughly than that he should be urged to nibble ineffectually at a large number.

I have written so far as though it were possible for the teacher to deal with these problems by discussing them with each child singly, one after the other. It is true that a child's difficulties and his rate of progress are so highly individual that this kind of face-to-face contact is uniquely valuable. But classes are large, even in the secondary school, and time for English is limited; some of the work on 'correctness' must therefore be done either with groups or with the class as a whole. Such teaching should be kept separate from the actual 'giving-back' lesson, and it has its maximum effect in the form of a brief spell of some ten to fifteen minutes devoted to a single carefully-chosen technical problem. One bite at the cherry will seldom, of course, be enough; the learning needs to be reinforced by reverting to the same topic two or three times at, perhaps, weekly intervals, until the skill in question is thoroughly mastered. What is absolutely essential is that the topic chosen should be one that a number of pupils are failing to cope with in their current written work; and to ensure this the teacher needs to keep a record, in his own notebook, of the mistakes that keep recurring. An alternative approach which can be recommended particularly for less gifted pupils is to shift some of this responsibility on to the children by providing, for each ability group within the class-room, a Mistake Box and a Spelling Box each brightly coloured, with a slotted lid, and provided with a neat pad of blank paper. Into the boxes . . . go the words that the children have mis-spelt, correctly written out on the paper provided, and the faults, corrected or explained. At intervals during the term, the boxes can be emptied and the contents discussed with the children who provided them. The Spelling Boxes will provide a basis for competitive Spelling Bees, in which each group is asked to spell a word drawn from its own box. It is interesting to notice how many a bad speller will quietly repair to the box to learn the words which his team may be required to spell, with no feeling of doing any extra work.[1]

Implied in all the above is a strong condemnation of the ritual which insists that no piece of writing shall be returned to its author until every single error has been underlined in red ink. Most teachers of English still spend many hours each week obsessionally 'marking' children's compositions in just this way; some have institutionalised the procedure by devising an elaborate code of symbols which are supposed to indicate to the victim the precise nature of each offence.

[1] Hobbs (1956) — an article which should be referred to for further discussion, in very practical terms, of the issues raised here.

Weakness in spelling is a rather specialised problem which deserves a brief note. According to Schonell (1936), poor spelling goes hand in hand with specific temperamental factors, among which the most important is the tendency towards a general disregard for details; at the same time case studies have shown that school experience has usually played a large part in establishing or confirming the weakness. Highly undesirable are the mixed lists of words haphazardly assembled which can still be found in many English course books, since these (a) waste children's time in learning words they either know already or will seldom use, and (b) actually lead to confusion between words as a result of chance associations. Much damage is done also by the practice of teaching together, on the same occasion, two words which are liable to be confused, such as *stationary* and *stationery*, *principle* and *principal*. Thus, bringing together in the same exercise or list *their* and *there* only strengthens the associative links between them; instead we should teach *they*, *them* and *their* together in one list, and *there*, *where* and *here* together in a separate lesson. Schonell (1932) recommends teaching spelling by grouping together in small units words which are allied in some way; he seems to be right in thinking that the most useful groupings are those which (i) associate words with a similar visual and sound pattern (e.g. power, shower, flower), (ii) words in which a similar visual pattern represents slightly different sound patterns (e.g. stove, glove, prove), and (iii) words containing the same silent letter (e.g. knee, knock, knob). The advantage of this kind of grouping is that it encourages the child to notice common spelling patterns, and hence to go on learning new words of similar structure in the ordinary course of his reading. Schonell, incidentally, reports that in all the cases he studied, educated adults with a spelling disability had done little out-of-class reading in school; the importance of incidental learning through reading has been demonstrated in other studies also, most notably that of Gilbert (1935).

More recent research has recognised the rather small amount of carry-over from rote memorisation of spelling lists, and has concentrated more on relating the learning of spelling to purposeful use in the pupils' own writing. One method, now widely used in the U.S. and also in New Zealand, is to have children compile their own learning-lists with the help of an alphabetic spelling-list in which the words are graded according to level of difficulty. For a fuller discussion, see Hildreth (1955), Patterson (1961) and Freyberg (1964).

It is no exaggeration to say that time thus spent is almost entirely wasted. The child who gets his composition back turns at once to the assessment (the letter-grading or numerical mark), and looks eagerly also for any crumb of comment on the content of what he has written. But since the target has by this stage been found or missed irremediably, he has no motive within himself to heed animadversions upon his way of expressing himself in an act of communication which is now over and done with; he can be compelled to attend to his past misdeeds only by threat or penalty, and in this situation his mental set will not be of the kind which favours learning. As a result the teacher finds inevitably that he is scoring through the same errors over and over again. (Moreover, extensive scoring-through can undoubtedly act as a disincentive; case-studies of backward pupils [e.g. Schonell (1948)] invariably show that 'negative marking' of this kind has played a part in the etiology of retardation.)

It is my own view that the red ink itself should be used selectively, and applied only to the mistakes that we believe the pupil is now 'ready' to learn about. The teacher who finds this unacceptable or hard to operate might try experimenting with other methods of reducing his 'marking-load'. (There are after all many other far more important things that he *ought* to be doing in his lunch-hour and at week-ends; all too often the 'marking' obsession seems to squeeze them out.) He might for instance content himself with correcting fully only a specified part of each composition—one week the first paragraph, perhaps, the next week the third paragraph, another week the final paragraph. Or he might try correcting a different aspect of technique each week—at one time punctuation, at another spelling, at another paragraphing. Such an approach keeps the techniques in a sensible perspective, while at the same time making clear that they have their importance and are not to be treated too lightly. The teacher should certainly explain to his class what he is doing, and why; and if he wishes to drive the point home, there is no reason why he should not award an additional grading or numerical-mark for 'technique', over and above the 'general impression mark' which should always be the staple form of assessment.

Better still, we may try to find ways of shifting some of this burden on to the pupils themselves. Gurrey (1958) includes in an appendix examples which show that many an eleven-year-old is perfectly capable of adding useful and sensible corrections to his neighbour's writing. Above all, however, what we want to foster is self-correction;

and we shall do this most effectively if we recognise that the natural time for this is *before* publication is complete. Wherever possible, we should arrange matters so that there is a further reading-public to be appealed to after the teacher's vetting has taken place. If the teacher can hand back a piece of writing with the comment that as soon as the flaws have been corrected this can take its place in the form magazine, or on the wall-display, then the child has a genuine motive for discovering his mistakes and producing a fair and faultless copy. By contrast the bad old tradition of compelling the pupil to write out his 'corrections' as a penance after the event is both irrational and ineffective because it ignores the question of motivation altogether; it is time it was abandoned, along with the other unthinking routines which still clutter up our 'composition lessons'.

Chapter 6

WHY TEACH GRAMMAR?

MY recommendation in this chapter is a radical one: I contend that no attempt should be made to teach children knowledge about the grammar of their own language until they reach the age of at least fifteen and preferably sixteen. I write this with full awareness that, if this advice were acted upon, some four-fifths of our children would receive no teaching about grammar at any stage of their education. Let me make clear, however, that this is not the same as saying that we should encourage our children to speak and write ungrammatically. Conscious knowledge *about* grammatical structures is a different matter from knowing *how to use* these structures; those of us who have been taught the grammar of our native language knew how to operate this grammar long before we learnt any grammatical terms, and our operational know-how continues, normally, to work at a wholly subconscious level, as a product of prolonged habit-formation. Nor is there any reason to think that knowledge about grammar is necessary for the highest level of achievement as a writer; as Ballard once put it, 'Plato never saw a Greek grammar, and Shakespeare never an English one'.

My reasoning in support of this heterodox viewpoint falls under three main headings. In the first place, if we are honest with ourselves we shall have to admit that most grammar teaching at present is patently ineffectual, largely because the subject of grammar itself is too difficult for children below the age of about fifteen. We teach it (often to the tune of one forty-minute period a week for four or five years), but our pupils do not learn it. For example, Macauley (1947) studied the outcome of grammar teaching in Scotland where children at that time were subjected to an exhaustive five-year grammar syllabus starting at the age of seven and a half. His simple test called merely for recognition of the five basic parts of speech, yet he found that few children below the age of fourteen succeeded in giving as many right answers as wrong, and that only the best of the senior secondary school pupils (aged fourteen to sixteen) were able to reach this distinctly unexacting standard. He concluded that 'a certain stage of mental maturity appears to be required for the understanding of grammatical function', and that children seldom reach this stage before the age of fourteen. His analysis of the test results suggested, moreover, that what children find difficult is the 'abstracting' or 'generalising' element in grammatical reasoning, and certainly this fits in with what we now know about the slow development in children of the capacity for abstract as opposed to concrete thinking. Particularly disturbing to Macauley was the thought of the widespread self-delusion among teachers about the knowledge supposedly built up on 'this non-existent foundation'. 'All our parsing and general and particular analysis,' he observed, 'must have been just so much hocus-pocus to the children.' Here no doubt lies the clue to the widespread unpopularity of grammar, as revealed in a number of surveys of pupils' attitudes towards school subjects. In one of these surveys a schoolboy summed up the situation in the memorable comment: 'I do not like grammar because I am not good at guessing.'

The second point to be made is that, even if English grammar were not only taught but also learned, it could not in the nature of things bring to children the benefits which are commonly claimed for it. Why do we, in fact, teach grammar? Are we motivated by anything more than an unthinking attachment to what has always been done in the past, together with a vague feeling that we would somehow be lowering the flag of learning, losing face educationally, if we left it out? (On one occasion when a former student of my own ventured to question the need for English grammar as a central element in the English syllabus, her headmistress drew herself up to her full height to utter the crushing rebuke: 'After all we *are* a grammar school!'; apparently she was blissfully unaware that on this argument from history the grammar obligatory for her pupils should be that of Latin.) I hope to show that of the three rational justifications sometimes advanced for the teaching of grammar, not one, when soberly considered, really holds water.

It is said, for instance, that the study of grammar provides an indispensable training in logical thinking. It is tempting to dismiss this as no more than a variant on the old theme of 'mental discipline!; the faculty psychology which underpinned this during the eighteenth and nineteenth centuries is now, of course, discredited, and the argument can in any case be used as a last line of defence for any subject which is at once unpopular and difficult. (Professor John Adams once suggested ironically that a good case could be made out on these lines for including burglary and petty larceny in the school curriculum.) But it seems likely that those who put forward this kind of argument on behalf of grammar have in mind (even if unexplicitly) a conception of grammar similar to that expressed by John Stuart Mill in 1867 when he said in his Rectorial Address at St. Andrews University: 'The distinctions between the various parts of speech . . . are distinctions in thought, not merely in words.' If it were indeed true that (in Mill's words) 'the categories of grammar are universal categories of human thought', the argument would need to be taken seriously. Unfortunately, however, the linguistic assumption has proved to be no more tenable than the psychological one. It was still plausible during the nineteenth century because up to that time the only grammar studied in the Western world was that of a few Indo-European languages with a structure fairly closely akin to that of Latin and Greek—the very languages within which (and out of which) the categories of traditional metaphysics had been formed. Since then, with the opening up for study of the whole range of world-languages it has become evident that there is an almost infinite diversity of formal patterns which human beings can use to categorise reality and to express their thoughts about it. As Robins (1951) puts it:

. . . the classical philosophical categories and structures which had always influenced the study of grammar, and in the work of the Modistae[1] had wholly supported the claim of Latin grammar to universality, were themselves found to be no more than reflexes of the formal patterns of particular languages (Latin and Greek), and therefore without claim to any general linguistic or grammatical applicability.

The most that can be said on behalf of 'universal grammar' is that 'no language wholly fails to distinguish noun and verb, though in particular cases the nature of the distinction may be an elusive one.' As far as the other parts of speech are concerned 'not one of them is imperatively required for the life of language'. (Sapir, 1921.)[2]

[1] The dominant school of medieval grammarians from the twelfth century to the Renaissance.

[2] For the detailed evidence which supports the assertions made in the paragraph the interested reader is referred particularly to Chapter V in Sapir (1921), as well as to the highly relevant discussion in Robins (1951). It may be of interest also to recall Sweet's comment: 'It must not be assumed that defective correspondence between logical and grammatical categories is necessarily injurious to language considered as a means of expression. On the contrary, illogical and ungrammatical constructions often add greatly to ease and even accuracy of expression.'

Nor is it any more acceptable, in the light of modern knowledge, to argue that the English teacher must teach grammar in order that his colleagues may be able to teach French or German or Latin. Each language has its own distinctive grammatical structure, and even the commonest grammatical terminology is seldom readily transferable from one language to another. In any case we now realise that a second language is best taught not by inculcating grammatical knowledge but by habit-formation which develops facility in handling the most frequently recurring structural patterns. Conscious analysis of the structure of the language is something which needs to be present in the mind of the teacher when planning his course, but not in the mind of the pupil.

In all probability, however, what carries most weight with teachers of English is the belief that one must learn grammar in order to acquire correctness of expression. The belief is unjustified. As we have already seen, the faults in our pupils' expression which we loosely call 'bad grammar' are not really a question of grammar as such. The native English speaker does not use non-English forms or structures. What he may do is to use forms which are *socially* reprehensible. The pupil may say, for instance, 'I done it', where his teacher would say, 'I did it'; the difference reveals merely that the teacher is more middle-class, not that he is more English. Each dialect, each variety of regional or sub-standard speech, has its own grammatical structure. Of its very nature, grammar cannot prescribe, it can only describe actual existing usage.

Moreover, the pupil's deviant form, 'I done it', has been embedded in his speech at a very early age, and is in consequence singularly resistant to any attempt to alter it which works only on the conscious intellectual level.[1] We often find that even when we have taught a child to know the relevant rule, his habitual pattern of speech remains unaffected – a fact of teaching experience which is aptly illustrated by Ballard's anecdote of the Lancashire boy who

[1] Wilkinson (1964) reviews concisely a number of experimental studies which indicate that learning grammar has no beneficial effect on children's written work. This conclusion is strongly reinforced by the work of Harris (1962, 1965) who studied the progress of writing skills in five matched pairs of forms over a two-year period from ages twelve to fourteen. In each pair, one form had a weekly lesson on English grammar, while the other spent the time saved in further practice of writing. At the beginning and end of the two-year period the children's compositions were assessed on a number of objective measures of structural skills (e.g. by number of words per common error, number of subordinate clauses, number of correct complex sentences, number of different sentence-patterns, etc.) The grammar lesson was found certainly not superior and in most cases inferior to direct practice in writing.

complacently told his teacher: 'Tom has put "putten" where he should have putten "put".' As Sweet was one of the first to see, theoretical rules have relatively little impact on usage as compared with unconscious assimilation and habit-formation:

We do not study grammar [he wrote] in order to get a practical mastery of our own language, because in the nature of things we must have that mastery before we begin to study grammar at all. Nor is grammar of much use in correcting vulgarisms, provincialisms and other linguistic defects, for these are more dependent on social influences at home and school than on grammatical training. (Sweet, 1891).[1]

The third and final count in the indictment against grammar teaching is in some ways the most fundamental. The plain fact is that the grammar which is expounded in school textbooks and prescribed in G.C.E. syllabuses is unsound, invalid, untrue. This, at any rate, is the almost unanimous view of those linguistic scientists who are best qualified to judge; and if we accept the expert verdict, we shall have to agree that on the whole it is just as well that our pupils don't in fact succeed in learning what we try to teach them. It must be made clear that the charge is not merely that many of the detailed factual statements in school grammars are false. What is claimed is that the procedures, principles and inner logic of school grammar are completely lacking in validity. Fries (1952), for instance, goes so far as to compare the 'false orientation' of 'conventional formal grammar' with that of the pre-scientific Ptolemaic astronomy; and suggests that in the twentieth century there is not much to choose, for value and usefulness, between the study of either.

It is easier to understand why this should be so when we realise that in its essential outlines the content of school grammar still follows that laid down by grammar-book writers of the late eighteenth century of whom the most influential was Lindley Murray; its procedures belong, in fact, to a period before there was in existence any developed scientific study of language at all. Since then, during the nineteenth century and even more during the twentieth century,

---

[1] It may be conceded that a few of the commoner grammatical terms may occasionally be useful time-savers when the teacher wishes to draw attention to a linguistic form which is unacceptable in its context. We can manage without them, however, and for most children the time taken up in acquiring an understanding of them is utterly disproportionate to their subsequent usefulness. They should perhaps be regarded simply as desirable vocabulary items for those who can pick them up without too much effort; one learns their commonly-accepted signification empirically, just as one can learn to recognise a sparking-plug without knowing anything about the working of the mechanical system of which it forms a part.

the science of linguistics has made immense strides forward; yet the work of such men as Sweet, Jespersen, de Saussure, Sapir, Bloomfield, and J. R. Firth (among many others) has made virtually no impact upon school grammar. During the present century, Nesfield (characterised by some scholars as the worst grammar-book ever) has enjoyed a wider circulation among school-teachers than any other English grammar, and was even reissued quite recently in a revised edition. It is only in the past decade or so that modern linguistic science has come to be included within the English degree syllabuses of some (but by no means all) universities; while into the work of the training colleges it has still penetrated hardly at all. As a consequence there is today an enormous gulf between the linguistic equipment and knowledge of the average English teacher and the up-to-date findings of linguistic study. I suggest in all seriousness that every teacher of English should impose a moratorium upon his own teaching of grammar until he has made a thorough study of modern grammatical theory. When he has done so, I suspect that in most cases his professional conscience will forbid him to resume the practice.

At this point we must turn aside for a moment for a brief (and necessarily inadequate) review of those features of modern linguistic science which distinguish it from the earlier pre-scientific study of language. Modern linguistics justifies its claim to be a science on the grounds that it is descriptive, inductive and empirical. Its raw material is 'people talking'—the unlimited number of diverse occasions when someone uses language to co-operate or interact with someone else. (The written form comes within the scope of these 'language events' because it draws its life from speech, and any written text carries within it the implication that it could be spoken aloud in some context of situation—even if only a typical and generalised one.) The method of study is descriptive because it is concerned solely to record and analyse the way people actually speak and write. Social, moral or aesthetic judgments are not part of the purpose of linguistic science; 'language is the way people talk, not the way someone thinks they ought to talk'. The method is inductive because it is concerned not with the individual and unique 'language event' as such, but rather with the attempt to form generalised hypotheses from a series of such events. As in any other science the research worker abstracts from the tangled complex of real events certain particularised aspects which he proceeds to study in isolation, one at a time. In thus trying to group together individual facts and state generalisations, he has to start by identifying the recurring patterns of regularity which can be observed in the ways people talk and write, within the specific language-community which is being studied. Finally, linguistics is empirical in the sense that it brings into play no fixed presuppositions imported from outside the language-material itself. Any hypotheses which may be formed are strictly provisional; and if it turns out that the facts of a language do not fit the categories which have been proposed, these categories must be abandoned or reconstructed.

Already the experienced English teacher will be aware of a contrast with the procedures of school grammar. School grammar-books are normally prescriptive, not descriptive; they assume the existence (somewhere) of a Platonic 'ideal form' for the language, and take it upon themselves to deprecate familiar contemporary idioms as an 'ungrammatical' falling-away from this. The ideal implied is invariably the written English of some earlier period, often in its most 'literary' form. As a result the pages are filled with highly unnatural sentences which call to mind irresistibly the waxworks figures in Madame Tussauds; it is impossible to imagine any situation in which a rational twentieth-century Englishman would utter them, and hard to conceive that any of his ancestors would have done so either.[1] Again, their method is deductive and not inductive; they start by giving an authoritative definition, and then instruct the reader to apply the definition to a number of carefully chosen examples. If as often happens the definition is at variance with the observable facts of the language, the list of examples is carefully screened to exclude any instance which would not fit; having defined a noun, for example, as 'a naming-word', your grammar-book takes care to shield its readers from encountering anything so inconvenient as the everyday phrase 'a King Edward potato'. Finally, school grammar, so far from being empirical in its approach, can be shown to be full of concealed presuppositions. The narrowest of these is the unspoken but pervasive assumption that the structure of modern English is bound to be more or less congruent with that of Latin. This belief has bedevilled the study of English grammar ever since the time of Ben Jonson, who assumed, in writing one of the earliest

---

[1] The following choice examples are culled from a single, but not wholly untypical, post-war textbook: *Thee will I repay. One lamp another lights. He answered me nothing. Answer me these questions neatly. What the King has done!*

English grammars, that the verb must have four conjugations, and was disappointed to be able to find only two declensions in nouns, as against the Latin five; its distorting influence is still apparent, in many school grammars, in their treatment of such topics as case and gender in nouns, or tense in verbs. More generally there are a number of presuppositions (often vaguely philosophical in origin) to the effect that language is, or should be, logical; that grammatical categories must correspond to distinctions in the real world 'or in mental processes (see, for example, the kind of distinction often drawn between 'concrete' and 'abstract' nouns); or that the system of a language must be one that can be fitted into a neat and tidy pattern. Typical of the school grammarian's readiness to distort his evidence to fit in with his expectations is his habit of saying (when it suits him) that in a given sentence a word or group of words must be 'understood'; thus 'I'll tell you what' is said to be a contraction of 'I will tell you what I mean' or 'I will tell you what I am thinking', though, as Sweet pointed out, *what* in this phrase is really a survival of the Old English *hwaet* which had the indefinite sense of 'something'. There can be nothing in common between modern linguistic science and an approach which is prepared to substitute for the actual language-material under discussion some other version which it is alleged the speaker ought to have said or must have meant.

Again it should be realised that traditional grammar confines its attention to only a part of the whole area of study covered by modern linguistics. Because language is a complex phenomenon, it has been found impossible to describe any piece of it 'at one fell swoop by one analysis at one level'; instead we must select and isolate the observable regularities on a number of different levels and study each level one at a time. The need for some such hierarchy of techniques is now universally accepted; it was indeed implicit in the traditional three-fold classification into phonology (the study of sounds), grammar (the study of structural patterns), and lexicography (the study of vocabulary). But although this three-fold classification has proved over-simple, there is still unfortunately no widespread agreement as to the number of levels needed, their precise status, or the terminology to be used for them. For the present purpose I shall take as sufficiently representative the hierarchy outlined by Firth (1957) in which there are five different levels.[1] The first and most abstract of

---

[1] I have omitted, as not immediately relevant, Firth's intermediate level of 'meaning by collocation'; for a discussion of this, see Chapter 15 in Firth (1957).

these is the phonetic level which is concerned to describe as fully as possible the sounds actually uttered by the individual speaker. But not all of the sound-features which can be thus described are significant in conveying meaning within the sound-system of the speaker's own language. The Englishman, for instance, has difficulty in recognising that the *l*-sound in *like* is different from that in *well*, because in English (as opposed to Russian) these two sounds are never contrasted one with the other to establish a difference in meaning. On our second level (it is open to us to call it either *phonological* or *phonemic*) we are therefore concerned only with those sound-differences which have contrastive value as part of the systematic sound-patterning which conveys meaning within the given language. On this level the function (and meaning) of the initial consonant-sound in *lug* is to be different from that in *rug* (a function incidentally which the Japanese speaker finds hard to grasp, since in his own language the difference between these two sounds has no contrastive significance). On the third or *morphological* level we study the scatter of forms in which the same word appears on different occasions, using the recurring regularities of pattern which we observe to assign the word to a particular morphological category or form-class. Thus, if we were to find that the nonsense-word *uggle* appeared in the forms *uggle*, *uggles*, *uggled*, *uggling*, we should be able on that information alone to assign it to the form-class traditionally designated as 'verb'. On the fourth *syntactical* level we study the structural relationships which can be traced between words (or to speak more strictly between categories of word) within a sentence; these relationships may manifest themselves in a number of different ways, among which the sequence of the words (word-order) may be no less important than the 'tied forms' of traditional Latin-based syntax. Finally we have the *semantic* level at which linguistic study is concerned with the utterance in its context of situation – a context which includes 'the human participant or participants, what they say, and what is going on' (Firth, 1957).

These five levels form a hierarchy in the sense that the technique of study at each of the higher levels may rely upon concepts or data drawn from a level below it (e.g. morphology upon phonology, or syntax upon morphology). It should be noted that although these levels when taken in ascending order become progressively less abstract, it is only the fifth or semantic level which is concerned with what we commonly speak of as 'full meaning'; only at this level does it become relevant to take into account the full human context in which the utterance takes place. Study at each of the lower levels can be carried on without reference to this. As Firth pointed out, a sentence such as 'My doctor's great-grandfather will be singeing the cat's wings' provides a sufficient context for phonetics, morphology and syntax (though not for semantics), and phoneticians and grammarians do in fact often find it convenient to use nonsense words or sentences for illustrative purposes.

It will be evident from the above summary that the school grammar-book, with its horizons bounded normally by 'parts of speech' and 'sentence analysis', limits itself to topics drawn from our third and fourth levels – morphology and syntax. Historical accident apart, there seems to be no compelling reason why these two levels should be singled out from the others as the only kind of linguistic study obligatory for all secondary school pupils. Some teachers would claim that, for the more verbally gifted pupil at any rate, levels one and two can provide some topics which are no more difficult and rather more interesting. And the kind of interest in language which children display of their own accord would certainly suggest that they are most likely to find relevance in the less abstract and more directly human issues associated with level five. In classifying a variety of different contexts of situation, in relating them to the different 'registers' or social categories observable in language (such as colloquial, slang, technical, scientific, journalese, literary), and in considering the different functions which language may serve in such contexts (e.g. exposition, narrative, quarrelling, gossip, persuasion), the pupils would be working at the level which is nearest to their own interests and their own capacities. The real difficulty here is that one cannot get very far at the semantic or 'context of situation' level without making use of classifications derived from the lower levels. Nevertheless there seems to be plenty of room for experiments in introducing this more vital kind of sociological linguistics into the class-room, and it seems obvious to me that the place where such experiment ought to start is the sixth form.[1]

[1] Some of the topics one would want to try out (the inter-relation of language, culture, and thought, the relation between speech and writing, the variety of 'group languages' within the complex entity we call 'English', the idea of 'correctness', the levels of language structure, the nature of a dictionary) appear in the syllabus proposed by Professor Randolph Quirk for an Alternative Paper in '*Modern English Language*' at the Advanced Level of the G.C.E. (*The Examining of English Language*, 1964, Appendix D). I should like to offer a warning, though, against an apparent assumption in this Appendix that the pupil would need to learn in some detail the systems describable

Before ending this chapter we must look more closely for a moment at the traditional subject matter of school grammar, which is located as we have seen on the intermediate levels of morphology and syntax. In English there are two main types of structural relationship which can be observed in operation at these levels. The first is that known as 'flexional', and its principle can be clearly illustrated by the Latin textbook sentence 'Balbus murum aedificavit', in which the relationship between the three words is conveyed wholly by their inflections (or variable endings). We should notice that in this kind of structure morphology and syntax are very closely tied together; we recognise a word as a noun on the morphological level by its particular set of inflectional endings, while simultaneously it functions as a noun on the syntactical level by virtue of these identical inflections. Flexion was the dominant element in Latin, and also in Old English, and it has been customary to treat modern English to a very large extent as though it were flexional on the Latin model. But in reality inflections in modern English are remarkably few in number; they are confined to nouns, verbs, and pronouns, and they account for only a relatively small proportion of the syntactical meaning of English sentences. Up to a point it is no doubt true to say that we use in their place a limited number of *form-words* or *empty words* (e.g. prepositions) which differ from inflections in their mode of functioning rather than in fundamental principle. Radically different, however, is the second main type of structure employed in English, that known as 'positional'. Word-order is, in fact, of prime importance syntactically in modern English; 'Man bites dog' is completely different from 'Dog bites man', whereas the most that a Latin speaker could do by altering the order of words in 'Balbus murum aedificavit' would be to produce a very slight shift in emphasis. Ever since Sweet the importance of positional structure in English has been increasingly studied, and some American linguists

within the grammatical and lexical resources of the language. An analogy with the teaching of biology may have some point here. At one time the pupil learning biology was expected to commit to memory a great deal of information about, at one level, the structure and functioning of tissues and organs, at another level the type system. The more modern trend is to focus on the living organism in its environment, illuminating this study where necessary by reference to particular tissues or organs, or by a selective 'dipping into' the type-system which enables the pupil to understand the system and to use it, without actually 'knowing' it in the older sense. It seems to me that similarly our linguistic studies in the sixth form should focus on language functioning in the human environment, illuminating this where necessary by a 'dipping into' the more abstract levels of syntax, morphology and phonology, which would enable the student to understand the nature and inter-relationship of these levels and to find his way around them, without actually 'knowing' the systems in detail.

have recently demonstrated at length the great complexity of the word-order patterns which we have all learnt to adhere to. One corollary of this which has some interest is the extent to which, in a language dominated by this type of structure, morphology has become disjoined from syntax. In a highly inflected language there is seldom any doubt as to whether a word is a noun or a verb, even when the word is isolated from a context; in English, on the other hand, and especially in its more colloquial modes, there is a remarkably large number of word-forms which can be either noun or verb, and which cannot be identified as one or the other until they are met inside the structural frame of a sentence. Thus two paragraphs (thirty-three lines of print) chosen at random from a story by Alan Sillitoe yielded the following instances (some of them used more than once in the passage): face, move, run, rope, side, post, clink, time, sense, wave, bark, mouth, beat, roar, gang, air, felt, drive, smell, sweat, gasp, knot, tape.

It is this disjunction between morphology and syntax which makes form-class analysis (i.e. discussion of the parts of speech) rather difficult to handle in English. On the morphological level a limited proportion of words may include some feature which signals their membership of a particular form-class; if a word ends in -*ation* or -*ness*, for instance, we expect to find that it is a noun. More generally on this level, we make use of information provided by the very small number of inflections which still survive in English to differentiate between, say, 'nouns' and 'verbs'. Given the set of forms *cronks*, *crunk*, *cronk*, *cronk*, *crunks*, *cronk*, *cronks*, *crunking*, *cronk*, *crunk*, *crunked*, we shall agree that morphologically *crunk* must be a verb, and that *cronk* is probably a noun. To continue the study of these two words on the syntactical level we should need not merely the forms but also a number of sentences or word-groups in which to observe the positions occupied by each word in typical sentence-patterns. If the material available included *Crunk this cronk for me, on the cronk, it kept crunking away, my cronk never crunks*, this would provide evidence suggesting that on the syntactical level also *crunks* is a verb and *cronk* a noun. Broadly speaking, categories defined at either of these two levels tend to converge; but we cannot assume that this is invariably so. After all, in English it is possible for almost any word to function syntactically, on occasion, as either noun or verb, as in the example, *But me no buts*.

In any case, it should be perfectly evident by now that for linguistic study at these two levels we do not need to refer to, or even to know, the lexical meaning of the words under discussion; the fact that we are unable to form a mental image of what a *cronk* might look like has not impeded our analysis in the least. The traditional grammar-book definitions which present a noun as 'the name of a person, place or thing', and a verb as a 'word which denotes an action, state or process' are therefore both irrelevant and misleading. They do not work in practice, even on their own terms, because they do not enable us to assign a previously unknown word-form to either of the categories defined; they leave us helpless in front of a sentence such as *But me no buts*, and distinctly puzzled when we attempt to apply them to many perfectly everyday utterances. The objection to them is that they have substituted a fruitless kind of speculative introspection for study of the actual characteristics of the linguistic material under review. It is only those aspects of meaning which are conveyed by recurrent word-forms and by the structural relationships between words in sentences that can properly be the object of linguistic study on the grammatical levels, and grammatical categories can be established only by reference to features which can be described in these terms. To take a slightly different example, we cannot decide whether *scissors* is a singular or plural noun by quasi-metaphysical argument as to whether what the word calls to mind is one object or two; what we are obliged to do is to examine a number of sentences in which the word appears, noticing in particular the verb-forms which go with it. To comment upon the relationship between grammatical categories and other categories, either in the real world or in human consciousness, is a perfectly legitimate activity *after* the grammatical categories have been established, but it cannot form part of the grammatical analysis itself.

When grammatical study is anchored firmly to its own levels, it should become less confusing, but it certainly does not become any less complex. Even at the twin levels of morphology and syntax, English turns out to be not monosystemic but polysystemic; in other words, we find not a single pattern of structure at work, but a considerable range of overlapping patterns which operate at different times or may operate simultaneously in intricately interwoven cross-patternings.[1] The native speaker has learnt to operate these

---

[1] In addition to the two main types of structural pattern already mentioned, flexional and positional, there are two other types which are relevant though less common in English. The first is that known as *agglutinative*, in which a word-base combines in a predictable order with a series of prefixes or suffixes each of which contributes an

cross-patternings without giving any conscious thought to them; when listening or reading he knows which signals to attend to and respond to at any given time, and in what order of precedence. But to make the patterns conscious, to isolate them and describe them systematically, is far more difficult. A measure of the difficulty is provided by the fact that no satisfactory comprehensive description of the grammar of contemporary English has yet been written, even for experts. We can reasonably hope that within a few years' time the gap may be filled by the *Survey of Educated English Usage* which is now going forward under the direction of Professor Randolph Quirk, but in the meantime the best recommendation one can make, for teachers, is the professedly incomplete and interim 'introductory textbook' by Strang (1962). The teacher who studies this (or the less satisfactory American alternatives by Fries [1952] or Roberts [1956] or Hill [1958]), will soon realise that the concepts and methodological approach now obligatory in the study of grammar are far too difficult for children below the age of sixteen; to find ways of bringing them within the mental scope of even the able sixth-former will be a formidable task calling for considerable ingenuity.

One cannot rule out the possibility that after several decades of experiment in teaching this material in the sixth form, there may emerge ways of simplifying some topics which would make them intelligible to, let us say, fourteen- or fifteen-year-olds. In the meantime, this chapter must end on the same note which opened it. At present the only sound advice for the teacher of English who contemplates teaching English grammar in the main body of the secondary school must be identical with that given by Mr. Punch to those about to get married. 'Don't.'

invariant element of meaning to the whole. This kind of pattern, which is a dominant one in certain languages such as Turkish, Hungarian and Malay, occurs only on a fairly small scale in English; one can, for instance, complain that someone is *un-get-at-able*, and it is conceivable that one might go a step further in the pattern-making and talk about his *un-get-at-able-ness*. The other type of structure may be known as either *incorporating* or *holophrastic*; its unit is a group of words which have become so indissolubly linked together that they cannot profitably be sub-divided for further analysis. Thus *How do you do?* is really a single unit which cannot sensibly be split up any further. One cannot say either *How did you do?* or *How does he do?*, and the appropriate response is not to embark upon an account of one's health or illnesses but merely to repeat the expression at the same time either bowing slightly or shaking hands; the piece of language has to be regarded as an item the parts of which are not related together by any analysable structure. It is customary to treat such holophrases as idioms, with the implication that they can be brushed to one side as 'exceptions' or 'special sentences'; but this seems to obscure the prevalence in English of word-groups which have in common this same characteristic (i.e. that what looks at first sight to be their internal structure proves, on examination, to be either dormant or fossilised).

Chapter 7

EXAMINATIONS AND
THE TEACHING OF ENGLISH

'PLEASE, sir, will we get this in the exam?'

We have all met this question; it is a revealing tribute to the influence of examinations upon the pupil's sense of priorities. When kept under the control of a wise teacher who understands the need of his own class, this lever can be a useful teaching-aid. It can, for instance, stimulate more intense effort in those aspects of the work which are the most important, or it can encourage steady application over the whole field of study, including those parts of it which some pupils, for one reason or another, have been inclined to neglect.

Unfortunately this kind of enlightened educational aim is seldom discernible in the examinations which really count in the eyes of both pupils and parents. These are external examinations, set, marked and administered from afar. They affect the education of a very large number of children directly. (Some 350,000 candidates now take the Ordinary Level English Language paper of the G.C.E. every year.) Their indirect influence is even more extensive, since they set the pattern, naturally enough, for the vast majority of internal school examinations, even those taken by secondary school pupils with a very much lower level of ability. Yet their influence is one which the best teachers of English view with acute uneasiness. And no wonder. The fact is that all past experience suggests the existence of a deep and inherent incompatibility between external examinations as we know them and the essential aims of good English teaching.

To say this is not to make imputations against the integrity or good intentions of the examiners, most of whom act as responsibly as they can within the terms of reference they are given. Any claim that all examiners are scoundrels, in league with the even more scoundrelly textbook writers, is a childish over-simplification; we must not fall into the error of adopting a 'conspiracy theory' of educational history. No, the incompatibility is built into the system, and arises mainly because the demand for examinations, and still more examinations, comes from outside the class-room situation itself. As the S.S.E.C.'s *Examinations Bulletin No. 1* said of C.S.E.: 'Society has made its wishes clear – the wish for more information about the attainments of a widening band of school-leavers.'

What society expects of examinations is, in fact, that they shall fulfil a predictive function. They are to act as a measuring instrument to foretell which boys and girls will succeed in particular types of job or at particular levels of employment; and they have proliferated so inexorably over the past century as part of the vast apparatus of vocational selection which seems to be required by an increasingly impersonal large-scale industrial society. The trouble is that the predictive role thus forced upon school examinations is necessarily in direct conflict with educational values – and nowhere more nakedly so than in the sphere of English teaching.

In the first place, if we want to improve the predictive usefulness of an examination we are compelled to bring the individual boy or girl into direct competition with a large number of others, so that the attainments measured may be comparable over the country as a whole. All the social pressures favour a large-scale external examination in which many thousands of candidates take the same paper, writing on the same essay topics or answering questions on the same set book. Secondly, if predictive efficiency is what matters, it is important that the results of the examination should be consistent and reliable; there is therefore a tendency to choose as yardstick those tasks which examiners can agree about among themselves and can mark with self-consistency. This happens whether or not the tasks which are easy to examine are also the most important educationally, and in the process significant areas of attainment which are hard to assess may be played down, or even (as in the case of spoken English and drama) left out altogether. Thirdly, it has been found that predictive reliability can be improved by setting a number of different short tasks rather than a few longer ones (context questions in literature, grammar and vocabulary questions in language); since the candidate may have his own inconsistencies, results based on a wide sample of his performances are less likely to be affected by the 'luck of the draw'.

The larger the scale of the examination, the stronger will be this drive towards comparability and standardisation. In the *mass examination* of today (Ordinary Level English Language is the most extreme example, and also the most hair-raising) the number of candidates taking the same paper is numbered not in thousands but in tens of thousands. The resulting flood of scripts is marked by a panel of examiners numbering sixty, seventy or even (for some English Language papers) a hundred and more. Each of these cogs in the machine has to process (in accordance with instructions given out at a briefing meeting) some 500 scripts within a period of about three weeks. The inevitable consequences of such a situation were first set out by L. C. Knights in an article published in *Scrutiny* in 1933. Under these conditions, he observed, standardisation and uniformity of marking can be achieved only by a system of markable points; the only markable points that are both recognisable at a glance and sufficiently objective to ensure uniformity among such a large panel of examiners are *facts* and *standardised opinions*.[1] To these we ought to add, in the case of English Language (not specifically mentioned by Professor Knights), *standardised mechanical skills*, such as spelling, punctuation, sentence structure and the like.

Obviously the accomplishments which can be reliably measured in a mass examination of this kind are not those which the good English teacher sets most store by. We value not so much the easily-assessed fragments of knowledge and skill which are common to thousands but, rather, those qualities of observation, imagination, perception, and judgment which are individual, which are rooted in the particular boy or girl's own experience and environment, and which relate to the concerns which really matter to him. We are interested above all in those moments when we light on something (a topic, a poem, a story) which engages and interacts with the inner world, so that the pupil's whole personality is involved and flowers in a use of language, which is for him a creative act, an enlarging of horizons. It is difficult to see how such moments can ever be planned for, in the abstract, for a faceless multitude. So much depends on the local environment, on the teacher's understanding of and sympathy with his own class, his awareness of individual talents and preoccupations, his sensitivity to

[1] Though this thirty-year-old analysis is still valid in its essential outline, some details in it would need modifying slightly today. Thus in English Literature papers most examining bodies have now abandoned an explicit system of markable points, at any rate for essay-type answers (markable points are still widely used for context questions). Instead examiners are instructed to give an 'impression mark' for different parts of the answer, or even for the answer as a whole. More is thus left to the discretion of the individual examiner, who can differentiate in his marking according to the quality of the response shown. Nevertheless, as we shall see later in this chapter, the circumstances and tempo of the marking—and above all the nature of the questions set—still ensure that what really counts are facts and standardised opinions; I believe any experienced examiner would confirm this.

the immediate psychological climate. How often do pupils have their spontaneous creative enthusiasm triggered off by an essay topic which has been cooked up (probably eighteen months beforehand) as a safe bet for a mass examination paper? (Usually, however hard the examiners may have tried, the response ranges only between the suppressed groan and the sigh of dutiful compliance.) And when it's so difficult to find a single work of literature which is 'right' for even thirty-five members of the same class, how often can an examining body hope to prescribe a set book which is suitable for tens of thousands of candidates at one and the same time?

Even so, this opposition of values would not be so unmitigatedly disastrous were it not for that invariable attribute of examinations which we started out from — what has come to be known as their 'backwash effect' upon teaching. The more an examination result matters, predictively speaking, the more inescapable is the constraint upon pupils to spend time and energy practising stereotyped imitations of the tasks they will be called upon to perform in the examination-room. The catastrophic effect of eleven-plus 'objective' English tests upon our junior schools is well-known; all too often English teaching has become a matter of shepherding the children every week round an unvarying obstacle-course of progress papers, test papers and spelling lists. If we may judge from the contents of the best-selling English course-books, it is clear that in all too many secondary class-rooms, too, what we shall find, masquerading under the guise of teaching, is no more than a prolonged repetitive practising of examination tasks which are artificial, limited, and trivial. Admittedly the good teacher, if he has steady nerves and confidence in his own powers, may be able to keep these pressures within reasonable bounds; and if his pupils are fairly able as well, there may be substance to his claim that they 'take the examination in their stride'. All the same, given the prestige and the material advantages conferred in our society by examination success, one may suspect that his values and goals will often be distorted, unconsciously, to a far greater extent than he would care to recognise.

Since the worst evils can be traced directly to the mass nature of our present external examinations, it seems inevitable that, however enlightened any syllabus may be, its good intentions will soon be frustrated if they have to operate within the framework of a mass examination. English is peculiarly vulnerable to this distortion by sheer weight of numbers, since it is a subject which, for most purposes, few pupils can afford *not* to attempt. At the G.C.E. examination in Summer 1962, 195,000 candidates were entered for O Level English Language, and 175,000 for O Level English Literature. From fairly modest beginnings in the first few years, it seems likely that C.S.E. entries in English will quickly rise to a comparable level — though in this case the numbers will be shared between fourteen examining bodies as compared to the present eight for G.C.E. The numbers taking Advanced Level English remain relatively small (26,000 in Summer 1962), but they have been increasing steadily; while it seems reasonable to predict that the new 'Use of English' papers will soon become a compulsory insurance policy for virtually all sixth-formers who hope to gain a place at a university. The urgent need (it must surely be felt in other subjects as well as English) is for more decentralisation of the examining process. As a first step the G.C.E. boards should be pressed to offer a wider range of alternative papers, and also to make it easier for schools or groups of schools to put forward alternative syllabuses of their own (a course of action which is already technically possible but tacitly discouraged). A slightly more radical solution would be to create more examining bodies. For G.C.E. the number of these is now the same as in the 1930s, although the overall number of candidates has increased several times over; some of the G.C.E. Boards (notably London and J.M.B.) are unquestionably far too large judged by any standards other than those of administrative convenience and economy. Moreover, although control of the examination by teachers is one of the proclaimed aims of the C.S.E., most of the examining bodies now in formation seem to cover far too wide an area to permit effective consultation with the class-teachers actually at work in the schools; as soon as the numbers of candidates make it financially feasible, they should be further sub-divided.

Nevertheless, whatever the amelioration such changes might bring, I believe that for English the educational need can be met fully only by adopting a system of internal examinations with external moderation. Despite what the cynics may say, this is *not* impracticable. The case for it, as a replacement of the old School Certificate, was argued in the Norwood Report as far back as 1943. It has been written into the constitution of the C.S.E. as one of the three possible forms of examination which must be offered, although unfortunately only a few of the examining bodies so far seem to be intent on making a working proposition of it. And the S.S.E.C. has now given powerful support by recommending experiments in 'externally supervised internal examinations' in English Language at O level as soon as possible (*The Examining of English Language, 1964*). What we stand to gain here is the liberation of good teachers from externally imposed shackles, and an immense impetus to all teachers to accept a fully professional responsibility for their own pupils. It would be worth paying for this by accepting some reduction in the predictive efficiency of the examination results; in any case it should be remembered that the reliability of our present external examinations has never been subjected to any kind of rigorous experimental scrutiny, is almost certainly much less than is commonly assumed, and is probably largely spurious anyway, since it has been gained by concentrating on inessentials (in other words, by sacrificing 'validity'). Apparently the social requirement at present imposed by employers and by competitive selection for further education is that the attainments of the more able half of the sixteen-year-old population should be graded into ten groups (the six grades of pass of the G.C.E. O level, the lowest of which will overlap with the uppermost of the five grades to be recorded by C.S.E.). Given a reasonably thorough co-ordinating system to iron out variations in standard between different schools and different teachers, I can see no reason why internal examinations should not be able to meet this fairly unexacting requirement with enough accuracy for all practical purposes. The real point is that the educational influence of examinations ought to take precedence over their grading, classifying and predictive role.

Nevertheless it would be naïve to suggest that all our problems would disappear overnight if we were to succeed in implementing A. N. Whitehead's principle that 'every question directly asked of a pupil in any examination' should be 'either framed or modified by the actual teacher of that pupil in that subject' [Whitehead (1932)]. The external nature and mass scale of our existing examinations in English are not solely responsible for all their defects, though they undoubtedly magnify and intensify them. We have, for instance, failed to carry over into our thinking about examinations that unified conception of English which increasingly underlies all our best teaching of the subject. The English teacher nowadays sees his objective as developing in children the ability to use the mother-tongue as effectively as possible, as sensitively and expressively as possible, in a really all-round way; in listening, speaking, reading, writing, and drama; for practical purposes of day-to-day living and also imaginatively and creatively; for communication with others and also as a means of coping with one's own experience of living. All these differing aspects are intimately related because language is so closely bound up with the whole personality. Yet our examining of English continues to split up and segment this unity. We find examination papers in 'English Language' (Ordinary Level, Use of English) which are based on the idea that 'practical English' can be isolated. In some questions it is covertly assumed that we can judge proficiency in writing even though the writer has nothing much he wants to say; in others that 'ability in reading' can be tested regardless of the value, importance and interest of the passage read. On the one hand the sixteen-year-old is asked to write a composition about *Boredom*, *Bells* or *An imaginary journey*; on the other he is subjected to routine comprehension and précis questions on a dull and worthless piece of journalism which is invariably (and, one understands, deliberately, since this is 'language' and must not therefore poach on the preserves of 'literature') of the kind politely described in *The Examining of English Language* as having 'meagre literary merit'. The other side of the coin appears in the belief that literature can be segregated as an optional 'subject', an aridly academic enclosure in which the books treated need make no real impact on the living human concerns of the pupils. For only in such terms, it seems to me, can one make sense of the choice of some of the set books prescribed, even today, for some Ordinary Level and Advanced Level Literature papers—for sixteen-year-olds, for example, Wordsworth *Selections* or *The Rape of the Lock*. I myself can clearly remember 'doing' *Paradise Lost*, Books I and II, as a boy, for School Certificate 'literature'—gaining high marks for it, too, although the poem had absolutely no meaning for me as an expression of human experience; over thirty years later these or other Books from Milton's epic are still being prescribed for Ordinary Level. And perhaps we should take a look also at the oddity of the situation in which 'English' at Advanced Level means exclusively a study of English Literature, a study moreover which is confined largely to a certain number of set books and in which creative or imaginative writing by the pupil finds no place whatever.

In all this the fallacy lies in seeing the mother tongue as an instrument, a tool external to the user, and not as an organic part of our human consciousness, the medium in which we have learnt to do our thinking and feeling and experiencing. The assumed dichotomy between 'practical and utilitarian' on the one hand, 'imaginative, creative and literary' on the other, is a false one, for if we observe children and observe ourselves we shall know that there is a constant interplay between the two functions within the one living personality. The 'literary and creative' modes of English feed the practical and the social, and we isolate the one from the other at our peril. Some encouragement can be taken from the fact that so far much of the planning for C.S.E. has stressed the unity of English as an examination subject. There must be an extension of this rethinking to G.C.E. Ordinary Level where the present unnatural and arbitrary division into Language and Literature is wholly indefensible; on this issue, unfortunately, *The Examining of English Language* has not had the courage to follow through the logic of its own argument. Advanced Level English, too, must not be seen merely as a preparation for an English Honours degree course at a university, but must represent a worthwhile educational goal for a wide range of sixth-form pupils; it should be an examination in English, not solely in English Literature, and should include opportunity for candidates to write imaginatively and creatively about life as well as about books. And if the universities insist on bringing into being a 'test in English' to provide an assurance that their entrants can use their mother-tongue effectively, they must be educated out of their short-sighted intention to restrict this to impersonal and expository forms of reading and writing.

In examining English we should, then, be trying to assess the pupil's ability to use his native language in an all-round way—this and nothing else. There can be no place for the linguistic parlour tricks which *The Examining of English Language* rightly condemns and which are given such a well-deserved trouncing in *The Excitement of Writing*; nor is there any room for tests of knowledge *about* the English language (except possibly at Advanced Level where there may arguably be a case for including some questions concerned with the study of the English language in the light of modern linguistic science). In general a justly conceived English examination will be confined to questions testing the candidate's power to express himself in English and to questions testing his ability to read English with understanding and sensitivity. To put it thus does not imply leaving literature out of account, but insists, rather, on giving it within our concept of 'English' the central place which rightly belongs to it, as the keystone which holds the arch together; what needs to be assessed, after all, is not knowledge *about* literature, but the power to read it and respond to it.

Of course, many examinations do already include an attempt to test reading capacity in the form of a short unseen passage with comprehension questions appended. It is hard to realise today that the introduction in the early 1930s of this kind of comprehension question into the School Certificate language paper seemed at the time to mark a real step forward, so rapidly did the innovation congeal into a standardised formula and so disastrous have been the back-wash effects upon teaching, as manifested by countless books of comprehension snippets thrown together with minimum thought and at minimum expense to provide examination practice for years beforehand. The stereotyping was enormously accelerated by the conditions of the mass examination, which favour, here as elsewhere, superficial questions (on the meaning of individual words or on trivial detail) which can quickly and confidently be marked right or wrong. It has been the outcome also of an unsound and over-narrow view of what is involved in reading. In the first place 'comprehension' has come to be thought of almost exclusively in terms of the *prose sense* of a passage, its informational or expository content, to the virtual neglect of those other aspects of meaning usefully classified by I. A. Richards under the headings of Feeling, Tone and Intention. This blinkering of vision reveals itself partly in the type of extract regularly chosen for the comprehension test, and partly in the examiners' predilection for the question which asks merely for some fact or idea to be restated in words different from those used by the writer. In the second place, reading has been regarded as no more than the adding-together of a series of discrete acts of word-recognition; as such it has seemed perfectly proper to test it by pulling out of the passage and holding up for inspection a number of items chosen almost at random (*Explain the meaning in its context of . . . Give the meaning in your own words of . . . Give a word or phrase of similar meaning to . . .*). Seldom has there been any awareness of the organic nature of the reading-process, as a building-up in the reader's mind of a related pattern of thoughts and perceptions; seldom has there been any attempt to clinch the questions on detailed points of meaning by a question which probes the extent to which the writer's over-all intention and purpose has gone home.

241

Once these misconceptions have been cleared out of the way, we shall find that it is by no means impossible to devise examination questions which test reading ability directly and in an acceptable way. As an example one might cite some (not all) of the questions set in recent years for the London G.C.E. Special Paper in Ordinary Level English Language on a syllabus originally submitted by the London Association for the Teaching of English; while among the papers (both Ordinary Level and even Use of English) set by certain other boards one can also detect evidence that a few of the more enlightened examiners have started to move in the same direction. To be judged satisfactory, the questions need to be based on an extract which is complete in itself, has genuine interest in its own right for the age-range undergoing the test, and possesses some real quality as a piece of writing. (No more shoddy journalism or vacuous belles-lettrism of the kind we associate with *The Times* fifth leader.) The questions themselves should arise out of the chosen extract, and should follow through the specific structure of idea and feeling which gives the passage its own coherence, its reason for 'being so and not otherwise'. In their wording and arrangement they should indeed actively *help* the examinee to reproduce in the examination room the movement of thought and response which the passage requires of the reader as he 'rethinks the ideas behind the printed page'. This means that they must eschew inessential detail or words chosen solely for their difficulty, and concentrate instead on 'the important elements of meaning in their essential relationship', culminating in one or more questions which sound out the reader's grasp of the central theme. In fact one might say that each passage, because unique in itself, should have a unique set of questions inherent in it. Finding these is a taxing, indeed a highly skilled, job; and I am afraid that *Examination Bulletin No. 1* ludicrously underestimates the complexity of what is called for when it naïvely suggests that candidates for C.S.E. should be asked to read a passage and then 'put down the main events, facts or ideas'.

In theory, of course, a question calling for a summary or précis of a passage ought to be capable of meeting our requirements; its whole *raison d'être* should be to test what Professor Gurrey has described as 'the power to grasp the essence of a speech or piece of writing, to note what is important and what unimportant, and to estimate the degree of relatedness to the central theme of the facts and ideas expressed' (Gurrey, 1954). In practice, as we know only too well, it seldom works that way. What is so stultifying about the conventional précis is the unvarying demand for the passage to be 'reduced to one-third of its original length'; the task is converted by this tradition to a mindless ritual in which word-counting takes the place of judgment. Some years ago one of my students returned from teaching-practice to report with bewilderment a comment made on a précis-lesson she had taken with a grammar school fifth form: 'Your lesson went off quite well,' the form's regular English teacher had said, 'but if I were you, I wouldn't pay quite so much attention to the meaning.' At the time I shared my student's baffled incredulity. Not long afterwards, however, I found myself in conversation with a Chief Examiner who was bewailing the difficulty of finding acceptable précis passages for his O Level English Language papers; apparently a long-standing local custom dictated not merely that two-thirds of the passage should consist of dispensable verbal padding, but also that each separate paragraph should be padded out in precisely the same proportion. On reflection, and after studying the past examination papers of his examining board, I could see that perhaps, after all, this grammar school English teacher had a point!

Nevertheless I would suggest that once these aimless examination routines have been safely buried we shall need to accept summarising as *one* of the alternatives whereby it is possible to test reading ability, provided that it is reserved for passages which really lend themselves to this approach.[1] Summarising should be demanded only when the extractable content of the passage is weighty enough to deserve extracting; since the point of the activity is to make judgments of relative importance, it is highly unreasonable to ask anyone to condense an argument which only an examiner would ever bother his head with. Ideally, summary-writing should be linked with some situation in which a digest of an argument might be needed for a specific purpose, thus providing the pupil with a guide-line which can help him to establish his criteria of importance. ('Your father is debating with himself whether to buy safety-belts for his motor-car. Write out as concisely as possible—for he is a busy man—the information in the following passage which would help him to make up his mind.') At the very least it should be conceivable that such a situation *could* exist in real life, even though no specific situation is indicated.

[1] For examples of suitable material, together with practical guidance for teacher and pupil, see my *Comprehension and Précis* (University Tutorial Press, 1956).

We must remember, though, that a question of this type cannot do more than test understanding of the Sense of a passage; inevitably, what is lost in the process of summarising is the Feeling and Tone of the original, since these are inextricably bound up with the writer's choice and arrangement of words. It is obvious that our tests of reading capacity need not and should not be confined to factual exposition or ratiocinative argument; they must be brought to bear also upon the non-intellectual use of language, including those which we call 'imaginative' and 'poetic'. It is encouraging that the question based on an unseen poem is now firmly established as part of A Level English, and has recently been introduced (hesitantly and in the face of fierce opposition) into some O Level papers as well. Here is one example from an Ordinary Level English Literature paper:

Read the following poem and answer the questions below it:

Winter: East Anglia

In a frosty sunset
   So fiery red with cold
The footballers' onset
   Rings out glad and bold;
Then boys from daily tether   5
   With famous dogs at heel
In starlight meet together
   And to farthest hedges steal;
Where the rats are pattering
   In and out the stacks,   10
Owls with hated chattering
   Swoop at the terriers' backs.
And, frost forgot, the chase grows hot
   Till a rat's a foolish prize,
But the cornered weasel stands his ground,   15
Shrieks at the dogs and boys set round,
Shrieks as he knows they stand all round,
   And hard as winter dies.

EDMUND BLUNDEN

(*a*) Refer to, and comment on, two details mentioned in the poem which emphasise the extreme cold of the scene depicted.

(*b*) What is meant by 'from daily tether' (l.5)?
In what way is this expression particularly appropriate here?
What is suggested by the use of the word 'steal' (l.8)?

(*c*) Explain the contrast drawn at the end of the poem between the rat

EXAMINATIONS AND TEACHING OF ENGLISH

and the weasel, and show by what means the poet conveys this contrast effectively.

(*d*) Point out and comment on two consecutive lines in the poem in which the sound of the word is important in helping to convey the poet's meaning.

(*e*) Do you think that the feeling conveyed by this poem as a whole is a cruel one? Give reasons for your answer.

There may be room for disagreement as to how far these questions succeed in their evident intention to sound out not only the reader's understanding but also his response to the nuances of feeling conveyed by imagery, rhythm, and 'the sound of the words'. Obviously it will never be easy in an examination question to treat a poem *as* a poem, and at the same time avoid offering an easy invitation to gush or waffle. I believe nevertheless that as experience accumulates of trying to frame such questions for sixteen-year-olds (both in G.C.E. and in C.S.E.) we shall find that the difficulties, though formidable, are not insuperable. Certainly it seems to me incontestible that in this kind of direct testing of the pupil's ability to read and respond on his own, independently of the teacher's guidance, lies the key to the examining of 'literature' at all levels.

There is no need to underline the contrast between this approach and that of the traditional examinations in English Literature. These, too, must have set out originally to assess pupils' ability to respond to poems, novels and plays; but, having abandoned as too difficult the attempt to do so directly, they now do it indirectly by testing 'knowledge' of a small number of set books. The procedure is based on an assumption that 'appreciation' of a work of literature and 'memory' of it go hand in hand. The assumption is often well-founded, but from time immemorial ways have been found of short-circuiting the process. In preparing for the 'set books' examination, as for the history examination, many teachers are convinced that the surest way to obtain good 'results' is to give out dictated notes – and, as a Chief Examiner once remarked in my hearing, 'I have examined some very competent teachers in my time.' This inherent flaw in the examining pattern is disastrously reinforced at Ordinary Level by the preoccupation with standardising which is characteristic of any mass examination. 'Facts' are what make standardising possible – 'facts' which the examiner's red pencil can tick without fear of disagreement; consequently memory for facts, even insignificant facts, takes on an absurd importance. Many questions ask for nothing else:

245

'Give an account of the wrestling scene in *As You Like It*'; 'Give the gist of Brutus' speech to the mob after Caesar's death'; 'Write an account of the great fire at Fishbourne'; 'To whom were these words spoken and under what circumstances?' Even if we discount the more extreme examples this kind of emphasis has a peculiarly unfortunate distorting influence upon teaching; it fosters a tendency to treat poems, novels and plays as though the valuable thing about them were their extractable content of event or argument—sometimes with the implication that it is important to remember quite small details. Yet after all the term 'facts' is a misnomer, since this is literature we are concerned with and not history; the *facts* which gain credit from the examiner are in reality *fictions* treated over-literally. What we observe in such an examination is indeed the creation of a unique class of mark-gaining item which we might call (borrowing a coinage from James Joyce) *ficts*. And how odd the results can be at times. 'Tell in your own words the story of Bottom and his friends'—as though anything but the alchemy of *Shakespeare's* words could have kept this particular story in circulation. 'What have you learnt from the play (i.e. *A Midsummer Night's Dream*) of the habits and characteristics of the fairies?'—a question which sounds as though it comes from an examination in natural (or should one say supernatural?) history. I can vouch for the authenticity of these two instances, though I do not claim that they are typical.

Even where *ficts* do not account for the whole of a question, they will certainly be allotted at Ordinary Level a high proportion (probably between two-thirds and three-quarters) of the marks; with the present rapidly increasing entry there are signs that in some Advanced Level papers, too, they have begun to loom increasingly large. The typical Ordinary Level question is made up of two parts—a body, asking for *ficts*, and worth 12 or 15 out of 20, followed by a smaller tail which calls for some kind of critical or personal comment. Since it is perfectly possible to pass (and even to gain a fairly high mark) by offering *ficts* alone, many candidates do not even attempt the 'tail'; about half of those who do make a very poor showing which scrapes up few if any extra marks for them. The 'tail' may ask merely for the expression of a personal reaction (. . . say which of the two poems makes the stronger appeal to you . . . which of the two characters you feel more sympathy with . . . how far these arguments [of Cassius] would convince you if you were Brutus); and at least there is implied here an expectation that the pupil's reading should have generated some sense of emotional involvement. More usually, some critical opinion about the writer's achievement will be either stated or implied, and the pupil asked to use his powers of inference, reasoning, and selecting evidence either to support or (in some cases) to disagree with it. Unfortunately only the small minority of exceptionally able Ordinary Level candidàtes are able to do this, under examination conditions, in terms which give the appearance· of being their own and not their teacher's. Can the examiners indeed have expected anything different? If they do, one wonders how much understanding of the sixteen-year-old mind can be credited to the examiner who, for instance, sets as an Ordinary Level question: ' "Justice is seldom done to the sheer beauty of Pope's poetry in *The Rape of the Lock*". Show, with quotation and reference, how far you think the poem contains beautiful poetry.'

As this last-quoted example may suggest, the difficulty of devising questions which test anything more than memory for *ficts* is closely bound up with the choice of set books. At present the texts prescribed at Ordinary Level fall into two rather disparate categories. On the one hand there are the established classics—Shakespeare, Sheridan, Jane Austen, Dickens, George Eliot, Hardy, Conrad. If we discount the occasional inert survival from the taste of a few decades ago (Drinkwater's *Abraham Lincoln*, for instance), these have genuine merits as works of literature; they are serious and complex enough to repay close study and repeated rereading. But even though they do not include their authors' greatest masterpieces (we shall find that, quite rightly, *Julius Caesar* is chosen and not *King Lear*, *Silas Marner* and not *Middlemarch*, *Typhoon* and not *Nostromo*), it remains true that the qualities we value in them are to the sixteen-year-old both adult and difficult; he can get near to appreciating them only by following and sharing the response of a teacher who acts as intermediary and guide. As a result his attempts to put this appreciation into words are necessarily fumbling, uncertain and lacking in confidence. In the second category of set book, on the other hand, we find contemporary fiction or autobiography which makes a strong appeal to the average sixteen-year-old; titles prescribed in recent years have included Grimble's *A Pattern of Islands*, Golding's *Lord of the Flies*, Forester's *The Ship* and *The Gun*, Orwell's *Animal Farm*, Churchill's *My Early Life*, Street's *Farmer's Glory*, Laurens Van der Post's *Venture to the Interior*. Enjoyable though they may be at the fifth-former's own level, such books have the disadvantages which often go with easy popularity; at best they are worthy but slightly second-rate, at worst they hardly amount to more than effective journalism. Certainly the average fifth-former would benefit from reading some of them—and it has to be admitted that, given the existing pressures on his time, he probably won't do so unless it is an examination requirement. But does it make sense when, say, *The Ship* forms one of the three books which make up a year's course, to be read at least three times, repeatedly written about, and solemnly committed to memory?

Some teachers, I know, have seen the set book system itself as the main enemy, particularly when the number of books required is small. In flight from the present pointless memorisation of *ficts*, they have suggested a syllabus which expects and encourages wide reading within a large, or even unlimited, list of authors and books; the questions the pupils have to answer would then be very general in form (variants on the formula: 'What have you found to enjoy in . . . ?') so that they could apply to a wide range of individual books, poems or plays. This solution has been tried out as an Alternative O Level English Literature paper by some examining bodies (though with rather few takers, I understand); it has also been widely canvassed as part of the preparatory thinking for C.S.E. The danger here is that, at any rate under the conditions of marking which prevail in any mass examination, the highest rewards will go to fluent reproduction of *standardised opinions*, so that more than ever the way is laid open for the 'prepared answer'. Such a paper is, in fact, highly vulnerable to the classic objection often voiced against *all* examinations in literature: namely that they set a premium on hypocrisy and encourage pupils to repeat 'mechanically and without reflection other people's judgments' (Huxley, 1936).

The dilemma can be resolved only by keeping clearly in mind what it is we are trying to test. As far as reading ability is concerned, we need a three-pronged approach. Any sound examination in English, at whatever level, must include first a test of the candidate's reading capacity, as measured by his unaided ability to read and respond to an unseen prose passage *and* an unseen poem. The only major limitation of such a test is that an unseen has to be short; it cannot assess the reader's staying-power, and if it were the only element in the examination it might induce teachers to concentrate unduly upon short poems and (even worse) short prose extracts. It must therefore be supplemented by some test of the candidate's ability to read a full-length work, a novel or play whose extended internal structure makes prolonged demands on the reader's attention and on his ability to hold in mind elements of meaning which though dispersed over the length of the book are nevertheless interlinked within the total pattern. There is a place here for the 'set book' so long as we insist that *the pupil must have a copy of the text beside him in the examination room when he comes to answer questions upon it*. After all, no reputable literary critic or reviewer would ever dream of committing his views to paper without having a copy of the text at hand to refer to and quote from. These are the normal rational conditions for writing about literature—*except* when writing for an examiner. To reproduce these conditions as nearly as we can is surely the only effective way, in a set-book examination, of taking the emphasis away from memorisation on to that relevant kind of familiarity with the book which makes it possible to turn up the evidence needed to support a statement or opinion. True, to avoid unfair advantage being taken, the examination-room copies would need to be clean ones, free from pencilled-in marginalia; the administrative difficulties of ensuring this should not be insuperable, unless for an examining body whose gigantism has lost for it all effective contact with its schools. And in any case the purpose of this part of the examination would be achieved by requiring answers on only a very small number of books. For C.S.E. and for Ordinary Level G.C.E. I suggest that one, or at most two, would be enough. For Ordinary Level the obvious choice would be a Shakespeare play (*Julius Caesar*, *Macbeth*, or *Twelfth Night*) supplemented possibly by a prose work of the calibre of *Pride and Prejudice*, *Great Expectations*, *Huckleberry Finn* or *Lark Rise*. At Advanced Level no more than three or four would be needed; a major Shakespeare tragedy, a long poem or a volume of poems (*The Pardoner's Tale*, *Comus*, *Lyrical Ballads*, Keats' 1820 volume or the poems of Gerald Manley Hopkins) together with a novel such as *Emma*, *Hard Times*, *The Secret Agent* or *A Passage to India*. For having thus safeguarded our assessment of the pupil's power of *intensive* reading, we must include as the third section of our examination some questions of a more general kind which will both test and encourage *width* of reading. It is true that questions of this kind (as already noted) carry with them some risk of encouraging the 'prepared answer'. Nevertheless so important at all stages is wide reading—and so shamefully is it neglected or even discouraged

I*

by the existing examinations—that I believe this risk has to be accepted in one portion of the examination. (It could probably be kept within reasonable bounds by a deliberate, and deliberately announced, policy of varying the type of question from year to year.) I should perhaps add that the books written about in this section of the examination would not necessarily be confined to *English* literature, nor indeed to that which could properly be called 'literature' according to the strict canon. Thus *The Kon-Tiki Expedition* or *The Diary of Anne Frank* would be perfectly acceptable for C.S.E. or for Ordinary Level; while at Advanced Level room would be made for translations of, say, *The Odyssey*, *Anna Karenina*, *The Cherry Orchard* or *Madame Bovary*.

It should be noted that the blueprint we have sketched out so far for our ideal examination in English would be perfectly feasible *either* as an external examination *or* as an internal examination with external moderation. If it were operated as an internal examination, the teacher would have more opportunity of using to the full his own knowledge of pupils in choosing books both for intensive and for extensive reading. On the other hand, it could be argued that since it is so inordinately difficult to set really satisfactory questions upon an unseen passage or an unseen poem, this part of the task would be better handed over to the presumed expertise of an external examiner.

When we turn, however, from the testing of reading to the next major area of our problem, that is, to the testing of writing, we find that the objections to the external method of examining come in at a more fundamental level. What has to be assessed here is the pupil's 'ability to express ideas and feelings' (*Examinations Bulletin No. 1*). But if we are to grasp the reality and not the shadow, these ideas and feelings must be his own—something he cares about and feels involved in. Is such involvement compatible with an external examination? As *The Examining of English Language* reports of Ordinary Level: '. . . many schools complain that the [composition] subjects chosen fail to connect with the candidates' studies or field of interest and the subjects are such that candidates too often have to give evidence of an artificial inventiveness rather than power to use language in the discussion of a subject of interest to them'. Surely this is almost inevitable. Each pupil is an individual, every classroomful of pupils is unique; a mass examination cannot hope to cater for their idiosyncrasies of interest and preoccupation.

If we fight shy of internal examining in this aspect of English, it must be because the marking of compositions is notoriously the most unreliable of all marking. Repeatedly it has been shown that even experienced markers fail to agree among themselves – and that all too often indeed the same marker doesn't agree with himself if he re-marks the same batch of compositions a few months later. For this reason, external examinations in English have, by long tradition, preferred to concentrate, in their methods of marking, upon the areas of minimum disagreement – in other words, upon spelling, punctuation, syntax, and paragraphing. The most common procedure is to use an analytic marking scheme, a fairly typical example of which would sub-divide a maximum mark of 40 into 15 for 'ideas', 15 for 'paragraphing, vocabulary, and sentence structure', and 10 for 'mechanical correctness' (the latter operated by providing a list of penalisable errors each of which leads to a deduction of half a mark every time it is perpetrated). The one thing that can be guaranteed is that, as with almost all analytic marking schemes,[1] the examiner's judgment of the value and interest of what is said will play only a minor part in the total assessment. (A similar dis-balance may sometimes be arrived at by a different route. One examining body using a non-analytic method of marking allocates a theoretical maximum of 50 for the essay, but instructs its examiners to mark within a narrow band so that virtually all the marks are clustered within the range between 25 and 30; meanwhile the effective sorting-out of candidates is accomplished by the 'short questions' where the marks occupy the full range from 0 to 15.) The freakish anomalies which may result from this are a matter of common experience.

Presumably few would contest that what really matters is the ability to write something that is worth reading. What we are up against is a readiness to give precedence to reliability of assessment (albeit spurious) even when it conflicts with a valid and widely accepted educational goal. The situation is closely analogous with that which prevailed for many years in eleven-plus selection, where tests of continuous writing' were replaced by 'objective English tests' on the grounds that these were more reliable and that the same

---

[1] e.g. Cast (1939 and 1940) who recommended sub-dividing a maximum mark of 25 as follows: 12 for content (thought and use of words), 7 for structure (accuracy and variety of sentence) and 6 for mechanics (grammatical accuracy and spelling). Steel and Talman (1936) went even further than this; holding explicitly that 'thought content' cannot be reliably assessed, they recommended a method of marking based exclusively on (*a*) vocabulary, (*b*) sentence linkings and (*c*) sentence structure.

children would do well in either. This ignored entirely the deplorable back-wash effect upon teaching, as a result of which many junior schools abandoned continuous writing altogether, and instead kept their pupils busy underlining words and filling-in blanks in practice tests. All justification for this state of affairs in the eleven-plus was long ago removed by Wiseman's experimental study of multiple marking. Professor Wiseman's starting-point [Wiseman (1949)] was a recognition of the fact that in assessing compositions individual markers differ from each other in their judgments. He was able, however, to find some experienced markers who showed a fairly high degree of *self*-consistency — enough to suggest that each had his own individual standard of judgment and was capable of sticking to it. Wiseman made the assumption, therefore, that in each case this standard was meaningful and did reflect qualities actually present in the pieces of writing assessed. Among the self-consistent markers if A differed from B this would presumably be because A attached more importance to certain qualities (say, choice of the right word, vividness, and liveliness) while B attached more weight in his own mind to other qualities (perhaps orderly organisation of ideas, or correctness and variety of sentence structure). In the experiments reported by Wiseman the eleven-plus compositions were marked rapidly (fifty to sixty per hour) by four independent self-consistent examiners; each examiner awarded each composition a mark out of 20, and the final mark was the aggregate obtained by adding the four marks together. By thus pooling a diversity of viewpoint the individual bias of each examiner was cancelled out, and it was found that as few as four examiners produced an aggregate mark that was highly reliable (a mark/re-mark correlation greater than .90).

This system has been used for a number of years in some eleven-plus selection examinations. In addition to the improvement in reliability its great advantage is that it builds on and uses the subjective element in assessment instead of ignoring or subordinating it. From the point of view of the English teacher it can therefore be expected to yield not only more reliable but also more valid results than other methods — in the sense of measuring the ability that it is relevant to measure. Why on earth then has this method not been tried out long ago in secondary school examinations? One can account for this only by the inertia and innate conservatism of the examining bodies, reinforced perhaps by their unwillingness to admit that there is anything the matter with present examining methods.

Britton (1963) has reported highly encouraging results in applying a variant of Wiseman's method to the marking of compositions written by fifteen-year-old secondary modern school pupils in a local school-leaving examination.[1] Yet even now the S.S.E.C. has done no more than recommend (and persuade the Ministry of Education to finance) further research 'upon a similar method of marking at Ordinary Level in the G.C.E.' 'We shall think further on't,' says officialdom. Surely it is time for teachers to reply, 'We must do something, and i' th'heat.'

But although the Wiseman procedure should prove a satisfactory way of dealing with the inconsistency of the marker, it will not, of course, do away with the inconsistency of the pupil. There can be little doubt that in the quality of their writing performance many pupils vary enormously from one topic to the next. Finlayson's study (1951) of eleven-plus marking showed somewhat greater discrepancies between performances on different topics than between different markings of the same topic; and Vernon and Millican (1954) working with essays by training college students found that, while the variations between the rank-orders of different markers were 'serious enough', the variations between topics were greater still. If the extent of this variability sometimes passes unnoticed by the class-teacher in the secondary school, this can only be due to the 'halo effect'

---

[1] One rather disturbing defect in Britton's experiment deserves comment. Whereas Wiseman pooled *four* independent marks each of which represented the examiner's 'impression of the whole performance', Britton's *three* 'general impression' marks represented assessments in which the marker had been instructed to leave out of account 'errors in spelling, punctuation and grammar, and "slips of the pen" '; he then added a fourth mark for 'mechanical accuracy'. This arbitrary modification in the direction of 'analytic' marking seems highly dubious on practical grounds alone, since it is unlikely that anyone can prevent his 'general impression' from being influenced in some degree by handwriting, spelling, errors, and blots. Nor is the theoretical justification any more convincing. Britton seems to have been influenced by a fear that Wiseman's method, unmodified, would not sufficiently take into account the 'attainment in teachable skills' which he considers more important at fifteen-plus than at eleven-plus. The fear does not seem to be warranted. Any teacher experienced enough to be a self-consistent marker would surely include in his 'general impression' mark such allowance for 'mechanical skills' as he judged appropriate to the age-level; the undoubted fact that teachers differ in their estimates of how much weighting should be given to this forms part of the rationale of Wiseman's procedure. It is not, in any case, true that (as Britton mistakenly states) 'Wiseman's method takes account . . . [of the fact that] . . . at eleven-plus a candidate's educational potential is more important than his mastery of the mechanics of writing'. The only point at which this consideration enters at all into the work reported by Wiseman is in the instructions to markers, which reasonably enough stress that what the marker is asked to do is 'to assess on evidence afforded by the composition the ability of the candidate to profit by a secondary education'. Any uneasiness felt about transferring the Wiseman method direct to the work of fifteen- or sixteen-year-old pupils should, in my view, be met by rewording these instructions, not by tinkering with the design of the method in a way which may impair its rational basis.

which results from prolonged familiarity with one's own pupils. Vernon and Millican, however, found that by combining a number of essays on different topics (seven in the case of the training-college students) it was possible to obtain a fairly consistent measure of an individual's writing-ability; thus there seems to be a strong case for including some course work as part of any assessment in English, so that writing ability may be judged on several pieces of writing done on different occasions.

Some C.S.E. boards have announced their intention of doing this. Otherwise, the farthest the examining bodies have been prepared to go is to demand two short pieces of writing on different types of subject, instead of one longer piece. If it is combined with some form of multiple marking, this may be expected to give a modest but useful increase in reliability, together with some gain in validity [Finlayson (1951); Oliver (1963)]. The snag is the price that has to be paid in back-wash effect—an emphasis in teaching upon the short-winded composition written at such speed that the writer has no time to get himself really involved. Ideally, what seems to be needed is an internally-set examination essay with external multiple-marking, *combined with* a mark for a fixed amount of course-work which would be marked internally, but subject to external moderation for standardising purposes. The first mark would be vulnerable to pupil-inconsistency, and the second to marker-inconsistency; but it is probable that the combination of the two would give as reliable and valid a measure as we can hope for without bringing in educationally objectionable back-wash effects. The procedure would, however, be cumbersome administratively, and probably rather more expensive. Here again the issue that has to be resolved is the conflict between predictive purposes and educational influence. Just how much reliability do we genuinely need in our examinations (at C.S.E., Ordinary, and university-entrance levels), and how far are we prepared to sacrifice our educational values in the pursuit of it?[1]

Finally a few words about the third area of English which has to be taken into account—that of speaking and listening. Here there is regrettably little that we can draw on in the way of practical examining

[1] The reality and seriousness of this conflict still needs to be hammered home over and over again; witness the following piece of myopic self-delusion from the pen of an influential Professor of Education: 'An examination is not a teaching syllabus or a textbook. Skill in the use of English may perhaps [*sic*] be best acquired by reading and writing and by discussing what is read and written; that is for the teacher to decide. The examiner's task is to examine, not to teach, and an examination is to be judged as a device for assessing the abilities and achievements of candidates.' [Oliver (1963).]

experience, or, for that matter, of experimental research. What can be said is that so long as we have examinations in English which leave out oral English entirely, the tendency to undervalue or neglect it in teaching will continue. Yet the attempt to bring it within the orbit of examining is full of difficulties. In the first place, there is little agreement as to what we mean by 'good spoken English'; until we have sorted out our confusions about dialect, received pronunciation, 'lazy speech' and 'elocution', there is a real danger that assessments of pupils' use of the spoken word will be not just unreliable but *wildly* unreliable. Secondly, there is even a lack of agreement as to the nature of the speech activities which ought to be assessed. Some existing or projected 'oral tests' do no more than require the candidate to read aloud a piece of *written* English (prose or poetry) and then take part in a question-and-answer conversation with the examiner about it—a perpetuation of the time-honoured 'foreign language oral' which is wholly inadequate for mother-tongue. The problem here is that in real life every use of the spoken word is very closely tied to a specific situation; consequently the appropriate criteria of effectiveness vary enormously according to the speaker's purposes and the nature of his audience. In an examination all one can do is to reproduce a few of the more regularly-recurring *types* of situation and hope that they will dredge up a moderately representative sample of the candidate's over-all capacities. But the choice of these situation-types can, at present, only be arbitrary. We may guess that it would be better to avoid on the one hand the artificialities of public speaking to a large audience and on the other an unrealistic confrontation with a single unknown examiner (where in any case the assessment will depend far too much on the degree of rapport between the two personalities). Our conclusion may indeed be that the most desirable audience would be a small group (between ten and thirty) of 'sympathetic listeners of a similar age, preferably fellow-candidates', if only because this comes nearest to reproducing the class-room situation in which oral English has to take place within the school.

Burniston (1962) has in fact suggested for C.S.E. a scheme based upon this premise which sounds a reasonable starting-point. Her draft falls into four sections:

I. A 'Personal Project' in which the candidate gives a prepared three-minute talk on 'some particular aspect of a school subject or hobby'.

II. Impromptu questions and discussion stemming from the talk.

III. The presentation of a short poem, passage of prose, or drama (not more than two minutes). Alternatively this may be a group item.

IV. The reading-aloud from a previously-read book of a paragraph chosen on the spot by the examiner.

One element in this which seems particularly to deserve extended trial is the idea of a group item involving dramatisation of, say, a ballad or a scene from a play. It is true that it might prove difficult to assess fairly the contribution of the individual to the group effort, but the wider considerations involved would make it worth while to persevere with this. The present written mode of examining gives an insistently non-dramatic stress to the study of Shakespeare and other playwrights; if the fifth or sixth form do find themselves acting a play this is because of their teacher's personal convictions and not because of the requirements of the examination. Some examiners do try at times to treat the material in dramatic terms, with questions which ask for discussion of how a scene might be produced, what advice the producer might give to an actor, or which elements would be particularly effective on the stage. But candidates always find such issues difficult to write about. Understandably, since it is only in the attempt to act that they really come alive.

It will clearly take a great deal of experience and experiment before we can tell whether Burniston's selection of speech-activities meets our educational need, and can at the same time be assessed with reasonable consistency. It does, however, have the merit of requiring and encouraging activities which are normal in the good school and desirable in all schools. And this, I am convinced, should be the overriding consideration. If reliability of assessment were all that concerned us, we could more readily go along with the approach which tries to break down the total activity (the two-way process of oral communication between speaker and audience) into its component parts, and then test these separately. There is, for instance, interesting work in progress [Atkinson, Davies & Wilkinson (1964)] on the construction of a battery of tests of listening comprehension, to consist of passages of speech recorded on tape and followed by multiple-choice questions. But my heart sinks at the thought of what would surely follow if such a battery became an established part of the C.S.E. — regular weekly practice periods in listening comprehension with the aid of commercially-produced tapes or gramophone records. The testing of spoken English must be holistic in approach if its inescapable influence on schools is to be beneficial instead of harmful; and it is (I repeat) the nature and direction of this influence that ought, more than anything else, to guide our decisions. Since there is such a wide range of speech-situations in which the pupil's capacities might be judged, it may turn out that the only satisfactory solution is to use continuous assessment by the class-teacher, supplemented by some kind of external moderation to bring standards sufficiently into line. This moderation might take the form of an annual visit by an examiner who would apply to a small sample of pupils the kind of test outlined by Burniston; it is difficult to see anyway how one could ever assemble a competent team of examiners with enough free time to test more than a fraction of the total number of entrants.

In these suggestions towards an acceptable way of examining English at all levels, I have tried to keep in mind both the ideal situation (internal examinations with external moderation) and the existing situation (external examinations over which the practising teacher has little effective control). It would be unrealistic not to recognise that for years to come external examinations are going to be forced upon many English teachers who would prefer to be freed from them, and I must therefore end by stressing how important it is to use every possible means of improving these examinations, even if only as an interim measure. Even the most mammoth of examining bodies can be influenced eventually by the demands of teachers, so long as the pressure is consistently applied. For G.C.E. there exists machinery (provided by the N.U.T. and the Joint Four) for making teachers' views known, but it is used only for complaints, and often seems most zealous in relaying complaints which are trivial or unintelligent. Enlightened teachers should use this machinery to the full, but they should also exercise their prerogative of writing direct to the board whose services they employ whenever they feel strongly about a syllabus, an examination paper, or an examination question. Nor should they write only at times when they need to complain. We all know that for children the most effective stimulus to improvement is not reproof for wrongdoing but commendation for doing right. Perhaps we should try a similar tactic with examining bodies — encouraging them whenever they choose a good prescribed book, a good unseen passage, or set a good question. I believe it might work.

Chapter 8

POSTSCRIPT

I HAVE confined myself in this book to the teaching of English under the conditions actually prevailing in the overwhelming majority of secondary schools in Great Britain today. Consequently, when I illustrate a teaching principle by referring to some practical example, this normally assumes the existence of a class of between thirty and forty children whose time-table sets aside each week for English some five to eight teaching-periods of thirty-five to forty minutes' duration. Though they are a fact of life which we are bound for the present to accept, these conditions are not ideal, nor are they immutable. Indeed, some of the directions in which they ought to be changed, and perhaps will be changed during the next few decades, are implicit in the argument of the preceding chapters.

Thus we have seen that good English teaching leads constantly outside itself. The effort to improve our talking and writing impels us continually to find out more about the subject-matter of our discourse; the quest for 'the right word' can never stop short at the level of words only, nor can we begin to judge whether an argument is 'well-expressed' until we know whether it is accurate, sound and true. The reading of literature involves us inevitably in wide-ranging questions of human conduct and values. The study of newspapers and advertisements cannot be isolated from discussion of cinema, television and popular music, or from a consideration of the social environment which has given us the mass media in the form we know them today. In short, the inner logic of English teaching itself seems likely to call increasingly for a breaking-down of the barriers which have grown up between English and other subjects—and between English and life. Reform may come about piecemeal through informal and *ad hoc* collaboration between the English teacher and individual subject specialists (the music teacher, the art teacher, the historian, the scientist, the teacher of rural studies or housecraft or social studies); or it may develop in a more planned way, in the form of project-work or team-teaching which deliberately cuts across the traditional subject-boundaries. The only danger in all this is that eventually, in losing its separate identity, English might lose also some of its indispensable intrinsic qualities.

Let me insist, therefore, that in any scheme for integrated teaching or unified learning the English activities I have been describing will have a necessary and vital place. Moreover the teaching principles I have tried to set forth will still apply, and must never be lost sight of. The fact is that English has for the English its own essential values; properly taught it imposes its own inherent discipline upon the mind and feelings. In this sense it remains true that 'English must be kept up'.

BIBLIOGRAPHY

List of Books and Articles referred to in the text

Abrams, M. H. (1953) *The Mirror and the Lamp: Romantic Theory and Critical Tradition.* New York: O.U.P.

Abrams, M. (1961) 'The Social Effects of Television', *Progress*, 48, 163–166.

Anderson, J. E. (1939) 'Child Development and the Growth Process' in *Child Development and the Curriculum*, The 38th Yearbook of the National Society for the Study of Education. Bloomington, Illinois.

Andrews, R. G. H. (1958) 'Newspaper Reading in the Secondary Modern School', *The Use of English*, IX, 190–192.

Angell, N. (1933) *The Press and the Organisation of Society.* Cambridge: The Minority Press.

Arnstein, F. (1946) *Adventure into Poetry.* Stanford University Press.

Atkinson, D., Davies, A., and Wilkinson, A. (1964) 'The Testing of Listening Comprehension for C.S.E.' *The Use of English*, XIV, 10–12.

Bantock, G. H. (1962) *Education in an Industrial Society.* Faber.

Biaggini, E. G. (1933) *English in Australia.* O.U.P.

Black, E. L., and Schofield, A. (1958) 'What do Girls Read?', *The Times Educational Supplement*, 586.

Breckenridge, M. E., and Vincent, E. L. (1960) *Child Development* (4th Edition). Philadelphia: The W. B. Saunders Co.

Britton, J. (1963), 'Experimental Marking of English Compositions written by Fifteen-Year-Olds', *Educational Review*, 16, 17–23.

Burniston, C. (1962) *What is Spoken English? Can it be examined in general education?* Liverpool: The English Speaking Board.

Burton, E. J. (1955) *Drama in Schools.* Jenkins.

Buswell, G. T. (1937) *How Adults Read.* University of Chicago Press.

Butts, D. (1963) 'What They Read and Why', *The Use of English*, XV, 87–90.

Cast, B. M. P. (1939–40) 'The Efficiency of Different Methods of Marking English Composition', *Brit.J.Educ.Psych.*, IX, 256–9, and X, 49–60.

Dewey, J. (1897) 'My Pedagogic Creed', reprinted in Dewey, J., ed. J. Ratner, *Education To-day*, London, 1941.

Druce, R. (1965), *The Eye of Innocence.* Brockhampton Press.

Finlayson, D. C. (1951) 'The Reliability of Marking Essays', *Brit.J.Educ. Psych.*, XXI, 126–134.

BIBLIOGRAPHY

Firth, J. R. (1957) 'Personality and Language in Society' in *Papers in Linguistics, 1934–1951*. O.U.P.

Ford, B. (ed.) (1960) *Young Writers, Young Readers.* Hutchinson.

Freyberg, P. S. (1964) 'A Comparision of Two Approaches to the Teaching of Spelling', *Brit.J.Educ.Psych.*, XXXIV, 178–186.

Friedlaender, K. (1942) 'Children's Books and Their Function in Latency and Prepuberty', *American Imago*, 3.

Fries, C. C. (1952) *The Structure of English*. Longmans.

Garrard, J., and Wiles, A. (1957) *Leap to Life!* Chatto & Windus.

Gilbert, L. C. (1935) 'A Study of the Effect of Reading on Spelling', *J.Educ.Research*, 28, 570–6.

Gordon, I. A. (1947) *The Teaching of English*. New Zealand Council for Educational Research.

Gray, W. S. (1956), *The Teaching of Reading and Writing*. Unesco and Evans Bros.

Gurrey, P. (1954), *The Teaching of Written English*. Longmans.

Gurrey, P. (1958) *Teaching the Mother Tongue in Secondary Schools*. Longmans.

Hall, R. A. (1950) *Linguistics and Your Language*. New York: Anchor Books.

Hall, S., and Whannel, P. (1964) *The Popular Arts*. Hutchinson.

Harris, R. J. (1962) *An Experimental Inquiry into the Functions and Value of Formal Grammar in the Teaching of English*. Unpublished Ph.D. thesis, University of London.

Harris, R. J. (1965) 'The Only Disturbing Feature', *The Use of English*, XVI, 197–202.

Hartley, R. E., Frank, L. K., and Goldenson, R. M. (1952) *Understanding Children's Play*. Routledge & Kegan Paul.

Hildreth, G. (1955) *Teaching Spelling*. New York: Holt.

Hill, A. A. (1958) *Introduction to Linguistic Structures*. New York: Harcourt, Brace & World.

Hobbs, B. M. (1956) 'Marking Composition', *The Use of English*, VII, 260–3.

Holbrook, D. (1961) *English for Maturity*. C.U.P.

Huxley, A. (1927) *Proper Studies*. Chatto & Windus.

Huxley, A. (1936) *The Olive Tree*. Chatto & Windus.

Isaacs, S. (1935) 'The Psychological Aspects of Child Development', *The Yearbook of Education for 1935*. Evans Bros.

BIBLIOGRAPHY

Jenkinson, A. J. (1940) *What do Boys and Girls Read?* Methuen.

Jordan, A. M. (1926) *Children's Interests in Reading.* University of North Carolina.

Kangley, L. (1938) *Poetry Preferences in the Junior High School.* New York: Teachers' College, Columbia University.

Kelly, M. (1948) *Group Playmaking.* Harrap.

Klein, M. (1960) *Our Adult World and its Roots in Infancy.* Tavistock Publications.

Knights, L. C. (1933) 'Scrutiny of Examinations', *Scrutiny,* II, 137–163.

Lawrence, E. (1964) 'Children's Tastes in Reading', *National Froebel Foundation Bulletin,* 147, 2–11.

Lazar, M. (1937) *Reading Interests, Activities and Opportunities of Bright, Average and Dull Children.* New York: Teachers' College, Columbia University.

Leavis, F. R. (1943) *Education and the University.* Chatto & Windus.

Leavis, F. R., and Thompson, D. (1933) *Culture and Environment.* Chatto and Windus.

Lewis, M. M. (1957) *How Children Learn to Speak.* Harrap.

Lewis, M. M. (1963) *Language, Thought and Personality in Infancy and Childhood.* Harrap.

Lowenfeld, M. (1935) *Play in Childhood.* Gollancz.

Luria, A. R., and Yudovich, F. Ia. (1959) *Speech and the Development of Mental Processes in the Child.* (Russian publication 1956, English translation 1959.) Staples.

Macauley, W. J. (1947) 'The Difficulty of Grammar', *Brit. J. Educ. Psych.,* XVII, 3.

Malinowski, B. (1923) 'The Problem of Meaning in Primitive Languages', in *The Meaning of Meaning,* by C. K. Ogden and I. A. Richards. Routledge & Kegan Paul.

Malinowski, B. (1934) *Coral Gardens and their Magic.* Routledge & Kegan Paul.

Mayhew, C. (1952) *Dear Viewer.* Lincolns-Prager.

Methold, K. (1959) *Broadcasting with Children.* U.L.P.

Morris, R. (1963) *Success and Failure in Learning to Read.* Oldbourne.

N.S.S.E. (1925) *The Teaching of Reading* (24th Yearbook of the National Society for the Study of Education, Part I.) Bloomington, Illinois.

N.S.S.E. (1937) *The Teaching of Reading: A Second Report.* 36th Yearbook of the National Society for the Study of Education, Part I.) Bloomington, Illinois.

BIBLIOGRAPHY

Oliver, R. A. C. (1963) *An Experimental Test in English*. Manchester: Joint Matriculation Board.

Patterson, A. C. (1961) 'A Review of Research in Spelling' in *Studies in Spelling*. Scottish Council for Research in Education.

Percival, A. (1963) 'Leisure Reading by Modern School Children'. *National Froebel Foundation Bulletin*, 143, 1–10.

Rankin, M. (1944) *Children's Interests in Library Books of Fiction*. New York: Teachers' College, Columbia University.

Reeves, J. (1958) *Teaching Poetry*. Heinemann.

Richards, I. A. (1929) *Practical Criticism*. Routledge & Kegan Paul.

Roberts, P. (1956) *The Patterns of English*. New York: Harcourt, Brace and World.

Robertson, S., and Cassidy, F. G. (1954) *The Development of Modern English* (2nd edition). New York: Prentice Hall.

Robins, R. H. (1951) *Ancient and Medieval Grammatical Theory in Europe*. Bell.

Sampson, G. (1921) *English for the English*. C.U.P.

Sapir, E. (1921) *Language*. Hart Davis.

Schonell, F. J. (1932) *Essentials in Teaching and Testing Spelling*. Macmillan.

Schonell, F. J. (1936) 'Ability and Disability in Spelling Amongst Educated Adults', *Brit.J.Educ.Psych.*, VI, 123–144.

Schonell, F. J. (1948) *Backwardness in the Basic Subjects*. Oliver & Boyd.

Scott, W. J. (1947) *The Reading, Film and Radio Tastes of High School Boys and Girls*. New Zealand Council for Educational Research.

Secondary Schools Examinations Council (1964) *The Examining of English Language*. H.M.S.O.

Slade, P. (1958) *An Introduction to Child Drama*. U.L.P.

Smith, M. K. (1941) 'Measurement of the Size of General English Vocabulary through the Elementary Grades and High School', *Genetic Psychology Monographs*, 24, 311–345.

Smith, H. L. (1956) *Linguistic Science and the Teaching of English*. Harvard University Press.

Steel, J. H., and Talman, J. (1936) *The Marking of English Composition*. Nisbet.

Stewart, M. (1960) *The Leisure Activities of School Children*. W.E.A.

Stott, C. A. (1947) *School Libraries*. C.U.P.

Strang, B. (1962) *Modern English Structure*. Arnold.

Sweet, H. (1891) *A New English Grammar*. O.U.P.

Tanner, J. M., and Inhelder, B. (1956a) *Discussions on Child Development.* Vol. I. Tavistock Publications.

Tanner, J. M., and Inhelder, B. (1956b) *Discussions on Child Development.* Vol. II. Tavistock Publications.

Tanner, J. M., and Inhelder, B. (1958) *Discussions on Child Development.* Vol. III. Tavistock Publications.

Tanner, J. M., and Inhelder, B. (1960) *Discussions on Child Development.* Vol. IV. Tavistock Publications.

Templin, M. C. (1957) *Certain Language Skills in Children: Their Development and Interrelationships.* University of Minnesota Press.

Terman, L. M., and Lima, M. (1925) *Children's Reading.* New York: Appleton.

Thompson, D. (1939) *Between the Lines.* Muller.

Thompson, D. (1943) *The Voice of Civilisation.* Muller.

Thompson, D. (ed.) (1965) *Discrimination and Popular Culture.* Penguin Books.

Vernon, P. E., and Millican, G. D. (1954) 'A Further Study of the Reliability of English Essays', *Brit.J.Stat.Psych.*, VII, 65–74.

Walder, R. (1933) 'The Psycho-analytic Study of Play', *Psycho-analytic Quarterly*, II, 208–224.

Walsh, J. H. (1965) *Teaching English.* Heinemann.

Washburne, C., and Vogel, M. (1926) *Winnetka Graded Book-List.* Chicago: American Library Association.

Weekes, B. (1929) *The Influence of Meaning on Children's Choices of Poetry.* New York: Teachers' College, Columbia University.

White, D. N. (1949) *About Books for Children.* O.U.P.

Whitehead, A. N. (1932) *The Aims of Education.* Williams & Norgate.

Whitehead, F. (1956) 'The Attitudes of Grammar School Pupils Towards Some Novels Commonly Read in School', *Brit.J.Educ.Psych.*, XXVI, 104–111.

Wilkinson, A. M. (1956) 'The Press and the School', *The Use of English*, VII, 167–171.

Wilkinson, A. M. (1964) 'Research on Formal Grammar', *N.A.T.E. Bulletin*, I, 24–26.

Williams, R. (1962) *Britain in the Sixties: Communications.* Penguin Books.

Wiseman, S. (1949) 'The Marking of English Compositions in Grammar School Selection', *Brit.J.Educ.Psych.*, XIX, 200–209.

INDEX

INDEX

Lowenfeld, M., 124n, 262
Luria, A. R., 13, 262

Macauley, W. J., 219–220, 262
Mailer, Norman, 174, 181n
Malamud, Bernard, 152
Malinowski, B., 158, 162, 262
Maturation, 17–19, 155–156, 173
Methold, K., 172, 262
Mill, J. S., 221
Millican, G. D., 253–254, 264
Morris, R., 71n, 262
Mother-Tongue, acquisition of, 11, 13–16, 154–161

N.S.S.E., 26, 31, 85, 262
Newsom Report, 41
Norwood Report, 237

Oliver, R. A. C., 254, 263

Patterson, A. C., 126n, 263
Percival, A., 40n, 263
Phatic communion, 158
Play, significance of, 20, 123–126
Poetry, the teaching of, 92–121
   ballads and folksong, 107–108, 131–132
   children's writing of poetry, 96, 174–177
   choice of poems, 95, 98–100, 119–120
   difficulties encountered by children, 93–94, 97–103, 113–114
   recommended anthologies, 99
   questioning techniques, 100–105, 110–119
   speaking poems aloud 95–96, 106, 107, 109–110, 114–115, 118
Précis, 90, 242, 243
Principles of English Teaching, 11–23, 258–259

Quirk, Randolph, 204n, 228n, 232

Rankin, M., 45n, 263
Read, Sir Herbert, 175
Readiness, importance of, 17–19, 21, 29–31, 160
Reading, the teaching of
   children's reading-habits, 40–44
   children's tastes in reading, 42–58
   class-readers, books suggested as, 83–84
   class-readers, work with, 24–26, 31–39, 58–60, 72–82
   comprehension, 69–72, 240–242
   encouraging wide reading, 31–32, 39, 68–69
   eye-movements, 27–28
   home-readers, books suggested as, 64–68
   home-readers, work with, 63–64
   phonic analysis, 28–29, 30
   prose-study, 75–81
   reading as thought-getting, 26–27, 84
   reading in the primary school, 26–31
   reading readiness, 29–30
   reading with discrimination, 55, 62, 84–91
   reading-lessons with 11–12 year-olds, 24–26, 31–39
   sequence of stages, 30–31
   use of libraries, 61–63
   value of reading in children's development, 45–58, 60, 212
Reeves, J., 174n, 263
Relation between speech and writing, 171, 211
Richards, I. A., 101, 183, 241, 263
Rickword, C. H., 81n
Roberts, P., 232, 263
Robertson, S., 203–204, 206, 263